Y0-EHZ-433

# THE PSYCHOLOGY *of* SCHOOL MUSIC TEACHING

*James L. Mursell*
PROFESSOR OF EDUCATION
LAWRENCE COLLEGE
APPLETON, WISCONSIN

and

*Mabelle Glenn*
DIRECTOR OF MUSIC
KANSAS CITY, MISSOURI

SILVER, BURDETT AND COMPANY
NEW YORK NEWARK BOSTON CHICAGO SAN FRANCISCO

*Printed in the United States of America*

# Preface

This book has been prepared in the strong belief that a competent knowledge of the established results of psychological investigations in the field of music can be of the utmost value to the working music teacher, and can further the cause of music education in America. A great many splendid music teachers in our schools are doubtless conforming to psychological principles through instinct, or through a personal study of the child and his needs. We believe that such teachers will find comfort and reassurance in the knowledge that their opinions have a solid basis of established scientific fact, and that a complete survey of the psychology of music may open up for them avenues of thought and practical approach which they might not otherwise consider. Others, again, may not have fully realized the importance and value of a psychological attack upon the practical problems of musical development; and these, we believe, may gain a great deal from an understanding of the viewpoint here presented.

Since it is the primary aim of the book to help the working teacher, we have been careful to avoid the more technical aspects and terminology of music psychology. But at the same time we believe that we have brought practically all the relevant studies into contact with teaching situations in school music work. We have constantly sought to show exactly how psychological results may be applied in the classroom. At the same time, when a certain method is recommended, it should be understood that we use it chiefly as an illustration, and do not insist that it is the only possible way in which a psychological principle can be applied. Teaching is an art, and freely takes and uses scientific results for its own purposes. Psychology can never dictate any teaching procedure as right to the exclusion of all others, though it most certainly can indicate that some *kinds* of procedures are wrong and that other *kinds* of procedures are desirable. It is our hope that an understanding of the psychological outcomes and principles here explained will enable the working teacher to fashion for himself methods of procedure and treatment of superior excellence.

JAMES L. MURSELL

MABELLE GLENN

# CONTENTS

## Chapter One

# Introduction

### How Psychology Can Help the School Music Teacher

The chief aim of this book is to bring together all the findings of psychological research which bear on the work of the school music teacher, and to show how they can help in dealing with the practical problems to be faced. There is a great deal of such material, and it is of the highest practical interest and value. But very few people in the school-music field know much about it. This is really not their fault, because the data do not exist in an available or usable shape. Much of the psychological research is reported in monographs or articles only to be found in the largest libraries. Even then such papers are apt to be so technical that without very special training it is hardly possible to get much value from them. Much of the best work is available only in foreign languages. Furthermore, the findings are reported in scattered fashion, so that it is not enough to know a few of them. One must be familiar with practically all, since they correct and supplement one another and need to be fitted together into a unified picture. Lastly, and in a way most important of all, the practical educational bearing of a technical psychological study is often not very obvious, and calls for a great deal of analysis if it is to be made clear.

It may help the reader to form a better idea of what is to be hoped from the following pages if we briefly indicate the fields of psychological research which are particularly inter-

## Chapter One

# *Introduction*

### How Psychology Can Help the School Music Teacher

The chief aim of this book is to bring together all the findings of psychological research which bear on the work of the school music teacher, and to show how they can help in dealing with the practical problems to be faced. There is a great deal of such material, and it is of the highest practical interest and value. But very few people in the school music field know much about it. This is really not their fault, because the data do not exist in an available or usable shape. Much of the psychological research is reported in monographs or articles only to be found in the largest libraries. Even then such papers are apt to be so technical that without very special training it is hardly possible to get much edification from them. Much of the best work is available only in foreign languages. Furthermore, the findings are reported in piecemeal fashion, so that it is not enough to know a few of them. One must be familiar with practically all, since they correct and supplement one another, and need to be fitted together into a unified picture. Lastly, and in a way most important of all, the practical educational bearing of a technical psychological study is often not very obvious, and calls for a great deal of analysis if it is to be made clear.

It may help the reader to form a better idea of what is to be hoped from the following pages if we briefly indicate the fields of psychological research which are particularly interesting and instructive for the school music teacher. First of all we should mention the extensive body of work in music psychology proper. Altogether something like three hundred items of all kinds,—books, monographs, and articles—have been devoted to this topic in its various aspects. While not all of them are practically important for music education, a great many are; and these will be discussed and presented in the following pages, and listed in the bibliographies at the close of each chapter, so that anyone who wishes to go directly to the sources will find it easy to do so. In particular, we shall find authoritative material relating to ear training, to the development of rhythmic grasp, to the musical interests of children, to the inheritance of musical ability, to the foundations of appreciation, to the nature of singing, and to the great problem of measuring both innate musical capacity and musical achievement. Obviously everyone at all interested in teaching music properly ought to know what has been found out in these directions, and should understand the practical bearings of the research material. Then there is a great deal of work bearing on the learning process which cannot but be valuable for the educator. Within the last ten years many American psychologists have greatly revised their ideas about how we learn. This new work has a far closer relationship to the problems of the school music teacher than did the older psychology of learning. We shall try to show how it applies. Besides this there are a great many special fields in which psychology has brought results of much value and suggestiveness for music teaching. For instance, our whole approach to the vexed question of technique will be made much more intelligent if we know what psychology can tell us about the nature of motor skill and its acquisition. Or again, the reading of music is usually a primary concern in school work, and so the data on the psychology of reading become valuable as a basis for wise, practical decisions. Then such topics as the psychology of individual differences, child psychology, and the psychology of feeling and emotion, have a relevancy to music education so evident that we need hardly point it out. Our task is to assemble all this material, to build it up into a coherent and understandable whole, and to indicate everywhere its relationship to educational practice.

To avoid possible misunderstanding and disappointment we should perhaps here indicate clearly one thing that psychology cannot do for the teacher. It cannot dictate a cut-and-dried method. Psychology can never tell the teacher that he must follow certain absolutely definite procedures in a certain absolutely definite order. As a matter of fact, it can do much better than this. It can formulate the principles upon which any and every good teaching procedure must depend. Methods in music education are often a snare and a delusion. Many school music teachers suppose that there is just one fixed right way of doing everything. This is absolutely false. But there are right ways and wrong ways, distinctions which psychology, and psychology alone, can make clear. The right procedure varies with the situation, with the child, and with the teacher. The ideal teacher is one who so clearly understands the mental processes he aims to guide and control that he can adapt his teaching techniques, often on the spur of the moment, to the particular human problem confronting him, and perhaps even invent new techniques there and then. Psychology can give vital help in such situations. It cannot furnish us with a ready-made method, suitable for all occasions; for as a matter of fact one of the chief things we can infer from the psychology of learning is that any ability or skill can always be taught and handled in a variety of ways.

### Why Many Music Teachers Are Skeptical of Science

A great many music teachers, both in the studio and in the school fields, are inclined to be doubtful about the value of scientific findings for their work. Inasmuch as this book is virtually an application of psychological science to music teaching, it seems well to discuss the grounds for this attitude of distrust.

1. One reason is that many music teachers have come across applications of science to music which may be all right as science, but have very little value for a working musician and even less for a working teacher. For instance, a great deal of very fine research has been done on the physics of music. A really wonderful technique has been developed for photographing the fundamentals and overtones in various musical tones. Studies of the dynamics of the piano mechanism have been made. Of course there is endless investigation in the general field of acoustics. Or to turn to another field, a great deal is known about the anatomy and physiology of the human voice, and about the intricate system of muscles and nerves that control it. Many serious-minded music teachers have turned hopefully to such work as this, looking for help. And they have come away disappointed.

2. Yet another reason is that quite a great deal of what has masqueraded as science applied to music is really not science at all. For instance, one of the best known and most important books on piano technique combines the insight of a really great teacher with a most lamentable mass of nonsensical physics. Many of the things written in the name of applied psychology about vocal action are positively shocking. Now alchemy and astrology will not help the music teacher. Indeed they will be hindrances. In a great many cases this is just about what has been offered. Not being altogether gullible he

perceives that the so-called science simply does not apply, and so forms a prejudice against all science which is really deserved only by pseudo-science.

3. Then, too, a great deal of the perfectly sound psychology which school music teachers in training have studied is very remote indeed from their problems. A course in general psychology often has a peculiar prestige with students. They come into it expecting much. But they quickly find that it seems to have no relationship at all with the teaching problems they know they will have to face later on. Naturally the connection is really there, but teachers and textbook writers in psychology often do little to bring it out. The student in training can hardly be expected to supply what the experts have omitted. So psychology remains remote from practice in music education, and the teacher comes to feel that science can give little or no help.

4. Besides the reasons just given, and partly because of them, we find also a general feeling that music is creative and a matter of sentiment, while science is just dust and dry bones. Often the musician actually prides himself on being "not a scientist." This is really a very unfortunate attitude, and yet it is quite widely held. When we talk about the application of science to education, what we mean is simply that education ought to take account of, and base itself upon, ascertained fact. No one, however temperamental and high-souled he may be, can afford to fly in the face of the facts that relate to his own work. The notion that there is a mysterious antagonism between music and science is absurd. It comes from the idea that science is essentially an affair of strange formulae and incomprehensible, dull processes, whereas its real essence is simply the discovery of fact. When the musician attacks and condemns science, he is in the position of a person who climbs

out on a limb and then cuts it down behind him. He undermines his own chances.

There never was a time when music education more urgently needed the help that scientific psychology can give. School musicians, in particular, are facing a really breath-taking opportunity. Through their effective public presentation of their case they have virtually asked the American people to give music a chance in the schools. The answer has been very favorable. This is the true meaning of the great progress in school music in the last ten years. It has not yet achieved final success. But it has secured a challenging and enlarging opportunity. Just at this critical juncture, mechanical appliances have transformed the whole situation in the music field. The machine has done in music exactly what it has done in other fields. It has rendered various procedures and viewpoints obsolescent, and at the same time it has opened the way for new developments. We see the first, and of course the darker, side of the picture in such changes as the decline of the traditional *virtuoso* concert, the transformation of motion picture music, the elimination of the weaker private teacher, and the depleted enrollment in music schools whose chief aim is the production of near-*virtuosi*. But these things no more represent a total loss than did the misfortunes of the handweavers when the power loom came in. The great constructive lesson is that human beings ought not to attempt to compete with the machine on its own ground; and that there are values in musical performance quite extraneous to display, technique, and mechanics. In other words, the machine is forcing us to recapture intimacy and sincerity in music-making. It is forcing us to re-evaluate music from the ground up, and to recognize that the elocutionary emphasis which has dominated music education for so long is impossible. We are face to face with an enormous job of musical reconstruction. Manifestly the day is with the teacher of music in the schools, who holds a position of unique strategic strength.

This is the reason why the work of the school music teacher is so significant today. It is also the reason why it is so important for this work to be founded on knowledge. Without an adequate background in psychology, the finest schemes for school music work lack solidity. Without psychological knowledge we have no authoritative basis for criticizing improper and inadequate methods and schemes. So we may define our task in the terms used by Pestalozzi long ago. It is our aim to psychologize music education.

### Plan of the Book

The plan of presentation here adopted has grown out of this central aim. First we deal with the foundations of music education. These are found first of all in the musical nature of the child, and secondly in the processes of learning and teaching. It will be shown that everything here indicates appreciation as the necessary central aim of music education, using the term in its most inclusive sense. Next we deal with the basic mental processes or abilities which music education must set up, and we find that there are three, all intimately related, —namely, skill in hearing, grasp of rhythm, and mastery of the musical score. Thirdly, we turn to the problems of executant music, which we approach by way of general discussions of technique and expression, passing on to a more specific analysis of the problems of vocal and instrumental music. Lastly, we deal with the measurement of musical mindedness and capacity, the evaluation of teaching materials in the field of music, and the basic aims of music education.

PART ONE

# The Foundations of Music Education

## Chapter Two

# *Music and the Child*

The problem of this chapter is to determine the relationship of musical ability, or what is often called "musicality," to the whole mental and cultural life of the individual child. Some of our questions are the following: What sort of a person is the musical child? Does musical ability commonly go with high abilities in other fields? Is musical ability largely inherited, or is it something the child acquires through education? What kind of appeal does music naturally make to the child?

We shall not undertake here to give any formal definition of musicality or musical ability. Indeed it may never be possible to do this. But as we go on, its general nature will become apparent enough. Two points of basic practical importance, however, must here be made:

1. A person may be musical, that is, may possess high musicality, without any great executant or creative ability in music. This is clearly recognized in the research studies, and notably by Révécz on the basis of his very careful investigation of the psychology of a musical prodigy. Here we have a conclusion involving the widest educational consequences. Specifically the following inferences are to be made. (*a*) We must not judge musicality merely on the basis of ability to perform. A single performance may be no better as an index of musicality than a single coached recitation of a poem would be of literary feeling. (*b*) Children lacking in executant ability or in creative ability may still be entirely suitable subjects for music education. This is true even with children who never show

any signs of becoming very good performers or creators of music. Such children may have a real talent for loving music and a keen sensitiveness to it; and they may reap immense benefit from proper musical opportunities. (*c*) The main emphasis in music education should be upon appreciation. This emphasis should penetrate the work in performance, which should aim at musical sincerity and feeling rather than technical perfection.

2. The possession of musicality in another can be quickly and certainly perceived by a musically sensitive judge. In a study made by one of the authors, teachers in a conservatory were asked to rate their students on musical ability and feeling, ignoring performance ability as far as they could. In some cases as many as five ratings were obtained for one student. There was a striking agreement in the ratings assigned students by the different teachers, all of whom worked quite independently. Clearly this seemed to show that judgments of musicality by these teachers were quite reliable. It often happens that the working teacher in school music has to try to pick out musical children for some purpose. Here, of course, we approach the whole subject of testing, which will be fully discussed later on. At this point, however, there are two things to say. (*a*) It is necessary for the music teacher to be a musically sensitive person. The musically stupid individual is very apt to be led away by unessentials when estimating musicality in another. The musical personality picks up all sorts of latent hints and small signs, ignores roughnesses due to poor technique and limited experience, and senses the underlying quality, often with uncanny accuracy. (*b*) If any sort of informal test is to be made, it should be a test of responsiveness to a genuine musical situation. For instance, in selecting children for a school choir, it is not enough to know that they

have voices of good quality. This may be a purely mechanical accomplishment. What we need for our choir is fine tone quality inspired and brought to life by a quick and sensitive musical mind. So we might test the child by having him sing back to us a melody of appropriate length. Or again, in selecting for instrumental ensemble, we cannot be satisfied with nothing more than a certain mechanical facility. We might test for melodic responsiveness again, or we might call upon the child to step or beat out series of rhythms of increasing complexity. In any case the thing to do is to discover the child's responsiveness to an authentic musical situation rather than his mere mechanical endowment.

Such are the two chief inferences from our finding that musicality is to be distinguished from performance ability and creative ability. *The general question with which we are dealing, namely, the meaning and place of musicality in the mental life of the child, is the most basic of all our educational issues. Our aim must clearly be education in music and education through music. That is, we seek in the schools to educate in music for the fullest and freest possible development of the human personality.* We desire to make our subject the means of creating lives that are happy, useful, and culturally rich. Above all, we wish for a type of music education in the schools which will produce men and women who continue to grow both musically and culturally after their education in school is over. This, in fact, is the educational meaning of our subject. But obviously we do not wish either to run our heads against psychological impossibilities, or to try to do through music what simply cannot be done in the very nature of the case. For instance, if musicality should turn out to be a very specialized ability, without any relations to any other field of culture, if the typical musical person were a dullard at everything else, we would certainly hesitate to recommend much in the way of correlation between music and other curricular subjects. Or again, if musicality should turn out to be inherited like the color of the hair or the eyes, so that a person either had it or did not have it by native endowment, then we would have to question such a slogan as "music for every child." But on the other hand, we emphatically do want a scheme of music education which capitalizes every atom of nourishment which music affords. We ask for no impossibilities, but for all the possibilities. And so while we want to know what cannot be done, we also want to know what can. We want to know, in a word, just what music actually has to offer in the way of educative value. Moreover, we must insist on ascertained, authoritative knowledge, for the whole issue is too serious for us to rest content with idealistic guesses. And so we turn to the research material to see what it can tell us, and base our conclusions on this alone.

### The Inheritance of Musicality

Is musical ability inherited, or is it acquired through training? Let us seek to assemble and interpret the data on this important point.

1. The most important contribution to this topic comes from Germany, and is constituted by the extensive questionnaire studies of Haecker and Ziehen and of Koch and Mjoen. These two pieces of work really belong together, as the method employed was very largely identical, and each dovetails into the other. The investigators sent out questionnaires to be filled in, regarding whole family groups. Some of the questions used were as follows: At what age was musical talent noted? Does the individual show much desire to hear music? Can he easily recognize music he has once heard? How ex-

cellent is his sense of rhythm? Does he hear mistakes easily? Does he easily sing back a melody he has heard? Can he readily hold a second part? Can he play readily by ear? Does he compose? Has he absolute pitch? What type of voice has he? What artistic talents outside music has he? Some of the above questions are of considerable practical interest to the school music teacher, for they certainly suggest methods of informally testing musicality when this is desired. Returns on these questionnaires were obtained for over 4,000 individuals from some hundreds of families, so that the results have a very respectable factual basis indeed. The authors classified the subjects on the basis of the questionnaire reports into five subdivisions—very musical, musical, neither musical nor unmusical, unmusical, very unmusical. Omitting various fine and small distinctions, the chief outcomes of interest to us are the following: (*a*) If children come from parents one of whom is musical, they will usually be musical. (*b*) Males are more musical than females. The authors suggest that this may be true in appearance rather than reality, and may arise from the superior activity and better opportunities of men and boys, which enable them to make a better showing. (*c*) If both parents are musical, the children are very likely to be musical. (*d*) If both parents are unmusical, there are still more musical than unmusical children. Offspring from two unmusical parents is much more frequently musical than is offspring unmusical from two musical parents. (*e*) The authors find it impossible to draw any definite conclusions as to the detailed biological mechanism of musical inheritance.

2. In this country Hazel Stanton has carried through a somewhat similar piece of work. She investigated 85 members of 6 family groups in which one member of each family was known to be conspicuously talented in music. She used

the first five of the Seashore Measures of Musical Talent together with supplementary questionnaires. She claims some slight evidence for hereditary musical ability.

3. A very important piece of work along slightly different lines is the extensive genealogical study by Feis. This author studies the families—parentage and offspring—of 285 musicians. He points out that the method has two serious limitations. First, data on the maternal lines of great musicians is very hard to obtain, so that the genealogical material is seriously incomplete. Second, the fewness of the descendants of famous musicians makes it hard to draw conclusions. The material he assembles unquestionably shows that musical ability tends to run in families, though it hardly proves specific and definite heritability. A very important point he brings out is that the parents of great musicians have often been distinguished in other arts or in literature. Thus it may well be that the influence of the family environment is quite as important as specific heredity in producing musicality. At least there is nothing in the work of Feis to prove the contrary.

4. Mention should here be made of Spearman's comments on the Seashore Tests. Using a very special technique, he has concluded that the tests do not reveal any special unitary factor of musical ability. Rather what we discover is the special aptitude measured by the particular test, such as pitch discrimination, time discrimination, and the like. The claim that musical ability, as such, is a composite of these special capacities, so that a person who possesses them in a high degree also possesses marked musical ability, is not proved.

5. The problem of racial differences in musicality is almost untouched. There is one important study, by Lenoire, in which 200 white and 200 colored children were compared by means of the Seashore Tests. The author finds the negroes very

superior in rhythm and tonal memory, and not inferior to the whites in the other four tests. If such results should be confirmed, so that we should find evidence of very definite racial differences in musical ability, it would be a supporting argument in favor of the contention that musical ability is innate.

This terminates our account of the research material bearing on our present problem. What conclusions can we draw from it?

1. We have no proof whatsoever that musical ability is inherited as a definite trait like hair color, skin pigmentation, and so forth. Indeed, the evidence on the point is negative, for if inheritance were so specific and unmistakable as this, it would surely have shown up in the studies. We cannot, then, in music education, take the position as to musicality that educators are inclined to take about the I. Q. We cannot say that nature gives the child a definite musical endowment, and that beyond this nothing can be done about it. Doubtless in music as in everything else, everyone has his limitations. But they are much more flexible limitations than in some other fields.

2. It is still true, however, that musical ability is quite specialized within family groups. That is, if we could collect and study all the very musical children who have gone through a large school system over a period of years, we would not find them distributed by chance among the families represented. We would find certain families contributing more than their "fair share" of musical capacity. But it is quite open for anyone to contend that this is due to home environment rather than to family inheritance. There is no decisive evidence either way.

3. By far the most important conclusion we would draw from the data, and more particularly from the works of Feis, Haecker and Ziehen, and Koch and Mjoen is that *dis-*

*tinctive musical ability is a manifestation of a general high level of all-round ability, and particularly of a high level of artistic and literary ability.* We are inclined to believe that it is this high level of all-round ability rather than a specific and specialized musical talent that is inherited from the parents. This high all-round ability becomes canalized in music by environmental influences. And so musicality becomes a general rather than a special inheritance. In the very musical child we are usually dealing with a human being of high all-round quality and excellence. Such a child, given a proper chance, could probably succeed very well indeed in many fields other than music, because what he inherits is general excellence, not special talent. This result, of course, is very significant indeed. *For it suggests that music, if taught in such a way as to do justice to its natural psychological connections, should be taught in close contact with a wide and rich range of culture. Musical ability is not a lonely ability. It has natural affinities for other excellences.* And music education should not be thought of as a specialized cultivation of specialized gifts, but as a broad agency for general culture.

### Musical Ability in Relationship to Other Abilities

This topic follows quite naturally from what has just been said. It is one aspect of a problem that has long interested psychologists and educators, the problem of the relationship of abilities possessed by the individual. At one time a theory known as the theory of compensation was maintained in this connection. This was the view that a person who possesses one outstanding ability is usually weak in everything else, because nature tends to even up her scores. Such a position, however, has never found any basis in fact, and it has long since been abandoned. Thorndike has put forward just the opposite theory, the theory of correlation, according to which high ability in one field is a probable index of high ability elsewhere. On this view, versatility and talent would tend to go together. It is clear that if one or the other of these views were proved correct the whole scheme of educational and vocational advice and guidance would be greatly affected. The fact is that neither is wholly substantiated in its pure and absolute form. It now seems likely that every individual has one or two fields where his ability is highest, and that he shades off from these by slow gradations to fields where he has but little talent. In any case our concern here is not to take sides in a controversy between these views, but to acquaint the reader with their existence, so that he may avoid being led astray. What is of interest to us is to assemble and interpret the facts about the relationship of musicality to other types of ability.

First of all we have the work of the Pannenborgs, and of Miller. The former, in their study, investigated the abilities of 423 musical adults, 21 composers with whom they used the biographical method, and 2757 school children between the ages of 12 and 18. It should be stated that they found a high measure of agreement between their three groups, so that we may conclude that musicality has about the same psychic and cultural characteristics wherever found. The latter (Miller) studied the school records of students in a teacher training institution where music was required, men only being investigated.

The characteristics of the musical personality as revealed by these studies are as follows. (*a*) The typical musical person has a high-grade mentality and shows much versatility, particularly in literary and artistic fields. (*b*) There is a close and definite correlation between musical and mathematical ability. (*c*) The musical person is likely to have notable linguistic ability. The work of Feis emphatically confirms this finding. (*d*) The musical person is likely to show qualities of effective social leadership. (*e*) He is emotional, unstable, and not very punctual or scientific. (*f*) He is physically healthy and active and endowed with strong appetitive tendencies. (*g*) He sometimes has definite neurotic or hysterical tendencies.

The general picture is that of a high grade, nervously organized and high-strung personality, urgently needing free and varied outlets for personal expression, and capable of great contributions, though these need not always be along musical lines. This is the personal type to be kept in the focus in music education.

Another point to be considered here is the relationship of musical ability to general intelligence. And here we find a sharp cleavage between the German and American studies. Feis, Révécz, the Pannenborgs, Miller, and others are unanimous in finding that musicality and high intelligence go together. Seashore on the other hand finds comparatively little relationship between these two functions. Hollingworth, again, using the Seashore Tests, finds no special musical sensitivity in children testing above 135 I. Q., which of course means a group of very high intelligence. How can we explain these seemingly flat contradictions? The answer is not difficult. The American work is all based upon the very special Seashore Tests, while the German work, as is clear from our description of it given above, takes a much broader, more functional, criterion of musicality. There may be no relationship between Seashore Test performance and intelligence, and still be a very close one between functional musical ability and intelligence. As a matter of fact, this is precisely our own opinion. We feel that there is ample justification for stating that musicality goes with high general intelligence.

Let us sum up our conclusions on this whole topic:

1. Musicality is one of the most valuable of all abilities of the humanistic type. It is not a highly specialized or lonely ability. It has natural affinities for a wide range of culture.

2. Clearly, then, music education should correlate with a broad cultural development. It should never be thought of as a specialized, limited scheme of training. Even for those whose vocation is to be music, much will certainly be lost in the way of refined musical intelligence unless their development is made broad as well as expert. And for music in the schools to fail to make connections with the other curricular subjects which are its natural brothers and sisters is a confession of very serious failure.

3. Music is specially important for the child of superior general ability. It is very probable that he possesses the capacities which make music a natural and easy expressive outlet for him. It is also likely that he has the sort of personality which urgently needs just such outlets, and greatly benefits by them. Above all, such a child can be educated not only in but also through music, for music makes contacts with the whole range of his cultural life.

4. *Music education should be planned, not in terms of technique and drill, but in terms of self-expression, emotional release, and the creative impulse.* Here we have a most inspiring picture of what music education can mean as a conserver and creator of human values.

## The Child's Musicality

The general proposition has been laid down many times by educators and psychologists that the child differs from the adult *in kind.* Immaturity, which is an unfortunate word, is not a state of lacking something so much as a state of possessing certain highly positive and very beautiful characteristics.

While this is well recognized in theory, it is not always translated into practice. As a matter of fact a great deal of work in education is dominated by a sort of worship of adulthood, which involves the viewpoint that the child is a seriously imperfect being, and that the best thing to do for him is to turn him into an adult in the shortest possible order. But a moment's reflection will show us that even the grown-up person cannot be considered as a finished product educationally. The most worth while people are those who still continue to develop and change, and who thus remain in a very real way, like little children. The kind of education we want is not an education which hustles children along towards a hypothetical perfect state of full "maturity," but rather an education which enlarges and beautifies their living *as children.* And this is supremely true in music education. A scheme of music education, properly conceived, is an organized plan for surrounding the child with a musical environment and bringing him types of musical experience which he can assimilate and enjoy, in which he can live and grow, and through which he will develop in his own way towards a richer, fuller, and nobler love and understanding of the art of music. So the teacher of school music most urgently needs a reverent comprehension of the mysterious miracle of the child soul.

Our general point of departure is that the child, as a musical personality, differs *in kind* from the adult, and that if we wish to educate him musically, we must understand his positive musical characteristics. Putting it a little more definitely, the child is naturally interested in and naturally responds to elements in the musical complex markedly different from those which concern the adult. If we try to call his attention to just the things in a piece of music that interest and delight the adult, the result will be confusion and stultification, for we are trying to force upon him something as yet alien to his nature. Thus we need to know what elements in a musical situation may be expected to appeal to the child, for these are the growing points of his musical mentality.

Unfortunately, we have not as much information bearing upon this matter as we could wish. By far the most important study is one carried on in Moscow by Sophie Belaiew-Exemplarsky. She very carefully studied the musical reactions of 29 children, 14 boys and 15 girls between the ages of 6.5 and 7.5. This age level was chosen because the children had just finished kindergarten, where they had had some musical experience, and because, while they were still at an uncritical age, they were able to answer questions intelligently. Various pieces of music were played to them, each composition being repeated three times. For the sake of motivation they were told that they were to listen to "musical riddles," and then to answer questions about them. From this work she was able to draw a number of very significant conclusions.

1. The element of what is known as tonal volume proved to be the chief musical interest of the child at this age. By tonal volume something quite different from intensity is meant. It is an idea which figures largely in the modern psychology of music, and we shall return to it again when we come to deal with ear training. It means essentially the fullness, the richness, the body, the exquisite enjoyableness of lovely tone. And according to this study, the child's interest in and love of tone as such is the first growing point of his musical life. To the child, music first and foremost means tone.

Here we have an idea full of practical suggestiveness. Free play with tone is a most valuable element in the musical education of the little child. One deeply sympathetic and perceptive psychologist has recorded an experience which is worth the reflective attention of every school music teacher. He took a little boy for a country walk, early in the morning, in the springtime, when the trees were full of singing birds. The child was enchanted with the music, and turning his head from side to side "gave back the bird tones with an inimitable sweetness." Surely our school singing would do far better by attempting to release something of this free, spontaneous joy in tone and tonal beauty, than by drilling everlastingly on technique and the intellectual elements of "note reading." Or again, if we watch a child at the piano, all alone, we can clearly see his natural preoccupation with tone as such. It is a matter of common experience that a child will enjoy sounding tones and groups of tones on the piano, and listening to the effects produced. This naïve and direct interest in the raw material of music is certainly very significant. It has not been capitalized as much as it ought to be in music education. We have perhaps been a little too apt to stress the tonal and rhythmic *pattern,* because this seems *to us* to be the chief interest in music, forgetting that the child's interest may not be identical with our own. To make it concrete, we would suggest the following lines of thought and approach, which doubtless the experienced teacher can readily supplement. In all vocal work, the element of good tone must be made central. And good tone, as we shall see later, does not mean hushed tone, or unnatural tone, but the tone produced by the free use of the vocal apparatus, expressing the mood and intention of the music. The children should, from the very first, know the joy of creating a living, beautiful tone quality, to which they are so exquisitely sensitive. Again, elementary piano instruction, beginning perhaps in the third grade, should, if possible, have its roots in mere tonal play with the instrument, beginning just as soon as the child shows an interest in it. The value for school music work of a piano in the home, and particularly of a good piano, can hardly be overestimated. But the *first* educational use of the piano should not be the difficult and formal business of creating tone patterns on it. It should be treated as an opportunity for free tonal experience. Then again, it may often be wise to provide children with other mechanical means for tonal play and experimentation. Toy orchestra work, using instruments of definite pitch, offers such opportunities. Mrs. Satis Coleman's plan, by which children in the early grades make and play their own simple instruments, should be thought through carefully from this angle. For the purpose of tonal play, instruments with a fixed pitch are obviously preferable, because they at once eliminate a serious mechanical problem. But apart from all instrumental agencies of tone production and tonal experience, we should insist on excellence of tone quality in all singing done by children, and should encourage children to listen to their own tone, and to the tone of the class.

It may seem very strange to give primacy to an interest in tone as such. We have been told so often that rhythm and melody are the fundamental musical interests of the child. But after all, have any good and sufficient reasons ever been given for this claim? Is it possible to watch a little child experimenting at the piano keyboard, or happily playing a small marimba, though with little thought of making formal musical patterns; or listening to the clear notes of water glasses tuned to the scale, without a rather uneasy feeling that surely there is something here very vital, something we ought to capitalize more effectively than we do? Of course the capitalization of such an interest means an exceedingly informal approach to music, and informality is the bugbear of many teachers, who always want to get a group together, give them a good drill on something that seems important to an adult, and shoot them through in lockstep. But we may here take occasion to say with much emphasis that, if anyone is serious about applying psychological principles to music education, this is just the sort of routine to avoid. A refusal to help the child to develop and build upon his natural love of beautiful tone, just because it is hard to plan such work in a school environment, is a lamentable surrender to the notion that the child exists for the school, rather than the school for the child.

2. According to Miss Belaiew-Exemplarsky, the second, but still important element in music which is of natural interest to the child, is the motor element. That is to say, the child is interested in sensing and experiencing music in terms of his own bodily movements. This expresses itself in two ways; first, as an interest in rhythm, which is felt in and through muscular action; second, as an interest in melody, which, she claims, is essentially felt as something *sung*. This last point is really of very great moment. It indicates that the child's natural feeling for melody is not a feeling for a pattern of tones or intervals primarily, but first and foremost a feeling for something he can carry with his voice and sense with his body. We would conclude at once that, beginning with the kindergarten, everything possible ought to be done to capitalize the free and spontaneous singing of the child. When the children listen while the teacher sings a new rote song, the aim should be, not to print something on their minds, but to make them want to possess and enjoy the beauty of the melody to the full, by singing it. Again, with some Mother Goose songs which the children bring to school as part of their musical vocabulary, the children may sing with the teacher, without any preliminary listening experience. Some teachers make an absolute

rule that children must never sing with the teacher. When stated in any such extreme and exclusive form, we believe this to be a mistake. The child's interest in the melody is not directed towards the abstract pattern of the sound, but to its singability; and that interest should be given the freest play.

3. The study also shows that the children were capable of a surprising intellectual grasp of the music. One of the questions regularly put was "What kind of music was that?" It was found to be quite intelligible. The children proved to be entirely able to apprehend the music as such, to single out its motor elements (tempo, melody, and rhythm) and to give an account of it in words. It was also found that the children rather failed to distinguish between their imagination, and the actual musical percept. They tended to think of music as being "about" things, *i.e.,* as telling stories, expressing ideas, and so forth. One other interesting result should be mentioned in this connection. Their teachers rated these children on musicality, and these ratings had a close relationship to the quality of the answers they made to the questions addressed to them about the selections they had heard. The conclusion drawn is that the ability to give a good verbal or intellectual response to music is closely associated with the real musical feeling itself.

We obtain here suggestive insights into two major fallacies in music education, intellectualization at the adult level, and the refusal to intellectualize at all. By all means children should be encouraged to have and to express ideas about music they have heard and enjoyed. And while it is necessary to use some tactful control to prevent the story-telling impulse from running away with the situation, yet the child's tendency to associate ideas with music, to feel music as "about" a star, a running brook, a lake, a bird, the forest trees, and the like, is a perfectly natural expression of his musical interest. Encouragement and recognition of this interest should take the form of giving the child an opportunity to say whatever he wants to say about music he has heard. It should not take the form of constantly prodding the child to make forced associations, to look always for a story or a definite idea back of the music. If we do this, we falsify all our values. We put into the center of our picture something that by no means belongs there, although it has a very real place of its own. The *ideal* educational situation here (and of course it cannot always be realized, even by the best of teachers), is one where the child's spontaneity is given free play, so that on the one hand the way lies open for a natural, exuberant bubbling up of imaginative and intellectual reactions, while on the other hand there is no compulsion to produce such reactions if the music does not supply the urge.

4. The study also indicates that young children have little concern with the harmonic content of music. There seemed to be no objection to very bad harmony even when played as an accompaniment to a familiar tune. This should not be taken to mean, however, that in music education it does not matter whether we give the child experience of fine harmonic material or not. The feeling for harmony possessed by the adult is very largely the result of training. This has been well shown by Moore and Valentine. Valentine in particular carried on an extensive investigation of the differences in preferences for chords among children and adults. He found that before the age of 9 the child shows no particular preference for concords as contrasted with discords, and that the adult scheme of preference is established at about the age of 12 or 13. He also showed that children from more cultivated homes and with better and wider opportunities for hearing music,

began to discriminate concord and discord earlier than others. So we would conclude that rich experience with good though simple harmonic content is valuable from the very first. But it is true that we must not expect to build a very living musical interest on this factor when dealing with young children.

Outside the extensive and well-conducted study whose results we have been discussing, there is very little of value bearing on child musicality. Agnew has shown that there are marked differences in the part played by musical imagery in children and adults. Stern deals with the natural manifestations of musical ability and interest in children at various levels, but his classifications seem rather theoretical. More interesting for us is his suggestion that the tendency to create melody spontaneously is one of the best indices of musical ability in the child.

### The Question of Musical Types

While we have no authentic answer to the question as to what types or kinds of musical personalities can be distinguished, yet the issue is so very important that we must devote a little space to it. Probably the most scientific and worth while approach to it is that of Miss Gaw, who made a survey of musical talent in a music school, using a large variety of tests and criteria. She discriminated four musical types. The first and best showed uniform high ability in sensitivity to musical stimuli (*i.e.,* in such matters as pitch discrimination, the sense of consonance, tonal memory, etc.), in motor ability, which showed up as a capacity to play accurately and in time and to sing pitch accurately, and in intelligence. The second type showed high level ability in everything but motor traits, in which they were average. The third type was high in sensory capacity, but low in motor capacity. The fourth type was above the average in sensory traits and average in motor traits. We should remember that these types were found among students in a conservatory of music, and that the range of differences in a grade school population is certainly very much wider. Probably many genuine musical types never get into a school of music at all. Still, the study has at least a suggestive significance.

In addition to this, Miller devotes some attention to the problem of types in the paper to which we have already referred. He speaks of the musicality of the poorly endowed person as a purely sensory musicality. The musical interests of such a person, while they may be very real, are somewhat superficial, and it may be that he can never learn to grasp and to love the greatest and most characteristic masterpieces of the art.

These are certainly very meager findings considering the obvious importance of the problem. It is a subject to which many teachers and supervisors could readily contribute much helpful material. About all we feel justified in saying is that differences of musical type undoubtedly exist. We should not suppose that every pupil is interested in music in the same way, or that the same things in music appeal equally to everyone. It is necessary to vary our approach as much as possible, to give the child as wide and diversified a range of musical experience as we can, and above all to encourage and cultivate his natural and spontaneous expressions of interest, rather than inhibit them for the sake of a convenient uniformity of procedure and administration.

### Is Musicality Universal?

Our position is that in a very real sense musicality is an almost universal natural endowment among school children. First, it is necessary to define this claim with care. Secondly, we must bring it into relationship with the ascertained facts which bear upon it. What we want is no windy, idealistic slogan, but a solid, scientifically based conclusion to guide us.

1. First let us consider the question of the so-called monotone. The position now taken by most progressive music educators is that the monotone is a problem case rather than a hopeless case, and that the nature of the problem varies with different individuals. In other words, the first thing to do when we are confronted with a monotone is to try to make up our minds just where the difficulty lies, and to what classification he belongs. It has been said that monotones nearly always fall into one of four classes:

(*a*) The child who has not yet found his singing voice,—that is, the child whose head tones have not yet been established. The proper treatment here is that outlined in the chapter on singing for developing the proper placement of the child voice. The difficulty experienced by monotones of this type is easily overcome by properly directed effort along the line of voice building.

(*b*) The child who is inattentive to pitch, or who fails to recognize changes in pitch. Here the indicated attack is by directing the child's attention to pitch changes. We may have the child motion up and down with the hand as the teacher or the class sings up or down. We may have him stand on his toes to sing high. We may use various devices and games in which the child tells which of two tones is higher. Such a story as that of the Three Bears may be used to call attention to three levels of pitch. Attention may be directed to wide differences of pitch level on the piano.

(*c*) The child who lacks coördinational ability in the vocal muscles. Such a case is harder to deal with. The procedure is much the same as with the second group, except that a more exacting effort of attention is required. The child may be required to *think* a tone very hard, and then to try to sing it. Such work as this should never be continued for more than a very few moments at a time.

(*d*) The child who is the victim of some physical defect, such as partial deafness, adenoids, or definite speech deficiencies of various kinds. Such troubles will not yield to anything less than medical treatment in most cases.

Other classifications have been proposed, and may be familiar to the reader. No such grouping is founded on indubitable research results, and the one here given may be as helpful as any. The essential outcome is that the entirely unmusical child is a rarity, and that music education has a mission and a responsibility to children who at the outset may seem rather hopeless cases.

2. One of the most important studies of poor musical endowment is Schüssler's investigation of 200 children classified by him as "unmusical." He gives it as his opinion that from five to ten per cent of all children fall into this category. Incidentally he finds that the "unmusical" and the "half musical" children do considerably worse in school work in general than the "musical" children. In interpreting his position, however, there are two points to be considered. First, his criterion of "unmusicality" was grade in school singing. We gather from his account that no particular attempt at remedial work, similar to that recommended above for "monotones," was made on behalf of the children represented in his study. The second point which calls for comment is his explicit statement that the "unmusical" children can still profit largely from musical instruction. Here of course we come back to our opening distinction between musicality and ability to perform. Because a child is not prospective glee club material we should not

assume that our scheme of music education owes him nothing. He may still have a keen and delicate musical sensitiveness which makes musical opportunities exceedingly valuable to him as educational avenues for self expression and development.

3. Another important piece of work in this connection is the study by Miss Copp. She argues that almost every child has musical ability, but that this is often lost through lack of training at a susceptible age. She bases her claim on the fact that 80 per cent of children, in her experience, can be trained to sing "center C" on demand, and to recognize it when they hear it.

4. The idea of musicality as something possessed by all but often dissipated by improper training and lack of opportunity leads to what in our own opinion is the most significant line of thought developed in this whole connection. Bernfeld discards all the more ordinary notions, and insists that musical progress depends on the individual's "will to be musical." In other words, musicality is a dynamic, not a static or mechanical affair in human life, and must be so treated in education. The musical child is not necessarily one who possesses a beautiful voice, or fine motor capacity, or an intellectual ability which gives him a ready mastery of the problems of musical theory. *The musical child is one who possesses an inner urge towards music.* Such a child may or may not possess the talents which will make him a fine executant artist or an effective composer. These talents of course are far from unimportant, but they are not the essentials. Musicality essentially depends upon will. If the will to music is lacking, musicality itself is lacking.

Now as Bernfeld clearly intimates, the will to be musical can be fostered or antagonized by circumstances. This is one great reason why, as we have already seen, children from musical homes are much more likely to rise to high musical achievement than children from unmusical homes. But we are particularly interested in the bearing of this idea upon music education in the schools. And the lesson is both clear and supremely important for a constructive practical philosophy of music teaching. It is this: *The primary business of the school music teacher is to foster and develop the "will to be musical."*

In a sense all the rest of this book is an expansion and application of just this idea. But we may pause here for a moment to make a few comments. Certain types of so-called music work in the schools definitely and obviously antagonize the will to be musical. This always happens where the chief emphasis is upon the mechanics of technique or intellectualized theory. For instance, the abrupt introduction of the musical score early in the grades as an explicit problem, nearly always means the substitution of a quasi-mathematical puzzle interest for a real musical interest. Again, if we put drill on voice production or on instrumental technique in the foreground, we imperil the pupil's interest in music. As far as secondary education is concerned, the surveys by Hutson and Scott on the musical interests of high school students are exceedingly enlightening on this point. The detailed statistical findings will not be reproduced here, though they well repay careful study. In general the outcomes of this work show a strong interest in and desire for music on the part of students in high school. This manifests itself in many ways, such as the persistent wish to take music lessons outside of school, the large numbers reporting a desire for further musical instruction (only 26 out of 240 seniors giving a negative reply here), and the fact that a steadily increasing liking for music is found with increased stay in school. What is especially notable for us is that by far the most important reason given for discontinuing music study outside school is the pressure of school work and the fact that music study receives no school credit. To be specific, 35 per cent of those who studied music previously discontinue their work during senior high school because of the pressure of school work, and 9.15 per cent of those who studied previously discontinue their work during senior high school because of dislike. Evidently then the music educator has on his hands the job of educating the traditional senior high school. *The primary business of music education in the high school is to organize a situation where the natural musical impulses of the pupils are adequately recognized, and where the school becomes the friend rather than the foe of the will to be musical.*

To clinch this whole point we may refer to the fact well established by Thorndike, that interest and ability tend to coincide. Interest in a subject alone is not necessarily a guarantee of high ability. One may be very much interested in a particular subject, and yet fail to do as well with it as some other person of greater natural endowment or better preparation. But if we drop comparison with others, we can say that an individual is likely to do his own best work in those fields where his interest is greatest. And this is particularly true if such an interest has been of long standing. Hence we would be justified in holding that a person's interests show the vital, growing points for his educational and personal development. If we can evoke in a child a keen enthusiasm for music, if we can sustain this interest over a period of years, and steadily build it up to higher levels, then even though he never becomes a *virtuoso* or a composer, he will have found himself and his personal happiness, and built for himself a better life and a wider personality through music. This is the chief business of music education.

### Summary. Outcomes of This Chapter

It is evident that we have reached some very important and widely significant outcomes. Let us now bring together all the elements of our picture of musical interest in the child.

1. What is inherited in connection with music is not a highly specialized musical talent which makes its possessor almost a psychological freak. The very musical child inherits a general high grade personality. This is the material which nature gives us to transmute into an enthusiasm for and comprehension of music which will be an energizing element in individual development and life.

2. Musicality is not a lonely thing in mental life. It is closely associated with a whole range of excellences. Thus music education must recognize always a reciprocal relationship between music and the whole body of culture, the one vitalizing and enriching the other.

3. Everyone needs music. The highly endowed need it as an avenue for noble and satisfying self expression, a giver of mental health. The less well endowed need it as an agency for enriching and humanizing a life which otherwise might be hemmed in by drab routines.

4. The simple yet exquisite musical interests and impulses of the child, so different in many ways from those of the adult, are the only proper bases for a glorious cultural structure which will be compromised and weakened if we try to erect it on any other foundation.

5. It is a fallacy to suppose that girls are more musical than boys. Probably the reverse is true. In dealing with the boy

we need to take pains that a tradition of spurious masculinity does not inhibit his will to be musical.

6. We must not expect everyone to develop musically on a common pattern. We must not despise any individual line of musical development, or any type of musical impulse so long as it is real and sincere. We must not set up any scheme of music education which nullifies or thwarts the sincere musical interest of any individual.

7. Musicality is dynamic, depending in the last analysis on the human will. Music education may either stultify and obliterate or foster and develop the essential will to be musical.

### Problems for Discussion.

1. Make an analysis of the personality, characteristics, and general school achievement of some musical children you know.
2. Suggest contrasts between musical and unmusical children in fields other than music.
3. Indicate some practical consequences for music education if musicality were entirely unrelated to any other human ability.
4. Show how home influences may produce in a high grade child sensitivity to and interest in music.
5. Assemble evidence from your own experience showing that musicality runs in families.
6. How might we explain Seashore's finding of the lack of relationship between musicality and general intelligence?
7. Suggest methods appropriate to various age levels for capitalizing the natural love of beautiful tone.
8. Should we expect the little child to enjoy absolute music? Give reasons.
9. Can Stern's suggested phases of musical development be applied in music education? If so, how?
10. What evidence have we that musicality is universal? What are some of the educational implications of this claim?
11. Suggest methods for conserving and fostering the will to be

musical. Discuss some procedures in music education which antagonize it.

12. Which of the questions used by Haecker and Ziehen and Koch and Mjoen seem to you useful as suggesting ways in which a teacher might quickly and informally estimate the musical ability of a pupil?

13. What would be some of the consequences for educational guidance in music if we adopted the theory *(a)* of compensation; *(b)* of the correlation of mental traits?

14. Pick out from the articles by Hutson and Scott the statistics which seem most significantly to show the presence and growth of a will to be musical among secondary school pupils.

BIBLIOGRAPHY.

1. AGNEW, MARIE, A Comparison of Auditory Images of Musicians, Psychologists, and Children, *Psychological Monographs,* 1922, vol. 31, No. 1, Whole No. 140, pp. 268-278.
2. BELAIEW-EXEMPLARSKY, SOPHIE, Das musikalische Empfinden im Vorschulalter, *Zeitschrift für angewandte Psychologie,* 1926, vol. 27, pp. 177-216.
3. COPP, E. F., Musical Ability, *Journal of Heredity,* 1916, vol. 7, pp. 297-304.
4. FEIS, OSWALD, *Studien über die Genealogie und Psychologie der Musiker,* Wiesbaden, J. F. Bergman, 1910.
5. FRACKER, G. C., and HOWARD, V. M., Correlation between Intelligence and Musical Talent among University Students, *Psychological Monographs,* 1928, vol. 39, No. 2, Whole No. 178, pp. 157-161.
6. GAW, ESTHER ALLEN, A Survey of Musical Talent in a Music School, *Psychological Monographs,* 1922, vol. 31, No. 1, Whole No. 140, pp. 128-156.
7. GRAY, C. T., and BINGHAM, C. W., A Comparison of Certain Phases of Musical Ability of Colored and White Public School Pupils, *Journal of Educational Psychology,* 1929, vol. 20, pp. 501-506.
8. HAECKER, V., and ZIEHEN, TH., Über die Erblickheit der musi-

kalischen Begabung, *Zeitschrift für Psychologie,* 1921, vol. 88, pp. 265-307.

9. HAECKER, V., and ZIEHEN, TH., Über die Erblickheit der musikalischen Begabung, *Zeitschrift für Psychologie,* 1922, vol. 89, pp. 273-312.
10. HOLLINGWORTH, L. S., Musical Sensitivity of Children Who Test Above 135 I. Q., *Journal of Educational Psychology,* 1926, vol. 17, pp. 95-109.
11. HUTSON, P. W., Some Measures of the Musical Training and Desires of High School Seniors and Their Parents, *School Review,* 1922, vol 30, pp. 604-612.
12. KOCH, HANS, and MJOEN, FRIDTJOF, Die Erblickheit der Musikalität, *Zeitschrift für Psychologie,* 1926, vol. 99, pp. 16-73.
13. LARSON, WILLIAM S., Measurement of Musical Talent for the Prediction of Success in Instrumental Music, *Psychological Monographs,* 1930, vol. 40, No. 1, Whole No. 181, pp. 33-73.
14. LENOIRE, Z., *Racial Differences in Certain Mental and Educational Abilities,* Thesis, University of Iowa Library, 1925.
15. MILLER, RICHARD, Über musikalische Begabung und ihre Beziehungen zu sonstigen Anlagen, *Zeitschrift für Psychologie,* 1925, vol. 97, pp. 191-214.
16. MOORE, HENRY THOMAS, The Genetic Aspect of Consonance and Dissonance, *Psychological Monographs,* 1914, vol. 17, No. 2, Whole No. 73.
17. PANNENBORG, H. J., and W. A., Die Psychologie des Musikers, *Zeitschrift für Psychologie,* 1915, vol. 73, pp. 91-136.
18. RÉVÉCZ, GEZA, *The Psychology of a Musical Prodigy,* Harcourt, Brace and Company, 1925.
19. RÉVÉCZ, GEZA, Über das frühzeitige Auftreten der Begabung, *Zeitschrift für angewandte Psychologie,* 1919, vol. 15, pp. 341-373.
20. SCHOEN, MAX, Recent Literature on the Psychology of the Musician, *Psychological Bulletin,* 1921, vol. 18, pp. 483-489.
21. SCHÜSSLER, H., Das unmusikalische Kind, *Zeitschrift für angewandte Psychologie,* 1916, vol. 11, pp. 136-166.

22. SCOTT, F. A., A Study of Applied Music, *School Review*, 1920, vol. 28, pp. 112-122.
23. SEASHORE, CARL EMIL, *The Psychology of Musical Talent*, Silver, Burdett and Company, 1919.
24. STANTON, H. M., *The Inheritance of Specific Musical Capacities*, Psychological Monographs, 1922, vol. 31, No. 1, Whole No. 140, pp. 157-204.
25. STERN, W. S., *The Psychology of Early Childhood*, tr. Anna Barwell, Henry Holt and Company, 1926, ch. 25.
26. THORNDIKE, E. L., Early Interests, Their Permanence and Relation to Abilities, *School and Society*, 1917, vol. 5, pp. 178-179.
27. THORNDIKE, E. L., The Correlation Between Interests and Abilities in College Courses, *Psychological Review*, 1921, vol. 28, pp. 374-376.
28. VALENTINE, C. W., The Aesthetic Appreciation of Musical Intervals among School Children and Adults, *British Journal of Psychology*, 1913, vol. 6, pp. 190-216.

CHAPTER THREE

# *Musical Learning*

Since all education is learning, the topic of musical learning has a fundamental place in music education. In this chapter it is our aim to see how children create in themselves the various abilities, mental, emotional, and motor, on which musical grasp and insight depend. To make it quite concrete let us list a few illustrations of the learning process in music education. We encounter it whenever we are building the power to hear and apprehend a specific musical figure, phrase, rhythm, melody, or harmonic sequence, or the ability to sing or play any of these. We encounter it whenever we are building an appreciative understanding and a fine and precise feeling for a whole composition, or the ability to play or sing it. We encounter it when we are building the capacity to apprehend the principles of tonal and chordal combination and relationship. We encounter it when we are building the capacity to recognize a phrase or a melody in the staff notation, or when we are building a general mastery of the staff notation. We encounter it when we are acquiring the particular motor controls demanded by a given composition, or when we are working towards a general control of the vocal mechanism or the muscular and nervous coördination demanded by some instrument. We encounter it when we are trying to build up general musicianly power and grasp. Thus the learning process penetrates every detail of music education. It may have to do primarily with creating aesthetic attitudes, visual or auditory skills, or motor abilities. Sometimes a piece of learning will last only a few minutes. But sometimes it may take years to complete. *Wherever and whenever we are aiming at an increase of power, there we are dealing with learning. Always its general characteristics are the same.*

## How Learning Takes Place

This is not the place to outline a general and complete theory of learning; but we must discuss certain current psychological issues in terms wide enough to define our own position for practical purposes. For much in the modern, general, theoretical literature on learning is full of practical consequences for music education. In particular, we are almost bound to criticize the older mechanical theory of learning which has been so very influential in American education, and which is so disastrous when carried over into the field of music. The two characteristic doctrines of the mechanical account of learning are: first, that we always learn by "doing," or repetition, and, second, that all learning is essentially the formation of fixed habits. Our full reasons for disagreement with both these propositions will emerge only little by little in the course of this and later chapters. But they are so important, they so persistently haunt the minds of so many teachers, and they have led to such unfortunate educational consequences, that we ought explicitly, though briefly, to review them here, and to show in a general way why we cannot accept the theory they embody and what alternative we propose.

1. Perhaps the easiest way to reach an intelligent conclusion regarding the mechanical theory of learning, with its twin doctrines of repetition and habit formation, is to see how it ever came to be set up.

(*a*) One of its roots is the early experimental work on

memory. The first scientific studies in this field (and we should remember that they represented a very real advance over what had preceded them), used carefully constructed lists of nonsense syllables. One of its most central problems was to find out how many repetitions it took to learn lists containing various numbers of these nonsense syllables. It was but a step from such procedures to the idea that memory itself is a mechanical affair of packing a certain amount of content into the mind by going over it often enough. While later work on memory has not discredited the earlier results, it has pointed towards a very different view. Instead of nonsense material, meaningful material of all kinds has been used, in which the subject can perceive various interrelationships, and about which he has various emotional reactions. We now believe that memory by no means depends on the mere brute packing of indifferent content into a passively receptive mind. Rather we think of it as the creation of a living structure or picture on whose clarity and stability our power to remember depends. Mere repetition comes to take a second or even a third place, and interest, attitude, and intelligence come to the front.

(*b*) Another historic root of the mechanical view of learning is the early work on animal learning. Thorndike in this country did remarkable pioneer work in studying the learning processes of animals when they tried to get out of problem boxes and cages so arranged that a certain sequence of movements was necessary to actuate the lock. The picture he built up was of a period of rather blind and often frantic fumbling, followed by a slow, painful, repetitious discovery of how to open the door. From this the inference has been drawn that all learning begins with blind trial and error, that little by little by long repetition certain successful procedures begin to define themselves, and that these are at last pounded into the learner's head. But critics have pointed out that when an animal is placed in a problem box, he is in a most unnatural and unintelligible situation, where there is really nothing much for him to do but blind scrambling and trusting to mere luck. Such an animal in his natural habitat will learn very differently indeed. He then learns because he wants to learn; and far from depending on endless repetition, it is quite likely that he will acquire the new attitude or skill the very first try he makes. *So in education in general, and music education in particular, we want the sort of learning that the animal achieves out in the woods, not the sort that takes place when he is condemned to escape from a problem box.*

2. Let us consider a little more closely the idea that learning depends primarily on repetition. We shall make two points in criticism of this view: first, that it is false to the facts; secondly, that it ignores a factor which education must consider vital.

(*a*) It has been demonstrated that there are factors in learning far more important than repetition. To mention one of the studies on which this conclusion depends, Peterson, taking a very complex piece of human learning, was able to show that in spite of certain mental connections being repeated far more often than others, these simply were not learned at all, and made no impression on the mind when they ran counter to the learner's interest and aim. So in musical learning, the attitude and interest of the learner is far more important in determining what he learns and fails to learn, than the number of times he goes over the ground. The dogma that we always learn by doing has been over-driven in music education to a point that is nothing less than amazing. For instance, we find systems of work in sight reading which consist in letting the class flounder through the song with nothing given but the initial pitch, and with an injunction against the slightest help from the teacher, as if this were the most shocking thing that could possibly happen! Such procedures are a travesty on psychological principles. We treat the pupils as though they were animals in problem boxes, and as though our main interest was in seeing how soon they could get out without the slightest assistance. Now one does not learn in any such way. One zealous, interested repetition will mean more than almost any number of mechanical and thoughtless repetitions. *Above all, one successful repetition, even though the teacher help with the success, means far more than any number of fumbles and failures.*

(*b*) The idea of learning as the result of mechanical repetition ignores the whole question of the origination of the learning process. But the origin of any piece of learning is a question of vital importance. It will almost certainly affect its quality and its final success. There is all the difference in the world between learning a song because a child loves it and wants to be able to sing it, and learning the same song because the teacher prescribes it. The number of repetitions has nothing to do with the situation. In the one case the chances are in favor of a psychologically successful and educationally fruitful undertaking, and in the other they are not. When we prescribe a song as if it were a dose of medicine,—good for what ails the pupil's reading, but nasty and stupid in itself—we set everything against proper learning, including learning to read.

3. Now let us consider the idea that learning consists in the stamping in of definite habits. This view has been enormously influential and has affected teaching in all kinds of

ways. But we are forced to regard it as a mere fiction, and a dangerously misleading fiction at that. The root conception is that whenever we learn something, a pathway or a number of pathways or connections is created in the central nervous system. Many people have picked up this idea in one way or another, and it has had a great influence in educational thought and practice. We here make two comments upon it. (*a*) The whole idea of neural pathways is a pure fiction. No one has ever seen such a pathway. It has just been invented to support and validate a preconceived view of the nature of learning. Modern neurology seems to be building up quite a different account of the action of the central nervous system. (*b*) As soon as we begin to find important and authentic instances of learning where the connections established are precisely those which are *not* most frequently repeated, the idea of neural paths worn smoother and smoother by use seems to go by the board. The conception of learning as depending upon the passage of an impulse again and again over the same chain of nerve cells is false to the ascertained facts.

So far from learning being a business of forming habits, it seems to be a great deal more like a business of breaking them. Suppose we follow the vocal development of a talented child from the kindergarten to a place in the high school glee club. When he reaches the glee club he has not so much perfected and polished certain vocal habits which existed in a crude state when he was in the kindergarten. *Rather his whole vocal skill has been transformed.* His vocal ability has become quite a different thing. He finds pitch, he produces his tone, he attends to quality and nuance in ways fundamentally different from those he adopted ten or twelve years previously. Research in vocal action leaves no real room for doubt about this. Exactly the same thing is true of every type of musical skill and every piece of musical learning,—improving the ability to read, apprehending melody or key, appreciating and enjoying musical compositions, and all the rest. Learning, improvement, is not an affair of polishing and refining a set of habits originally present in a crude form. It is a process of transformation, of creating something entirely new.

Perhaps all this may seem a little abstract and theoretical, and the reader may welcome one or two concrete and practical illustrations. While a great deal that will be said later on will really illustrate this account of learning and help to make its meaning clearer, yet it may be brought home more intimately and forcefully by a couple of examples here. First, let us see how our analysis of learning as transformation bears on a problem which concerns a great many music teachers,—the famous problem of so-called practice in error. What attitude shall we take towards mistakes made by the pupil, and particularly towards somewhat persistent mistakes? If we regard learning as mechanical habit building we shall feel very badly indeed about such mistakes. They indicate wrong habits, and these habits may be permanently ground in. So before we let the pupil go a single step further, we must eradicate them at all costs. But this is precisely not our point of view. For us it does not matter if the pupil makes mistakes at an early level, so long as he also makes progress. He will not learn the wrong way if only we can keep him moving, and above all if we can keep him zealous to do better. For he is not mechanically building upon his present low-level habits. He is working out of them, just as the butterfly works out of the chrysalis.

So much for our first illustration. Our second is that of

formal drill. The idea of learning as habit formation,—the idea that a great skill is a sort of complex structure of fixed habits—evidently implies the use of plenty of formal drill. We want to form first one habit, then another and another, to make them all facile and smooth-running, and then put them together. Our account of learning is wholly opposed to this. For us learning depends on interest and impulse. It is a transformation brought about by zeal. The pupil who is eager to learn tends to make discoveries, to find for himself new and better methods. Hence, we place all our emphasis on making the task before the pupil interesting and meaningful, and use formal drill work only in the most incidental way as an aid which the interested, zealous pupil will recognize as necessary and so will appreciate.

To sum up, we regard learning as the active creation of a living structure, a process of transformation and discovery. This is not possible without repetition. But repetition is not the essential, central agency. Moreover, it is not possible without forming certain fixed routine habits. But again these belong at the circumference, not the center. For instance, vocal and instrumental pupils need to be habituated to a certain pose; ensemble groups need to be habituated to direct steady attention to the conductor. Every living process carries with it some mechanical concomitants. But the vital essence of the skill does not lie in such things as these, any more than the power of a great writer lies in the way he holds his pen. The essence of all learning is creation. The essence of all great skill and power is not in habituation or routine at all, but in the capacity to meet flexibly and intelligently the complex, shifting demands of real situations. This is the account of learning which we must now seek to develop and apply in detail.

### The Course of Learning: Analysis and Synthesis

Whenever a person learns anything we always find that he begins with a crude and imperfect synthesis, and passes by complex and fluctuating processes of analysis to a progressively better and better synthesis. We see this when we watch a little child learning to talk. He does not begin with the logical phonetic or grammatical elements of the language. He begins with crude total efforts to make language sounds. Little by little he comes to discriminate sounds and words more and more sharply, and comes to know the subtle feel of various types of vocal movement. Here we see the process of analysis, the process of attention to the component elements of the synthesis. Through this analysis there emerges a better and better synthesis, a better and better total language response. We see the same thing in learning any game, such as golf. The first step is not detailed drill on the component elements of the swing; it is the actual making of a crude and awkward swing; it is a synthesis. Progress depends on taking our synthetic, total effort to pieces, as it were, improving it here a little and there a little, and organizing the improvements back into the total response. So again we see that learning is not a matter of adding habit to habit, but of organization and progressive transformation. Anyone who has had the privilege of watching a painter at work has a fine and instructive example of the nature of human learning. First we see the picture dimly and vaguely indicated. Next the artist concentrates here on one detail, there on another. Little by little, through this piecemeal process, the total effect builds up. This is exactly what happens in all learning. Here we have a conception full of meaning and practical value for music education. Let us work out and apply it in detail.

1. The proper starting point for all learning is a meaningful, synthetic experience. Two points should here be noted. (*a*) This does not mean beginning with "trial and error." Trial and error is a mechanistic concept derived from observing the antics of unfortunate animals placed in problem boxes. This we wish particularly to avoid. The pupil should not be merely thrown on his own resources. He should be given a sense of a meaningful problem from the very first. For instance, there is no reason in the world why the teacher should not deliberately help the pupil a great deal in learning a rote song or in mastering a little instrumental piece. What we want is not mere action from the pupil. He does not learn just by doing. He learns by vision. We want to start him off by giving him a vision of his task. (*b*) Our claim does mean that we should cut down pre-drill to an absolute minimum. Some teachers begin a new song by drilling on its difficulties with the idea of avoiding prospective mistakes, and so avoiding "practice in error." We have seen the fallacy in this. Sometimes, as in certain approaches to instrumental music, a little pre-drill and pre-analysis cannot be avoided. But we should always question it, and reduce it to a minimum. Its function is not to avoid forming "bad habits," but to give the pupil a meaningful synthetic experience at the earliest possible moment.

In general our claim that we must begin with synthetic experience means that *learning naturally starts with the learner's recognition of the presence of a meaningful, interesting problem*. Examples here are more illuminating than much exposition, and we will now try to supply them.

(*a*) *Learning the rote song*. The proper beginning is to give the pupil a conception of the song as an aesthetically meaningful whole. This may be done by the teacher singing the song through and entering into some discussion of its meaning and appeal with the class. This at once sets up a project for the pupils, and all the rest of the learning consists in realizing this project. The opposite approach would be by drill first on some of its rhythmic and melodic constituents, its meter, or the more difficult intervals that it contains, and similar intellectual and technical considerations. Here we see contrasted the idea of learning as habit building, and as creation through a process of synthesis-analysis-synthesis. (*b*) *Learning to play an instrument.* Here the vital thing is to begin with actual music making on the instrument. A great many instrumental "methods" are open to the criticism of being mechanical and aiming at habit building. The material given the beginner cannot possibly constitute a meaningful aesthetic project, for it is obviously designed to bring out technical problems. Perhaps the ideal instrumental method has not yet been perfected. In any case what we want is to start the pupil off with a vision of the instrument as a means of music making and musical pleasure and self-expression. (*c*) *Learning to read the score.* The synthetic approach here means helping the pupil from the very first to see the score as a picturization of significant and interesting musical ideas. But the mechanistic approach through habit building is very often found. The score is taught with primary emphasis on lines and spaces, clefs, key signatures, bar lines, note lengths, and in general on musical grammar rather than on meaning. Such procedures are defended by saying that the child must form the proper habits from the start. This is entirely contrary to the modern conception of learning, which insists that the child must perceive functional meanings from the start. (*d*) *Learning to listen intelligently to a composition.* Here we come upon a very interesting and instructive qualification of our doctrine. Beginning with synthesis does not necessarily mean making a class listen to a whole new composition as the first step of the listening lesson. Very often this cannot possibly be done without hopelessly losing attention. Here would be a very stupid literalistic interpretation of our contention, which would really destroy its meaning and value. Remember that what is wanted is to give the pupil the sense of a project, to create an appetite. An appetite for a meal will be created much better by a menu card than by samples from each of the courses. Perhaps in music we may use a few samples. Perhaps we may play parts of the composition, not for separate study as yet, but to indicate its spirit and interest. On the basis of this experience we may enter into a discussion of the music to be enjoyed. In this way we set the stage by creating the sense of a synthetic, total, meaningful undertaking. This is analogous to the teacher's first presentation of a beautiful rote song, when he creates the tonal beauty which awakens interest and musical desire in the child.

2. The next phase of a properly directed learning process is the singling out of critical elements of the synthesis for study. This is the analytic phase. It differs from what we shall frequently refer to as "formal drill" in the following respect. Formal drill on a technical or notational problem in music means working on such a problem entirely for its own sake, in isolation from any musical application or aesthetic meaning. The analytic phase of learning means the selection of some aspect of an actual musical undertaking for specific and directed study. This procedure occurs when a new problem, reviewed in a familiar song, is discovered, named, isolated, drilled upon, and then applied in new contexts,—synthesis, analysis, synthesis. Always the critical point is the learner's consciousness of a vital connection between the special prob-

lem and the actual making of music. Thus a child who is set to practicing scales is being put through formal drill, because he just learns scales. But a *virtuoso* who practices scales, is not drilling in our sense of the word, because he is consciously attacking one of the problems of music making. Or again, vocalizes in the first grade would be pure formal drill. But with a senior high school glee club they may be felt and apprehended as directly contributory to producing a desired musical result,—as one element in the analysis of a total synthetic experience. Thus there is nothing mechanical or formal in our conception of analysis. There are no external signs by which the teacher can tell when it is proceeding properly and when it is becoming dissociated from musical experience. Everything depends on the pupil. Instead of speaking of this phase of learning as drill, therefore, we shall speak of it as the *study phase* of learning.

Here again a few illustrations may help. In the rote song, the study phase may concentrate on such elements as rhythmic pattern, phrase structure, tonality relationships, vocalization, and the like. All these are present vaguely in the earlier synthesis. Any of them may be made focal. An improvement in any or all will result in a better synthesis, *i.e.,* a better grasp of the song. In teaching the score, we begin with a vague total notion of the picturization of music. From this point we can go ahead and little by little analyze all sorts of detail,—clef, key signature, time signature, bar lines, note lengths, and so forth. As the pupil focalizes upon these in some organized order, he builds up once more to a better synthesis, a clearer and more definite apprehension of the score as a picturization of the sound, as he successively apprehends new problems and masters them in new contexts. Further applications are so obvious that they need hardly be elaborated. The analytic or study phase of learning is remarkably like what happens when we put a photographic plate into a developing solution. First one detail and then another emerges, and at last all of them fuse into a perfectly articulate, meaningful picture.

There is one general principle which should be laid down here before we go on. *The study phase of learning must always be directly related to the preliminary and to the final synthesis.* That is, the pupil must not merely concentrate on detail. He must realize, while he works at the detail, that the synthetic picture is clearing up. This is why it would be contrary to our view of learning to present a rote song as an aesthetic project, and then instantly turn to a drill on the note names involved, or to present an instrumental melody effectively and then do nothing but study the finger techniques it involved. In such cases we have a concentration on detail, but we do not have an analysis of the synthetic picture. The attention is switched entirely towards the note names or the finger movements, and away from a better grasp upon the composition and its meaning. Such a criticism may certainly be directed against the abrupt introduction of drill work on the score in the second grade, thrown in as a new problem instead of as an agency which the child can instantly feel as valuable in helping him to sing better and enjoy more completely.

3. The next phase in learning is the final constitution of a better synthesis. It is this at which the learner has been encouraged to aim from the first, and it should be the definite culmination of the study phase of learning. One of the most valuable, and indeed essential, elements in properly directed learning is the sense of specific achievement. It is not enough for *the result-minded teacher* to feel that every day the class is getting better and better. It is not even enough for *the*

*teacher* to prove this to his own satisfaction by the application of some test or other criterion. What is required is that *the pupil himself* shall recognize that he has made progress; that he is now able to do something he could not do before. Of course it is perfectly true that the sort of synthesis achievable by children will not be finally satisfactory. They will certainly not learn to sing a song or play a composition to a high standard of artistic excellence. But after all, the greatest *virtuosi* are not usually quite satisfied with their own achievement. What is important is that the learner shall feel himself to have started somewhere and to have arrived somewhere. The bad thing is study leading nowhere, a process of "habit building" that just meanders on and on pointlessly so far as the learner is concerned. For this reason *it is always desirable to push every learning undertaking to a definite achievement level as high as the pupil's age and capacity will permit.*

Certain types of work in school music are open to the criticism that they never push through to a final synthesis, and so fail to give the pupil a clinching sense of achievement and mastery. For instance, some teachers "put their pupils through" a long series of songs of equal grade of difficulty and often of quite indifferent value, with the idea of building sight-reading habits. So we are back once more to the days before the flood, and again recognize our old friend the mechanical theory of learning. The answer is that we do not develop power and mastery in any such way as this. Improvement is brought about by adopting definite undertakings involving problematic elements, analyzing these elements, and working through to a definite level of achievement. What educates the child musically is not so much the number of songs he has "read" through as the excellence with which he has performed them. Once we give up the idea of learning as a mechanical adding of habit to habit, and adopt the view that it is a process of creative growth, there is simply no reason or excuse for neglecting to bring about a final synthesis, and insisting upon a relatively finished product.

4. Our view of learning involves a very serious reconsideration of the famous dogma that one should always move from the simple to the complex and from the known to the unknown. As a matter of fact, in all the vast research literature on learning there is really no authentic proof of the validity of this claim. Indeed, at least one important study—that by Hull listed at the close of the present chapter—indicates that it is far from absolutely true. It certainly has a close affinity with the mechanical theory of learning, and looks a great deal more like the dictum of a mechanistic pedagogue than a proper part of the creed of a creatively-minded teacher and guide of youth.

Obviously we must not overwhelm the child with new and complex experiences which far transcend his powers. To do this is simply to produce bafflement and to prevent all learning because effort and hope both fail. But we must always remember that the mind grows through real experiences, not through a pretty, logical sequence from simple to complex. Also we must remember that the better the teacher, the higher the type of material he can handle. Suppose we have a song which is appropriate for children, beautiful and appealing, but which might be considered too difficult from several angles. Suppose we have every reason to believe that the class would love it, and love trying to sing it. Shall we deprive them of this experience simply because we remember that we ought to go always from simple to complex? Certainly not. Let us set it up for them and help them through its tonal, rhythmic, and interpretive intricacies. It will make a real demand upon the teacher, and be for him a true test and challenge. Moreover, the pupils may not achieve anything like final perfection. They may gain a somewhat sobering sense of their own limitations. But they will have made a real educational advance, because they have acted in terms of a real desire and a real ambition. Far from believing that everything ought to be simplified to the limit, and that difficulties ought to be introduced only in the most imperceptible of homeopathic doses, our conception of learning indicates that the mind grows and power increases through tussles with real, intriguing problems which seem worth while.

In practice, uncritical worship of the entirely unproved simple-to-complex, known-to-unknown dogma has two unfortunate consequences. (*a*) It involves the over-organization of educational content. When school music materials are organized with this idea primarily in mind, the tendency is always to make them so exceedingly simple that they lose all musical interest. When this happens, they also lose all educational value. (*b*) It involves the idea that the teacher may start the pupils off, but that he must never help them through. Of course this depends also upon the notion that learning is brought about by doing, whereas we hold that it is brought about by interest and will. Obviously we need very simple material if the class is to have no help from the teacher in singing a song. The "hands-off" policy, pure and simple, is impossible if we propose to introduce much interesting material that is unavoidably somewhat difficult. Our whole view is that the pupil does not learn through his *unaided* effort, but through his *interested* effort. If the pupils have zeal and a real desire to achieve an intriguing goal, temporary help from the teacher will not spoil the educative process in any way.

5. Lastly, a word should be said about the relationship of our conception of learning to instinct. It used to be the fashion to urge teachers to build all their work upon the

natural instincts of the pupil. But there are now very few psychologists who would hold that human beings are endowed with a definite set of clear-cut, instinctive drives. The advice to build teaching on instinct has broadened into the principle that we should deal with children in the light of what child study has revealed about their emotional, mental, and physical characteristics.

Thus we cannot say that the school music teacher should seek to capitalize human instincts as definite drives in certain directions. Our position is that human tendencies are not given by nature, but created by learning. All learning worth the name is a process of discovering and releasing what is natural to man. *When a great artist sings or plays we are not dealing with an artificial stunt. We are not dealing with a sort of trick produced by training. We are face to face with a supreme release and a supreme manifestation of human nature.* When a class learns to sing a song with beautiful tone and a fine sense of nuance and values, we have something altogether different from the performance of a pack of trained animals. What has been achieved is the natural utterance of musical ideas. Hence, instead of thinking that learning must be driven from behind by natural instinctive tendencies, we should regard it as a release, an achievement of what is proper to human nature.

## The Learner's Attitude

The next thing brought to light by the research on learning, is the attitude of the learner. This has been demonstrated to possess enormous importance.

1. **Participant and spectator attitudes.** Miss Heidbreder, in her study on rational learning, has brought out a very interesting and important distinction between participant and

spectator attitudes in learning. Let us explain these ideas, and see how they apply to our problems.

(*a*) Let us begin with participant attitudes. Miss Heidbreder found that in the learning process she investigated, attitudes of this kind were regularly present. Their essential mark is that of a definite, positive attack on a problem, with a desire "to do something about it." This is typical of the successful learner. The analysis of this kind of attitude is then carried further along two lines. First, it means a healthy attitude towards partial failure. A learner with a strong and positive participant attitude will tend to meet a temporary failure with a shift of method, or an effort to find the causes of lack of success. Here we see once again that mistakes in musical learning do not matter so long as the learner has the proper orientation. While this is preserved, the tendency will be to transform the whole approach in order to get rid of the failure or mistake. So we would say that in order to deal with mistakes the thing to do is to work for a positive and hopeful attacking attitude. Secondly, Miss Heidbreder finds that the participant attitude leads to the capitalization of success. Success is ardently desired, and when it comes it is recognized and repeated.

The creation and maintenance of participant attitudes is thus of very great importance in musical learning. When a new song is to be undertaken, everything should be done to avoid making it a mere routine affair. The stage should be set to give the class a sense of a worth while and engrossing undertaking. The spirit should be that it is a privilege and a joy to learn to sing a beautiful, interesting, and expressive piece of music. When a listening lesson is being undertaken, again, mere routine should be avoided at all costs. The teacher should use every possible device to give the sense of a deeply enjoyable experience that is to be had, to arouse keenness and interest in the study phase of the learning, and to reach a point where the class can listen to the whole composition with real pleasure and effective concentration. Again, a rhythm play should be no mere lackadaisical running off of conventional evolutions. The children should be encouraged to try to catch the spirit of the music, and to express this in spontaneous and yet well-timed movement. So we might continue, but the point is clear. *Every piece of musical learning should be presented to and undertaken by the class as an appealing project.* The evidence showing how important this is, is overwhelming. Without it learning will simply not take place, no matter how much rote, mechanical repetition we may have.

(*b*) Now as to the spectator attitude. This is found in those learners who are just "going through the motions." Nearly always it is a poor attitude. Yet Miss Heidbreder finds that it has its occasional uses. It sometimes happens that a passive, nonchalant attitude, temporarily assumed, will lead to the discovery of new and better methods of attack. This may take place after a hard try which has failed. Then one relaxes for a moment, and quite unexpectedly success arrives. One of the very great dangers which the studies reveal in much of the most zealous learning is conservatism of method and attack. Sometimes the learner will try again and again, only to fail, and even though the teacher shows him that his procedure is hopeless, and points out a better way with great care, yet he almost instantly slips back into the old groove, and continues battering his head against the same place on the wall. It sometimes happens that relaxation of tensions, and the temporary adoption of a mere routine attitude will bring about the shift we want. Once more we must remember that learning is creation, and that difficulties and errors are overcome by organizing around and beyond them. Anything which can help to bring about a transformation of the response system to a higher level is all gain.

2. **The will to learn.** Another of the ideas regarding attitude in learning brought out by the research studies is that of the "will to learn." This happy and suggestive phrase was coined by Book and Norvell, but the notion itself was brought out in one of the earliest and best of all the learning studies —one from which much can still be derived—the work of Bryan and Harter on acquiring the telegraphic language. The statement emerges from these and other studies that "it is intense effort that educates." In other words, learning depends on directed will and is impossible without it.

Here again we see the essential importance of making every piece of learning towards which the class is directed, in spirit a true project. That is, we should always set up the sense of a well-defined, appealing task. Otherwise learning will not take place, unless indeed some pupils guide themselves better than we teach them, and create this sense of task or project on their own account.

It would no doubt be instructive to work out various illustrations of techniques for arousing the will to learn in various situations in music education. But we think it better to try to show the teacher just why it is supposed to be so important. What happens in the actual details of the learning when the will to learn is effectively present? The research results render possible a very definite and practically suggestive reply. (*a*) The will to learn, aroused at the outset, sharpens up the whole analytic or study phase of learning. Suppose we have a class which urgently wants to learn a song. This desire operates to make them follow keenly every suggestion we give them leading to improvement. It is relatively easy to get them to attend to tone quality, to the phrase units, to the melodic curve, to the rhythmic pattern, and to the indications for nuance. This whole study phase functions far more thoroughly and efficiently than if they have the attitude that here is just another song. (*b*) The will to learn tends to produce annoyance with failure. If the pupil really does not much care whether he ever gets the song right, he will not be greatly worried when he gets parts of it wrong. Now it is far better to have a situation where the pupil is annoyed at the mistakes he makes,—and at those made by others—than to correct errors made by apathetic learners. Such then are the concrete results of a strong will to learn.

In connection with the idea of the will to learn, Book and Norvell, and Bryan and Harter have also taken up the very interesting question of why learners fail to learn. The following cases of failure and breakdown are brought out, all of which deserve the thoughtful attention of the school music teacher. (*a*) Learners fail to learn because they feel that the task before them is not worth while. *Thus we are reminded that the vital thing in music education is not to work out a carefully graded scheme of habit building, but to create musically worth while situations in which the pupils can actively participate.* (*b*) Learners fail because of "quasi-desire." It is only half the battle when we have brought a pupil to the point of vaguely liking a piece of music we wish him to understand or become able to sing or play. What we need is an aggressive, positive attitude, a definite desire for mastery. (*c*) Learners fail because of badly directed analysis, and concentration upon the wrong problematic elements. Here is one of the chief responsibilities of the teacher, and it is at this place that expertness is most essential. For instance, if we begin a new song with an effective, positive attitude in the class, and then pass on to a study phase constituted of an elaborate consideration of the vocal technique involved, of its harmonic structure, or a note-wise rather than a phrase-wise approach, the task of really learning to sing the song well may be made so gratuitously difficult as to be beyond the reach of all but the most talented pupils, with the result that our original excellent impulse is dissipated.

In all this we are coming to see more and more impressively the importance of dynamic elements in learning, and also to enrich our insight into the claim that learning depends on intelligence and will, rather than on mechanical habit building. To avoid a possible misunderstanding we should perhaps point out that the will to learn is something much more than a mere general mood. Always it must take the form of sentiments such as these: "Let us do *this:* Let us sing *this:* Let us enjoy *this:* Let us achieve *this:* Let us master *this.*" It is always a specific attitude of attack upon a specific project.

### Blockages and Spurts in Learning

Just as a child does not grow physically at an absolutely even rate month by month and year by year, so learning, which in itself is a process of living growth, shows periods when no advance is made, periods when there may be an actual retrogression, and conversely, periods when advance is exceedingly rapid. When a piece of learning is graphically represented by a learning curve, these periods take the form of what are known as plateaus, retrogressions, and spurts. We have already made some reference to these phenomena in discussing the will to learn, and have insisted that they must be explained in dynamic terms. But they have attracted so much attention from psychologists, and a knowledge of their conditions and meaning is so valuable for the music teacher, that a separate and longer treatment is indicated.

1. Blockages in learning, which show up as plateaus in the learning curve, may arise from inadequate earlier learning. The study by Bryan and Harter, to which reference has already been made, is the chief source of information on this point. They found that persons learning to send and receive the Morse Code on a telegraph instrument always show long periods of practice in which no progress takes place either in speed or in accuracy. The explanation they gave was substantially as follows: A beginner at telegraphy will find it necessary first of all to think about each separate letter in each word. For a little time his facility will increase, but soon he will reach a level which persists in spite of practice. If he continues, however, he reaches a stage where the letters are so automatic that he finds it possible to attend to the words themselves as units; and with this there comes a sudden increase of skill. Again there is a prolonged plateau, but at last words themselves come to be so very familiar that he is able to work in terms of phrase units of increasing length; and once more a marked progress is made. Their inference was that the aspiring telegrapher must wait and work for the "mechanization of the lower order habits," and that if he tries to push on too soon without proper foundations, he will defeat himself.

While we do not accept the general theory of learning which dominated the phraseology of these investigators, and so would put their claim in somewhat different words, their general result stands unchallenged.[1] As a process of learning

[1] It should be observed that Bryan and Harter's findings were made in connection with telegraphy, a very special skill, and that the prolonged mechanization of the lower order habits which they recommended has not been shown to be essential in certain other types of learning. For instance, some authorities would question it in the case of typewriting.

goes on, the skill transforms itself, and the controls become more efficient and more economical. It is just at these moments of transformation that we may look for a rapid advance. Before they come, we may find the learner on a plateau. If we neglect fundamentals and push on too fast, we may defeat our own ends.

What Bryan and Harter's results imply for music education seems to be this: Many troubles and much delay and even frustration in musical learning may be avoided simply by seeing to it that a genuine synthesis is achieved at all points. That is, it is exceedingly important that the learner always do as well as he can at whatever level he is working. This is one of the best guarantees against disappointment later on. *What the learner does, he should do well.* Synthesis is then continuous, and the learner will not long remain on a "plateau." In other words, he should not scamp a job, and then hurry on. This is a further reason for bringing every song sung and every piece learned to as high a level of artistic finish as the capacity and age of the pupil will allow.

2. Another great cause of blockages in learning is loss of interest and will. This is particularly apt to occur in the middle of learning—during the study phase—when the initial impulse has been lost and final success is not yet in sight. The teacher can do a great deal to avoid plateaus due to this cause, by skilled motivation, a matter which will be discussed at some length in the following chapter. Incidentally, we are reminded of a very valuable principle for the proper management of learning. *All learning should proceed in terms of objectives limited to the range of the pupil's vision and desire.* If we are dealing with mature people, we may have very remote objectives. For instance, one very distinguished musician now before the public changed from the violin to the piano comparatively late in life. For him it was

possible to set up the aim of facility with the new instrument, and work consciously and powerfully towards it over a period of several years. But for the child this is not possible. We must set up aims which can be achieved in relatively short order. *This is why facility with reading or mastery of a technique cannot function as aims for learning in the child's mental life.* This does not for a moment mean that he cannot move towards an acquisition of these things, but only that he cannot set them up as long-distance, motivating goals. As we shall see later on, they are to be learned *incidentally.* The immediate conscious aim of the elementary music pupil must be to sing a particular song, to play a particular piece, or to enjoy a particular composition, analytically attacking and solving only the problems that will directly contribute to the desired result.

3. Another cause of plateaus is wrongly directed analysis. For this the teacher is usually definitely responsible. We know that a child may study music for years, and get practically nowhere. This is due almost wholly to stupid teaching, and more specifically to stupid analysis in learning. A study phase in learning is always bad when it is carried on in isolation from meaningful and interesting synthesis. For instance, we have bad and stupid music study when the child is forced to deal with notes and note names, with the make-up of the staff and its notation, with musical theory, or with executant technique apart from immediate musical meanings and achievements. It is precisely work of this kind that is responsible for many failures to make progress.

4. Another cause of plateaus—and even of regressions in learning, is over-forcing. This is brought out in the work of Snoddy, one of the most significant of the more modern studies on learning. Snoddy had his subjects trace with a

stylus a six point star which they could only see reflected in a mirror. He found that if the learner in the earlier phases of his work pushed for speed, he never made any progress at all. His reason is so interesting that we may state it briefly here. He considered that in learning to trace the star, a response pattern was being created. If the learner was pushed and tried to make speed, so that he was tense and agitated, this pattern never crystallized, and the fruits of effort were never reaped.

There are many instances of over-forcing in music education. For instance, if we assign music that is hopelessly difficult, and do not give a great deal of help, or if we demand an impossible standard of achievement, it is apt to take place. Improper vocal demands are a common source of over-strain; for instance, excessive pitch or intensity demands from young children, or the arbitrary classification of boys whose voices are in transition as belonging to one definite part in the ensemble. Again, in instrumental work, we find that a premature insistence on speed, or in some wind instruments on extreme range, is open to this criticism. In general, a learning situation ought to be genuinely problematic, but as soon as it leads to an attack in terms of desperate straining for effect or achievement, it becomes of negative educational value.

5. Lastly, let us discuss the converse of all this, and see how the sudden advances which are so characteristic of much learning take place. On this point Book gives the following advice. Choose a day when the pupil is working well at his ordinary level. Start him off and let him become well "warmed up." Then push very hard for a higher level of achievement. The spurt usually takes place due to the sudden extra push when the skill is already working fluently and well.

By way of showing the bearings of this idea, let us apply it to two concrete cases. Suppose we have a monotone of the second class discussed in the preceding chapter,—that is, one whose trouble is defective attention to the factor of pitch. We would carry him along for part of the period with the class, perhaps making a special effort to rouse his general interest, and would watch carefully to see if he were trying to participate. We would select, if possible, a moment when he seemed to be particularly "in the vein," and choose this for a little individualized attention. Our aim then would be to secure a supreme instant of concentration on the pitch factor, and we would use any one of the devices previously discussed, or perhaps some other, to achieve our end. We would not continue until his attention flagged, but work urgently for some sort of immediate, definitive success. In other words, we would try at a favorable moment for a radical transformation of his musical-mental skill to a higher level.

Another illustration would be what often happens in school classes when work begins for an important and exciting public appearance, such as a music festival. Class ability to read and sing has already reached a definite level. Then the new and interesting material is presented, with the special urge behind it, and often there is a very marked rise in capacity, so that the new work is very speedily mastered, and a permanent gain results.

To sum up the outcomes of this section, we see that the skilled teacher, familiar with psychological principles, can nearly always obviate serious plateaus and regressions in learning. Where they must occur, he can see to it that they are made the foundations of future progress. He can avoid trying for a premature advance which can only result in a rapid crumbling of the weak and inadequate structure. He can deliberately seek to set up the conditions for those rapid, definitive, and striking advances which are always so delightful to teachers and pupils alike.

### Standards

Another most impressive point brought out in the research literature of learning is the enormous importance of standards in producing high achievement. Thorndike in an eloquent passage has said that in many of our ordinary performances,—adding numbers, reading language, remembering names, and so forth—we commonly work very far below our maximum level of possibility, for the mere and simple reason that we are content with mediocrity. Book gives an instructive illustration along the same line. He tells of a world's champion typist who in 1906 wrote 82 words a minute, and said she believed that this would never be surpassed. Yet this same person later raised her own record successively to 87 and then to 95 words. And at the time he wrote, the record stood at 147 words a minute. One of the most necessary things for a teacher to believe is that human beings can always do better. Once the learner is content, once he ceases actively to try and begins merely to repeat, improvement stops. If we expect little, we shall achieve little. If we expect much, we shall achieve much. One of the most necessary words in education is "excelsior."

This is true precisely because learning is not mechanical. If improvement beyond the level of singing in the first grade were a mere matter of polishing and refining the vocal habits of the pupils in that grade, there would be a very definite limit to the process. But improvement is a matter of discovery, of finding new and better methods of control and attack. It consists essentially in transforming the skill into something different and more efficient. Permanent and final stoppages and plateaus are always evidence of misconceptions about the nature of learning working through into educational practice. The person who types 147 words per minute has not just refined the same habits that operated in typing 82 words per minute. The whole nature of the skill has become different and risen to a better level. This is the reason why we can never speak of an absolute upper limit for any complex skill, for always new methods may be found which will yield results previously thought impossible. *Musical learning, in a very real sense, consists in the discovery by the learner of the feasibility of new and better achievement.*

1. In order to be effective, standards in musical learning must be properly mediated to the pupil. (*a*) Standards cannot be made real to the pupil merely by words. It is not enough to tell the pupil to do better,—to produce better tone quality, to sing with better rhythm, or to be more accurate in pitch placement. The trouble here is that the words may stand for nothing in the pupil's experience, and so may be meaningless for him. (*b*) To be effective, standards must be actualized. That is, the child must have an actual instance of what is wanted. This may be done in many ways. For instance, the teacher may sing over the song or the phrase to show its possibilities in the way of nuance, rhythm, tone quality, and the like. Or the better pupils in the class may be used as agencies for standard setting, as is sometimes done by working out schemes of pupil teaching, where the abler children help out the weaker ones. Here is one argument against sectioning grade school groups in music work on the basis of ability, for it may mean that the weaker pupils lose the incentive of the presence of those who can most effectively set a high standard of work. Or again, the listening lesson may

be a means of revealing to the children what musical performance of high excellence really means and of giving them a contact with and concept of music beyond their ability to perform. (*c*) To be effective, standards must be brought closely into contact with the actual musical projects on which the children are at work. What they need is not so much general instances of fine singing, but rather the fine singing of the song on which they are working. (*d*) Mediating standards by words, *i.e.*, telling the class to sing with better tone, improved placement, etc., is quite proper if done on the basis of sufficient actual concrete experience so that the meaning of the words is perfectly evident. But even so, there is constant need for examples of work of superior quality. *In general our aim must be by a combination of example and precept to lead the child to see the possibilities latent in his own performance.*

2. One of the most characteristic and necessary methods of setting up and using standards in all education is to work for perfection. For instance, in a course in English composition, the value of writing many mediocre themes is far outweighed by that of writing a few really good ones. Thus, once again, we return to our claim that the songs children learn in the grades, and the compositions they have in instrumental work should always be carried as far as possible along the road of perfection and artistic finish. Only in this way does the full force and meaning of a standard become apparent to a person. This at once implies three things about procedure in music education. (*a*) It is necessary to have song material and instrumental material with enough musical value to bear careful work. Futile and trumpery compositions, written to give practice in reading or in technique, will not yield the result we want, because the natural impulsion to perfect such things

is necessarily lacking. (*b*) When a new song or a new piece is learned, it should be pushed to the standard of an effective musical achievement, and then dropped for the time being though, as we shall insist, the pupils should return to it later. Working for perfection does not mean everlasting lingering on a single song or a single composition. (*c*) An essential part of a well planned sequence of work in music education should be *creative reviewing*. This is directly implied by the previous point. We should return now and then to work already learned with the purpose of seeing more in it and getting more out of it. When pupils find that they can now take a song learned some time ago and sing it more easily, more expressively, and with more enjoyment to themselves, they effectively recognize the fact of their own advance. Only in this way can we get all the educational nourishment out of fine song material.

To sum up this whole idea, each song should be carried as far as possible towards artistic perfection both for its own sake, and because this is the only means of capitalizing it for musical improvement. *Every song and every piece the children undertake should be at once a goal and a stepping stone.*

3. The last thing to say about standards is that they are never truly effective until they have been made internal. The imposition of standards really means the effort to make the pupil constructively critical of his own efforts. Thus we should definitely encourage initiative in all matters connected with musical performance. For instance, as a song is being developed, the class may be asked to make suggestions about how it should be sung, and to pick out the various analytic points such as expression, rhythm, phrase structure, and the like, on which its effectiveness depends. Or criticisms of the class effort may be invited and encouraged. The use of the

toy orchestra in the primary grades, where the children themselves decide how to orchestrate a composition, is a case in point.

## Incidental Learning

It is very important to understand that while all learning follows the general rhythm of synthesis-analysis-synthesis, it is not always a fully conscious or completely explicit process. A great deal of learning may be treated incidentally. Kirkpatrick performed a very interesting experiment on this point. He had two groups learn to multiply, using a special multiplication table consisting of large numbers. One group memorized the table, while the other simply used it from the start, with no effort to learn it by heart. It was found that the second method yielded the best results in the matter of increasing skill. He says, "The results indicate that in many lines of teaching there has been a tremendous waste of time, energy, and interest in first memorizing, then later practicing the use of what has been learned." And again, ". . . there can be no doubt that there is no need to have children *memorize* any tables." Incidental learning is largely involved in the direct method of teaching foreign language (*i.e.,* teaching the language by its actual use rather than through a grammatical approach), and in various modern systems for teaching the reading of English. There is no doubt that it can be used in music education. And also there is no doubt that if we are to have a dynamic, creative scheme of music education, it *must* be used.

There are two chief places in music education where incidental learning is indicated. One is the acquisition of mastery of the score, and the other is technique. Let us try to make quite clear just what this means. (*a*) It means that we never set up the notation or technique as definite, isolated, unitary study problems, to be attacked directly. For instance, some music teachers begin calling attention to note names, lines and spaces, note symbols, clefs, sharps and flats, and all the rest of it, quite early in the grades, and build up a knowledge of the score as a learning unit. In school music we rarely find such processes as this directed towards vocal technique, though some tendencies along such lines may appear. Such procedures as those described above are wrong. Notation and technique should be handled incidentally. (*b*) We set up a series of musical projects, consisting of songs to be sung, compositions to be played, and perhaps music created by the pupil around some interesting idea. In carrying through these projects, the pupil finds it necessary to use the score in various ways. That is, the score enters into the analytic or study phase of his learning when he learns the new song, etc. Here we give him just enough explanation to enable him to use the score as a tool for bringing about a desired musical result. The kind of explanation to be given will be discussed in the chapter dealing with the mastery of the score. Here we may say that we do not tell him the note names, or go into the minutiae of the symbolism, but begin with the actual picturization of the phrases. *Thus the pupil builds up his mastery of the score not by directly learning it, but by using it in actual musical situations.* (*c*) But it will be said that we cannot expect the pupil to achieve mastery of the score unless we specifically call his attention to its details,—to the five lines and the four spaces, and all the rest of it—and unless we make sure that he "knows" them. The reply is all contained in Kirkpatrick's findings. *Working mastery can be achieved without memorizing and without direct attack.*

It is profoundly regrettable that some school music teachers still put the cart before the horse in this connection by making the song incidental to reading and technique. The pupils are put through a mass of song material of indifferent quality, without anything being carried to a high standard of artistic excellence, in order to give practice in reading. Besides the objections we have already mentioned, the following criticisms are in order here. (*a*) This is not the best way of securing functional mastery. We may build up a good theoretical, intellectual, problem knowledge and grasp of the score, and yet fail to build power in reading. Such a theoretical problem mastery may and probably will measurably fail to transfer to actual musical situations, where the pupil has to use the score to produce musical results. This is the direct inference from Kirkpatrick's study, and it is borne out by the experience of language teachers who find that a knowledge of grammar by no means guarantees language mastery, and who therefore propose that grammar shall be made incidental to language use; and by the work in elementary reading, where the alphabet is handled incidentally with very beneficial results. *The score should be taught as an incident to music making, not as an end in itself.* (*b*) It involves a deflection of interest from music to a series of quasi-mathematical problems. Proponents of the direct teaching of the score are fond of insisting that children become keenly interested in working with the various problems involved in it, learning how to make up key signatures, how to handle note symbols, and all the rest of it. Doubtless this is quite true. Doubtless it would also be true that if in the music period we performed a striking chemical experiment, the class would be interested. But it would not be the kind of interest a music teacher ought to arouse. The presence of interest is not enough. *The whole problem is towards what that interest is directed. If it is not directed towards music itself, we have falsified our values in music education.* (*c*) It involves a precise inversion of the obvious demands of the situation. To use music to teach the score would be like using Shelley's "Skylark" to teach grammar. It would be substituting means for ends.

### The Management of Practice

Only a small part of the extensive work done on such topics as the distribution of practice, the length of practice periods, the interpolation of rest periods, and whole and part learning, is relevant to the problems of the school music teacher. But some conclusions seem important enough to warrant their mention here.

1. Prolonged practice is less effective than an equal amount of time divided into briefer periods. Just how long practice periods ought to be it is impossible to say. There is no general "best" length, for this varies with different kinds of learning, and for different learners. The younger the learner, the shorter the practice period ought to be. On the basis of the studies the following advice may perhaps be safely given. (*a*) A work or practice period should not be so short that the pupil has no chance to "warm up" and adjust himself to the task in hand. In the special case of intensive work with a monotone, or of a strenuous push for a higher adjustment, warming up is provided for before the brief vigorous effort is demanded. (*b*) A work or practice period should never continue to the point of lassitude and loss of interest. Under these conditions, learning stops and negative attitudes are set up. Thus it is often well to devote the music period not to a single type of activity, still less to a single song, but to draw upon a number of diversified activities. Each separate activity constitutes a separate practice unit.

2. Effective practice is impossible without zeal and interest. Learning does not depend on mere repetition, but on a directed will. Hence when we "lose the attention" of a class or an individual, we may be quite sure that learning itself has stopped.

3. The effectiveness of practice can be completely destroyed by over-strain. The aim of practice is to create a clear-cut, definite structure of response, and if the learner is under a heavy strain, this structure will never form at all, or will be deformed from its birth. In order to learn well, it is necessary to pay the most careful attention to the details of the learning. If the pupils are hurried or tense or make a distracting effort, this cannot be done. What we want in the learner is intentness coupled with ease. Here we come upon the celebrated question of fast and slow practice. We do not particularly advocate slow practice as such. *But we do advocate easy, thoughtful, attentive practice.* In a great many cases, and particularly in instrumental music, this cannot be other than slow. But it is not the slowness that helps the learning. It is the facile thoughtfulness, the keen attentiveness to getting the right "feel" of the skill. Certainly it would be very unintelligent to argue that because a passage must ultimately be played at a certain tempo, it ought to be practiced at that tempo as soon and as often as possible. The capacity to play fast, to go to extreme ranges, to modify dynamics with precision and effect,—all these things depend on having a well-consolidated and clearly defined response pattern, which is created only by thoughtful and attentive care. This in turn is not possible if we push for speed. If the response structure is forming, speed will take care of itself. If we destroy this creative process by working prematurely for speed, we only get crude scurrying without control.

### Musical Memory

The last topic we consider here is that of musical memory.

1. Memory in general is not a process of stamping in, but a creating of a response structure or pattern through analysis and synthesis. That this is so has been conclusively shown in many of the modern studies, among which we may particularly notice that of Gates on the importance of recitation in memorizing. Gates points out in effect that when we memorize some verbal material by going through it once or twice, then trying to recite it, then working over the weak parts, and so on, we are setting up what some psychologists would call a "trial and error" process, but what we would call a process of analysis leading to a final synthesis from an imperfect synthesis. Actually we nearly always do memorize in just such a way as this. We rarely repeat a poem or a prose passage again and again until we are perfectly sure we know it. We run over it a few times, and then try it out, and so on. In other words, we are not so much adding one bit to another as creating a structure, a totality. When we forget, we have no mere process of subtraction. Forgetting is not as simple as all that. Some parts of what we have learned stick with us in an uncanny fashion, others get distorted out of their original sense, and still others are almost completely lost. So what happens is that a structure disintegrates rather than that habits are lost.

The practical outcome of all this research is that we should never regard memory in general or musical memory in particular as a mechanical affair. Whenever we memorize we should proceed in terms of meaning and interest. We should make memorizing a definitive project. Moreover, memory properly treated has a very important place in progressive education. When we memorize a structure of any sort, whether of words or tones, we come to understand, grasp and feel it better than we can in any other way. This is true only if we memorize in terms of and for the sake of interest and comprehension. Memory so managed cannot be ignored in any scheme of education.

2. The most important work on musical memory proper is that of Kovácz and Juhácy. Kovácz in particular undertook to find out whether some of his presumably quite advanced pupils memorized music better by playing it through or by studying the score and imaging the music. He found the latter to be the preferable procedure. It is quite true that this will not directly transfer to music work in the schools. But his general conclusions are of decided value to us. He infers that musical memory depends primarily on a direct imaging and thinking of the music itself, *i.e.,* the tonal structure of the composition, and that remembering note names, or key transitions, or visualizing the score, or calling up the feel of the music on some instrument, are all adventitious aids and not the central thing. This leads to two practical considerations. (*a*) In order to memorize music well, we must analyze and study it well. The trouble with a great many pupils is that they never really hear the music in all its detail. It is this hearing and imaging of the music that is the true basis of musical memory. (*b*) Memorizing may be of real value in musical development, precisely because in order to memorize effectively we must listen carefully and attend accurately to the detail of the music. There is really no particular value in playing or singing from memory merely for its own sake. We believe that this holds true all up and down the line from the youngest child to the greatest artist. The fashion of playing and singing from memory has been elevated into a really preposterous fetish. But we repeat that memorizing has a real

value in music education. *The value of memorizing is that it is a first rate agency for getting the child to attend to the music.* This arises from the contention that musical memory depends first and foremost on musical grasp.

### Summary: Outcomes of This Chapter

1. We have insisted that learning is not a process of habit formation and that it does not depend on repetition. Repetition is necessary in a great deal of learning, but it is neither sufficient nor central. Fixed habits are unquestionably formed when one learns, but they are the incidents, not the essence, of the process.

2. For us learning is a process of growth, through which a living, flexible pattern of response is created. It proceeds by a combined, interweaving movement of analysis and synthesis. This view leads us to abandon the notion of a movement from the known to the unknown, or the simple to the complex, as characteristic of all properly directed learning, and also to feel unable to advise teachers to base all learning on instinctive drives.

3. Learning depends essentially on insight, interest, and will. This is seen in the primary importance of the learner's attitude, in the proper method of diagnosing and overcoming blockages in learning, in the almost magical effect of standards, and in the proper management of practice.

4. We have insisted that learning involves not so much the perfection of early habits as a transformation of the whole skill to a new and higher level. This is why we cannot set definite limits to possible achievement in any complex skill.

5. Educators should recognize clearly the possibility and the value of incidental learning. In order to build up a functional mastery of a complex symbolism or a set of relationships, it

is not by any means always necessary to use the direct approach and proceed in terms of explicit memorizing.

6. Memory itself, which is so often regarded as a mere routine affair, is seen to involve all the characteristics of creative learning, and thus to have a very necessary and valuable place in any scheme of progressive education.

7. Perhaps our widest and most important outcome is the idea that children learn music through musical projects. In any project we see the rhythm of synthesis-analysis-synthesis associated with a definite and directed will to learn. A musical project may be along the lines of listening to music, performing music, or creating music. All the musical-mental abilities classified under the heads of ear training, rhythmic mastery, and mastery of the score are developed in connection with musical projects along these three lines.

## Problems for Discussion.

1. Discuss some procedures in music education which seem based on the mechanical theory of learning.
2. Assemble and discuss some illustrations of improvement in musical capacities due to analysis leading to final synthesis.
3. Why does a child often fail to learn something in spite of many repetitions?
4. Suggest methods of arousing the will to learn *(a)* in connection with a rote song; *(b)* in connection with a study song *(i. e.,* where some special musical problem is being studied); *(c)* in a rhythm play; *(d)* in a listening lesson.
5. Have you ever noticed anything in your own experience or elsewhere that would indicate the value of spectator attitudes?
6. Make a list of some songs that might be considered somewhat too difficult for some given grade, but which you think it would be educationally valuable to teach to that grade because of their unusual appeal.
7. Discuss possible sources of over-strain *(a)* in vocal work; *(b)* in instrumental work.

8. Bring together from your experience instances of the abrupt improvement of a skill due to strategically-timed, intense effort.

9. Have you ever noticed yourself or your pupils moving on a "plateau" in musical learning? How would you diagnose this condition? How would you try to overcome it?

10. Suggest methods of encouraging self-criticism in children.

11. What reasons are there for and against having children memorize their songs and compositions? Would these reasons apply equally *(a)* to a glee club preparing for public performance; *(b)* to an individual pupil preparing for a recital or appearance?

12. Are there any important phases of musical development besides technique and reading which might well be handled incidentally?

BIBLIOGRAPHY.

1. BOOK, WILLIAM F., How to Develop an Interest in One's Tasks and Work, *Journal of Educational Psychology,* 1927, vol. 18, pp. 1-10.
2. BOOK, WILLIAM F., *The Psychology of Skill, with Special Reference to its Acquisition in Typewriting,* The Gregg Publishing Company, 1925.
3. BOOK, WILLIAM F., and NORVELL, LEE, The Will to Learn, *Pedagogical Seminary,* 1922, vol. 29, pp. 305-362.
4. BROWN, W., Whole and Part Methods of Learning, *Journal of Educational Psychology,* 1924, vol. 15, pp. 229-233.
5. BRYAN, W. L., and HARTER, NOBLE, Studies in the Acquisition of the Telegraphic Language, *Psychological Review,* 1897, vol. 4, pp. 27-53; 1899, vol. 6, pp. 345-375.
6. CASON, HULSEY, Criticisms of the Laws of Exercise and Effect, *Psychological Review,* 1924, vol. 31, pp. 397-417.
7. GATES, ARTHUR I., *Psychology for Students of Education,* The Macmillan Company, 1923, chs. 10, 11.
8. GATES, ARTHUR I., Recitation as a Factor in Memorizing, *Archives of Psychology,* 1917, No. 40.
9. HEIDBREDER, EDNA, An Experimental Study of Thinking, *Archives of Psychology,* 1924, No. 73.

10. HULL, CLARK L., Quantitative Aspects of the Evolution of Concepts, *Psychological Monographs,* 1920, vol. 28, No. 1, Whole No. 123.
11. JORDAN, A. M., *Educational Psychology,* Henry Holt and Company, 1928, chs. 3, 4, 6.
12. JUHÁCY, ANDOR, Zur Analyse des musikalischen Wiedererkennens, *Zeitschrift für Psychologie,* 1924, vol. 95, pp. 142-180.
13. KIRKPATRICK, E. A., An Experiment in Memorizing *vs.* Incidental Learning, *Journal of Educational Psychology,* 1914, vol. 5, pp. 405-412.
14. KOFFKA, KURT, *The Growth of the Mind,* Harcourt, Brace and Company, 1924.
15. KOVÁCZ, SANDOR, Über das Verhältniss der erkennenden und mitteilenden Gedächtnisse auf musikalischen Gebiet, *Archiv für die gesammte Psychologie,* 1917-18, vol. 37, pp. 283-299.
16. KOVÁCZ, SANDOR, Untersuchungen über das musikalische Gedächtnis, *Zeitschrift für angewandte Psychologie,* 1916, vol. 11, pp. 113-135.
17. MURSELL, JAMES L., *Principles of Musical Education,* The Macmillan Company, 1927, ch. 12.
18. OGDEN, R. M., *Psychology and Education,* Harcourt, Brace and Company, 1926, chs. 14, 15.
19. ORDAHL, L. E., Consciousness in Relation to Learning, *American Journal of Psychology,* 1911, vol. 22, pp. 158-213.
20. PETERSON, JOSEPH, Learning when Frequency and Recency Factors are Negative, *Journal of Experimental Psychology,* 1922, vol. 5, pp. 270-300.
21. PYLE, WILLIAM H., *The Psychology of Learning,* Revised Edition, Warwick and York, 1928.
22. RUGER, H. A., The Psychology of Efficiency, *Archives of Psychology,* 1910, No. 15.
23. SNODDY, GEORGE P., An Experimental Analysis of a Case of Trial and Error Learning in the Human Subject, *Psychological Monographs,* 1920, vol. 28, No. 2, Whole No. 124.
24. SNODDY, GEORGE P., Learning and Stability. A Psychophysi-

ological Analysis of a Case of Motor Learning with Clinical Applications, *Journal of Applied Psychology,* 1926, vol. 10, pp. 1-36.

25. Thorndike, E. L., *Educational Psychology, Vol. 2; The Psychology of Learning,* Teachers College, Columbia University, 1914.
26. Wheeler, Raymond H., *The Science of Psychology,* T. W. Crowell Company, 1929, chs. 10, 11, 12.

## Chapter Four

# The Teaching of Music in the Schools

### The Nature of Teaching

Teaching has been defined as the guidance of learning. This indeed is the only possible way to think about it intelligently and constructively. Thus what we have to say here follows on directly from the discussion in the previous chapter. Music teaching simply means creating and maintaining a situation where musical learning can take place properly.

Music teaching in the schools is a business which involves the coöperation of a great many different people who discharge diversified functions and duties. Much of the work has to be done by the grade teacher, so it is imperative that she have some musical training as part of her preparation, and absolutely necessary that the supervisor help her to a better understanding of the ideals and methods of music education. The attitude and interest of the building principal will greatly affect the classroom situation, so that the needs of the music program must be clearly and convincingly set before him. The superintendent will have much to do with determining budget appropriations and time schedules, and here once more a sympathetic understanding is highly important. The task of the supervisor or director is to work out a constructive program on solid principles, and to secure the coöperation required to make it effective. If there is a serious weakness at any one of these points, the musical interests of the pupils are directly threatened, and the whole teaching function is made weaker and less effective.

Two general points arise out of all this. (*a*) Music teaching in the schools is a coöperative venture. This involves the danger of divided responsibility. If things go wrong it is relatively easy to "pass the buck." But everyone interested in music education, and particularly the working supervisor, should see that though responsibility be divided, it nevertheless exists. A unitary task is to be performed. Learning is to be guided. The essential thing is to build up a working organization which will really take care of the situation. (*b*) Music teaching in the schools means a great deal more than the classroom contact between the teacher and the class. This of course is the essential focus. But no individual teacher can possibly cope with bad conditions in the school or the system as a whole. Everyone who has anything to do with the plan of music instruction must understand its purposes well enough to be able to do his or her share in making the whole scheme as effective as possible.

For these reasons it seems very desirable to approach the problem of teaching music from a broad viewpoint. *We have a favorable situation in music education when all the conditions favor the carrying on of the three kinds of musical projects—listening, performing, and creating—through which musical development takes place.* It is our task in this chapter to show what conditions must be met for this result.

## The Music Program as a Whole

Our first task in creating and maintaining good teaching conditions is to see to it that the music program as a whole is properly administered. To repeat, teaching means a great deal more than the immediate classroom contact. It means the creation of opportunities for real and effective musical experiences and projects. This makes it necessary for us to think in terms of the program as a whole. In this connection there are four points to be considered,—adequacy, correlation, grading, and materials.

1. **Adequacy.** We can hardly pretend to lay down in advance an adequate program of music work for any given school system. But it will be helpful to present and briefly discuss what is actually being done along these lines.

The following types of work and activity should be considered as having a place in any complete program of music education. (*a*) Singing, which is the core activity as far as the end of the sixth grade. We shall see later that this is much more than an administrative convenience. It is psychologically and educationally desirable, for almost all other types of musical activity have a natural basis in song. (*b*) Appreciation work in the grades, and in the junior and senior high school, leading naturally into the history of music. (*c*) Instrumental work beginning with the grades, and moving towards ensemble performance of artistic merit in the junior and senior high school. This should include both band and orchestra. Class instruction in instrumental music should be given in as many different fields as possible. (*d*) Toy orchestra work, primarily for the sake of ear training and appreciative discrimination, in the primary grades. (*e*) The making and playing of instruments, in the primary grades, as a creative project to arouse interest in music. (*f*) Definite encouragement of improvisation and original composition as soon as the children have a vocabulary of motives and figures to be recombined in new contexts. (*g*) Opportunities for activities of the type of eurythmics, *i.e.,* rhythm plays, rhythmic expression, folk dancing, or eurythmics proper, large bodily activity for the sake of rhythmic training being the thing desired. (*h*) Choral and glee club work in the junior and senior high school. In the seventh and eighth years in junior high school, chorus is often required, but this is rarely so in senior high school. (*i*) Courses in theory and harmony late in senior high school, developing directly out of the earlier work in singing, instrumental music, original composition, and ear training. (*j*) Recognition by the schools of individual instruction in music. Sometimes this is done by giving private lessons as part of the school program. Sometimes it is done by setting up music examinations for school credit. The accreditation of private teachers by the schools hardly seems necessary or desirable, as shown by results so far obtained.

All these factors in the program will be discussed much more fully later on. It will be noted that we have said nothing about ear training as a separate element in the program. This is because we believe that ear training should be carried on in every and any kind of work with music, so that it does not exist as a separate unit. The nearest approach to its separate consideration is the high school harmony course.

We do not say that every system ought to provide for all the activities here listed. But we do believe that if any are omitted, a good educational reason ought to exist. The problem of school credits and of college entrance requirements often makes it hard to put through an adequate program of music education. But these and other difficulties are things we must work to overcome in the interests of our subject and of the children themselves. We sometimes find systems where the program is hopelessly defective and inadequate due to the tendency of the supervisor or director to invest enormous amounts of the pupils' time in drill activities of the habit-building type. For instance, we may find a whole program for the grades aimed primarily at teaching reading. The quasi-mathematical problems which then must be set up are so difficult that they absorb a great deal of the time assigned to music, and all sorts of other activities, absolutely indispensable to proper musical development, have to be eliminated. To this we are wholly opposed on principle. We believe that in the light of what we know of the psychology of musical learning, *no program of school music can be considered adequate which fails to provide ample and varied opportunities for musical experience and for the carrying through of appealing musical projects.*

2. **Correlation.** A program of music education must be correlated in two senses. It must be internally homogeneous, and it must establish its natural contacts with other phases of school work.

(*a*) The internal correlation of the whole program of music education is a matter of great importance. If any musical activity exists in isolation from the rest, it is a sure sign of something wrong. It means that educational principles are being violated, that the teaching function is weakened, and that the pupil's musical development is imperiled. Let us indicate a few of the problems in this connection. First of all, appreciation must be integrated with all the rest of the work in music. It sometimes happens that the setting up of certain kinds of appreciation courses, and the rigid apportionment of time for appreciation lessons threatens good correlation. This leads some teachers into the fallacy of supposing that appreciation in music education belongs only to a certain kind of course or lesson. Such a viewpoint means that appreciation itself is not properly handled, and moreover, that other types of work lose educational value. If we think of musical development as arising out of musical projects within the fields of listening, performing, and creating, appreciation tends to disappear as a definite educational unit, and to merge with all the rest of the work. This is what we want. Appreciation always means much more than listening, and reciprocally, work in appreciation should transfuse and irrigate all musical projects in performance and creation. Secondly, the vocal and instrumental work needs to be fused into a close and effective unity. Often we find that the instrumental and vocal teachers have very different viewpoints and methods of attack. This means that there is something wrong with the vocal program, the instrumental program, or both. Vocal work is the natural foundation of instrumental work. Indeed, a creative approach to instrumental music is rendered very difficult, if not altogether impossible, without a functional basis of properly directed vocal experience. Thirdly, the work in theory and harmony should develop in natural sequence from the whole body of musical experience which the pupil has had before entering high school. High school harmony presented as a theoretical subject, pure and simple, has little value. The introduction of this subject into our secondary schools constitutes a great opportunity for making it what it ought to be but which it has not been in this country at any rate,—a summing up and systematizing of a living wealth of musical experience.

(*b*) In our second chapter we saw that music has natural affinities with a wide range of culture. This is our basic reason for insisting that the work in music should be intertwined with other fields of interest. The natural educational relatives of music are history, geography, art, science, and physical education. If effective contacts between these various subjects and music are established, they reciprocally vitalize one another. We do not of course mean that a highly formal scheme of correlation should be worked out, particularly in the grades. What is wanted is a music teacher of culture wide enough to see the relation of what he is doing to other fields, a classroom teacher sufficiently musical to perceive the relationship of other fields to music, and teaching material which lends itself directly to the making of these contacts. If we fail to secure correlation between music and other subjects, our music program is impoverished in itself, and will not yield its full value as an agency for developing the personality of the pupil.

3. **Grading.** Under our system of education it is almost essential to map out some sort of grade-by-grade program fairly definitely. The principle must be that of actual living experiences with music, and vital musical projects of steadily increasing scope and complexity, organized into a sequence which makes their administration possible. There are two general points to be considered here. (*a*) We should not make any particular grade sequence a fetish. There is no perfect fixed sequence of natural musical development. Moreover, we cannot gain aid and comfort from the dogma of moving from the simple to the complex and from the known to the unknown. All we can do is to mediate to the pupils genuine musical experiences, and to give them increasing opportunities for undertaking musical projects more or less within their capacity, in some orderly sequential manner which makes assimilation and success possible. (*b*) We should make provision for the exceptional child by special classes and special assignments, by electives, and by shifting from grade to grade. One of the great vices of our schools is the failure adequately to care for the very able child. To do this should be one of the express aims of the music program.

In this whole connection we suggest that a definite course of study in music should be drawn up. This is of value in regularizing the whole situation, and for purposes of publicity.

4. **Materials.** Here we have the question of the room, the musical equipment, and books. Many rooms which must be used for music work render certain parts of a complete program very difficult. For instance, with fixed seats, good rhythm activities are very seriously impeded. Most American classrooms are constructed obviously on the theory that education consists in sitting still and attending to teacher. But we need something different from this for ideal conditions in music education. As to music materials, instruments, and so forth, distinctive quality is a thing greatly to be desired. If children have no experience with superior instruments, it unquestionably affects their musical standards. With regard to books, this question is so important that it will be discussed later in a separate chapter.

All in all, then, the music program in the schools should be considered as a program of activity and opportunity. Its aim is to open the way for fruitful and interesting musical projects through which the musical development of the child may be brought about.

### The Creation of Favorable Attitudes in the Pupils

We now go on to discuss more specifically the classroom contact, and to see just what the teacher ought to attempt to do when dealing with the pupil directly instead of when programizing for him, or building up an administrative structure in his interests. The first thing we would say is that he should undertake to produce favorable attitudes in the class. We have seen the importance of attitude in learning. Every piece of learning should be directed as a specific project, and a definite will to learn should be aroused in connection with it. This is brought about by proper motivation, originating from the teacher. Let us see what sources of motive are available for the music teacher.

1. The first great source of motivation is the attitude of the teacher. A number of studies have been made, the most important of which are listed at the close of this chapter, showing that learning is favored most by attitudes of approval on the part of the instructor. That is to say, we want a positive tendency, a tendency to look for and appreciate good work, rather than a tendency to look for and blame poor work. Part of the art of teaching lies in taking this point of view without at the same time sacrificing standards, and relapsing into a totally uncritical geniality. When this tendency emerges, the value of a helpful attitude is eliminated, for then the pupils have no real idea whether they are doing well or badly, and the will to learn is lulled to sleep by indiscriminate praise. In general, we would suggest that the teacher should look for and appreciate effort and willingness rather than pay somewhat insincere compliments to a musical result which in and of itself may be rather mediocre.

2. Another source of motivation is the presence of a group. This affords a definite opportunity which ought to be recognized and capitalized to the limit. In some fields the class situation may be a little unnatural, and better work might result from an individual contact between teacher and pupil. But in music, group work and the group interest are perfectly natural. It is musical instruction wholly or largely limited to the private individual contact that is more or less unnatural. Music is an art which naturally expresses itself through group activities, and in music education we may confidently try to avail ourselves of group motivation.

A group is properly capitalized as a means of motivation

only when the following dynamic trends are utilized. (*a*) *The natural desire to conform.* It will often be quite a revelation to a child to find that other children with whom he is associated really enjoy listening to and making music. A musically interested and active group has a definite and most valuable impact upon the individual child. It is a primary and natural source of motivation in singing, in instrumental work, and in appreciation. Moreover, the presence of a group can often stimulate musical creation, for, when a child sees others working out musical ideas, he is moved to do likewise. (*b*) *The desire to excel.* It is perfectly natural for the child to wish to measure himself by others, and to do as well, comparatively, as he is able. For this reason the music group should be organized and seated in such a way that this tendency is recognized, without producing, however, unfortunate rivalry. The seating scheme often used of grouping the best singers at the back of the room has much to recommend it. It can hardly be criticized as an unnatural and artificial procedure, like that of a spelling bee, because it exists largely for a legitimate musical purpose,—that of making the class tone audible to the poorer singers. Also, it gives a certain recognition to merit, and this after all can hardly be open to much objection. (*c*) *The desire to coöperate.* If we can lead a child to feel that he is contributing something to the total effort of the group, we shall have set up a good positive motivation and built the will to learn on a natural and proper foundation. One such plan in music education is that of assigning certain pupils as teachers to help the weaker children during class singing. Sometimes, too, the problem of a monotone may be effectively attacked by having another child help him under the direction of the teacher. (*d*) *The desire for group approval.* There is no inherent reason why the wise and tactful teacher should not capitalize this motive, which again is a perfectly natural and proper one. The opportunity to show the class what he can do may turn out to be a very effective incentive to the individual, and may also have an appreciable effect on the whole group.

While dealing with this topic we should say that in music groups in school the children should be habituated from the first to individualized work, so that when called upon they can sing a phrase, express a rhythmic idea, or comment on music they have heard, in the presence of the group naturally and without embarrassment.

3. The third type of motivation is that which comes from a sense of increasing mastery. It has been conclusively shown that learners always do better if they have before them an objective record of their own progress, and the more specific and detailed this record, the greater its effect. In other types of school work this is one of the great arguments for frequent testing. In music, however, it is a good deal harder to apply the principle. Here we see the great danger of mere amiability on the part of the teacher. It is very important for her to take a positive and appreciative attitude, and to avoid scolding and fault finding. But it is quite equally important for her to remain effectively and wisely critical. There are in general two directions in which we can work in seeking to give children in school music a definite impression of their progress. The first is the use of what we have called "creative reviewing." One should return frequently to songs already learned, —a procedure which will at once give the class a sense of the progress they have made. (It may be remarked that this makes it essential to have songs worth returning to.) The second is the constant effective mediation of a high standard of performance by the teacher.

4. The last, and by far the most important type of motivation in music education, is that which is derived from the music itself. If we lack this, we most certainly shall not have good motivation. Davison, in his book on music education, has remarked that while music naturally expresses itself through group activities, the primary emphasis must be on the music rather than the sociability, if even this value is to accrue. What we should always aim at is to give the class the attitude of singing a song with a definite musical meaning and value, listening to a composition full of interest and beauty, or creating an expressive musical idea. *In other words, music teaching must be founded on the direct, intrinsic interest and appeal of the music itself.* Here once more we see how essential it is to use good music, irrespective of the fact that it may be somewhat difficult. Lack of interest condemns far more fatally and completely than lack of difficulty can recommend.

All these motives should be used in such a way that every new musical project is undertaken with an effective participant attitude, an effective will to learn, and also in such a way that each individual in the class feels an inspiration to attack the project.

### The Setting of Effective and Functioning Standards

This is the second great element in the work of the teacher in guiding learning. We have seen its psychological importance as a condition of effective learning. Now we may briefly consider it from the angle of the teacher who has the job of standard setting actually before him. Let us see what means for setting standards are available in school music.

1. A teacher may set standards by personal example and demonstration. In effect we may say that every music teacher

ought to be a personal embodiment, a personal revelation of the possibilities of music to the children. Part of his business in guiding learning, and a most essential part, is showing what it means to put through a musical project with finish and beauty. It is worth noticing that what is involved is not imitation. In psychology the idea of an instinct to imitate has been quite definitely exploded. No such general tendency exists at all in human beings. This should be obvious enough to the most superficial observation, for otherwise the children would tend to talk when we talk, stand up when we stand up, and walk away the moment we go out. So in music work, the teacher is not giving the pupil a copy,—he is giving him a revelation. When the child follows the mannerisms and parrots the faults of the teacher, it is because these details are not distinguished in his mind from the artistic idea the teacher is trying to inculcate. It is important to see that children do not really learn from a teacher by copying. *The mechanism is not imitation but inspiration.* This is the true reason for performing for the class, and for doing it beautifully. We believe that these procedures are too little used in music education.

2. The second method of setting standards is by criticism and verbal analysis. The thing to be avoided primarily is a mere intellectual attack upon musical problems, such as just telling the class to produce better tone, to attend more to pitch, to bring out the rhythm more effectively, and so forth. To avoid this, the verbal criticism should always be concentrated on a particular point in a particular musical effort that the pupils have made. Furthermore, such criticism should not primarily be negative, and even when it is necessary to tell the class that something has been poorly done, the general aim should be constructive, and they should feel that they are being shown a better way rather than merely blamed for a fault.

In other words, verbal criticism should be along the line of showing how a piece of music may be made better and more effective. Standards are set in this way not so much by a correction of errors as by a conquest of them.

3. Lastly, standards may be set by creating real situations in which they are imperatively demanded. Here we see the educational value of public occasions at which the children appear. Such opportunities for group and individual appearance in public should definitely be provided as part of the music work. They should not be so frequent as to become trivialities, and yet should come often enough really to affect the work. They should not be used as chances for display (as is too often the case in producing operettas, particularly those of inferior text and music), but for the making of beautiful music and the giving of pleasure. Handled in this way they may be a highly effective means of musical growth, because public performance is the musician's most natural and most drastic test, and of all the experiences which come to him the one which probably has the most potent effect upon his own personal standards in his work.

### Dealing with the Pupil's Difficulties

This is the third great function of the teacher in contact with the class. To some extent this problem is taken care of by the proper grading of the materials of music education, so that the songs are reasonably within the compass of the class. But no scheme of grading will carry all the way, particularly if we give up the idea that we are bound to follow a rigid simple-to-complex order. There is no doubt that the introduction of difficult song material calls for superior expertness on the part of the teacher. It is far easier to teach a simple song, used to illustrate certain reading problems or other points, than to handle an art song of greater artistic appeal which involves some points really difficult for the class to compass musically. Usually a situation where there is complaint of a song being "too hard," can be analyzed to show that the music itself is not too difficult for the children, but the teacher is too poorly prepared to direct the learning properly.

In dealing with the difficulties encountered by pupils in their music work, there is no substitute for living, personal insight on the part of the teacher. He must be an individual sensitively musical, and aware, though perhaps not in a technical way, of the psychological peculiarities of musical learning. What is required of him is ability to recognize the sources of failure in such fields as rhythm, tone production, note error, and so forth. Such work on the part of the teacher is of indispensable importance, because it means the steering of pupils away from blind alleys where motivation and impulse would die.

One other point should be mentioned before passing on. How much help should a teacher give a class in going through a song? It will depend on the purpose, to a large extent, for which the song is used. However, some people suppose that no help at all should be given, particularly in the reading process, and that the teacher should never sing with the pupils as they are learning. Perhaps this may be good advice to give some very crude beginning teachers who have no well defined idea of the meaning and nature of the educative process, and who tend simply to carry the class along on their backs all the time. But it should not be taken as an absolute prohibition. To set it up as such, means a return to the idea that "we learn by doing," from which it is inferred that the learner alone must "do." The amount of help the teacher will give cannot be decided beforehand. Such a choice rests on art and insight. We would say that in a difficult song a great deal ought to be given. Perhaps the following principle might be suggested. Where routine difficulties exist, as in the singing of a difficult reading song undertaken out of a love for its artistic value, help may well be given. On the other hand, wherever the initiative and individual choice of the pupil is involved, the policy ought to be "hands off." For instance, in deciding upon expressive nuance, blocking out a rhythm pattern, marking the beginning and ending of phrases, and so forth, it is very easy to show the children what to do, and quite fatal to yield to any such temptation. Whenever it comes to the spirit, the meaning, or the mood of music, whenever the problem is that of understanding the music, the pupil should be thrown upon his own choices, even though the teacher clearly sees a better way, and longs to point it out. On the other hand, when it is a question of conquering a difficulty otherwise insuperable, and yet routine in character, which has been introduced for good pedagogical reasons, there is no objection whatever to help.

### The Teacher as a Musical Personality

The whole scheme of music education now vaguely envisaged, which we are to develop and explain, clearly requires the music teacher to be a truly musical personality. There are some plans of music education before the public whose deliberate intent seems to be to make it possible for musical ignoramuses to give musical instruction. They are exactly like the good old plan by which a teacher who knows nothing about geometry, let us say, can "teach" it (*sic*) by putting pupils through a textbook—a plan which every treatise on classroom procedure criticizes with the most deserved harshness. Doubtless any reasonably intelligent person can make such a system work, even though his musical insight and grasp is practically non-existent. The only trouble is that these systems do not really teach music at all. One thing is very certain. A creative scheme of music education cannot possibly be carried through except by musical personalities. How can an unmusical person possibly undertake to initiate, advise upon, and judge musical projects in the way of listening, performing, and creating? Often such work demands real musical expertness as well as keen artistic sensibilities. For instance, such a task as teaching a difficult song to a grade school group is no job for an unmusical person. The unmusical grade teacher must stick probably to the type of songs—used solely to illustrate a technical point, or a notational problem, and to afford a drill opportunity—which are so simple that he cannot possibly go very far wrong with them. In such cases, the class is receiving only a routine type of musical experience unless the supervisor on his visits is able to supply, at least in part, the musical deficiency. Again and again we shall see that certain teaching procedures are indicated, and indeed demanded, which imperatively require a real musicianship on the part of the teacher. To give one illustration, it may be possible to teach rhythm in terms of note lengths and time signatures without having any rhythmic sense at all. But one certainly cannot convey to a class the direct sense of the rhythmic structure of a piece of music, without any reference to the symbols of the score, unless one has a keen and definite feeling for rhythm, which is built up only by musical training. In the absence of adequate teacher training background, the textbook material must help the musically uneducated teacher to grow.

So we insist that to obtain creative results, the teacher and supervisor of school music must be musical personalities.

They should stand as representatives of what music can and should mean in life, and this is the heart of their power in the classroom. They represent music to their colleagues and superior officers, and it is the heart of their power to secure the coöperation necessary for a well-rounded program. They represent it to the public, and it is the heart of their power to enlist that popular support without which no great things can be achieved in school music. Here then we come to the very center, the mainspring of music education in the schools.

### Some Questions for the Music Teacher in the Schools

We close this chapter by suggesting a few questions which the working school music teacher may well put to himself by way of self-criticism and assessment.

1. *What are my own musical deficiencies, the limitations of my own musical experience and horizons, and what am I doing to make them good?* For instance, one may be a poor reader, or have a defective rhythmic grasp, a limited repertoire of pieces one knows or of pieces one can perform, or one may have absolutely no contact with some important branch of music. Such deficiencies are not things to be ashamed of in themselves. But emphatically they are points at which the effort of the teacher should be directed, for the sake of increased professional competence and ability to serve.

2. *Am I seeking and capitalizing opportunities to hear the best music?* Harlow Gale reports that in a city of 300,000 where there were about 500 private music teachers, only 20 per cent were regular concert-goers. This is a condition of professional indifference and self-complacency which the school music teacher should never permit himself.

3. *Am I steadily increasing my ability as a performer of music?* We do not believe that any musician can really grow

without serious music study. This is of very high importance for the working teacher, who so readily gets into an easy rut unless he adopts strenuous and exacting measures of musical self-discipline. Daily exacting practice with a definite musical goal in mind should be part of the routine of the working teacher who really desires the best personal development. Membership in an informal ensemble group, again, can be an agency of great value and refreshment.

4. *Am I coming steadily to a better understanding of music?* The point here is the great value of regular professional reading in the history, the theory, and the psychology of music. Even though such reading may not seem to be immediately practical, yet many connections will be made later on in the mind which is constantly enlarging its horizons and enriching its resources.

5. *Am I gaining more information and insight as to educational practices in school music?* It is astonishing how many school music teachers simply stay in the groove where their teacher training work pushed them. In spite of the fine work of the professional associations and conferences, many of these teachers have an exceedingly limited knowledge of methods and ideas other than those they themselves use. We have known school music teachers of long experience who had never even heard the name of Jaques-Dalcroze and did not know that eurythmics existed. This cannot but mean a serious professional weakness. "He who dares to teach must never cease to learn."

6. *What definite reasons have I for believing I am contributing to the musical wellbeing of my community?* That is, for instance, are there individuals to whom the teacher can point who owe their love for and understanding of music to some extent to his work?

One of the very hopeful signs in American music is the willingness of school music teachers to face just such questions as these. Undoubtedly the growth of music in our schools is fraught with great possibilities for advance in the whole profession of music teaching.

### Questions for Discussion.

1. Check over the list of activities to be included in an adequate program. If any were to be omitted, which would you choose to leave out? Why?

2. Would you add any items to the above mentioned list?

3. Discuss the values of drawing up and publishing a course of study in music. Would there be any disadvantages?

4. On what points would you expect vocal and instrumental supervisors to be at variance?

5. To what extent should the schools give credit for private music lessons? How should this matter be administered?

6. Discuss methods *(a)* of seating and handling the class; *(b)* of dealing with the individual in order to capitalize group motivation.

7. Why is group motivation more natural in music than in some other fields?

8. Discuss the statement that without motivation arising out of direct interest in the music, the whole scheme of motivation will fail.

9. Do you know any schemes of music education which do not demand a high standard of musicianship from the teacher? Do you think the scheme here presented calls for high grade technique in the teacher?

10. Collect and discuss instances of how the teacher can help the child in a difficulty with music.

11. To what extent may the teacher legitimately "carry the class" through a song?

12. In view of the position we take, how much time would you allot in the training of a school music teacher for general culture, for school music methods, and for music?

BIBLIOGRAPHY.

1. ARPS, G. F., Work with Knowledge of Results vs. Work Without Knowledge of Results, *Psychological Monographs,* 1920, vol. 28, No. 3.
2. BAKER, EARL, and GIDDINGS, T. P., *High School Music Teaching,* George Banta Publishing Company, 1928.
3. BEATTIE, JOHN W., MCCONATHY, OSBOURNE, and MORGAN, RUSSELL V., *Music in the Junior High School,* Silver, Burdett and Company, 1930, ch. 15.
4. BOOK, WILLIAM F., The Rôle of the Teacher in the Most Expeditious and Economic Learning, *Journal of Educational Psychology,* 1910, vol. 1, pp. 183-199.
5. DAVISON, ARCHIBALD, T., *Music Education in America,* Harper and Brothers, 1926, ch. 2.
6. DYKEMA, PETER W., Music in the School Survey, *Music Supervisors' Journal,* October, 1930, vol. 17.
7. GALE, HARLOW, Musical Education, *Pedagogical Seminary,* 1917, vol. 24, pp. 503-514.
8. GEHRKENS, KARL, W., *Introduction to School Music Teaching,* C. C. Birchard and Co., 1919.
9. HUGHES, J. M., A Study of Intelligence and of the Training of Teachers as Factors Conditioning the Achievement of Pupils, *School Review,* 1925, vol. 33, pp. 191-200, 292-302.
10. HURLOCK, ELIZABETH, The Value of Praise and Reproof as Incentives for Children, *Archives of Psychology,* 1924, No. 71.
11. MURSELL, JAMES L., *Principles of Musical Education,* The Macmillan Company, 1927, ch. 11.
12. SURETTE, THOMAS WHITNEY, *Music and Life,* Houghton Mifflin Company, 1917, ch. 3.
13. SYMMONDS, PERCIVAL M., Methods of Investigating Study Habits, *School and Society,* 1926, vol. 24, pp. 145-152.

Chapter Five

# Appreciation

Appreciation may be defined as that force in music education which seeks to arouse in the child a love of music, and to make that love deeper and wiser. We might almost say that the business of appreciation is to evoke musicality, for Révécz defines musicality as ". . . the ability to enjoy music aesthetically." The whole tendency of our chapters on learning and teaching is to show that appreciation so understood is absolutely central in music education. It has been pointed out as an established psychological principle that no learning takes place without the will to learn. Also it has been shown that the intrinsic motivation which comes from a direct love of and interest in music is not only the best sort of motivation to arouse, but also absolutely necessary, in that without it none of the extrinsic motives really amount to anything at all. Putting these two claims together, we can arrive at only one result. Music education must be founded upon the appreciation of music. Appreciation furnishes the motive force. And the goal of music education can only be better and deeper appreciation.

In our treatment of this topic we shall take up three main points. First of all, we shall discuss the psychological foundations of the love of music. We shall find that psychology has been able to show from what sources musical pleasure is derived, and information on this point is clearly to be desired. Secondly, we shall raise the question of the educational means by which these sources of musical pleasure may be utilized and rendered effective. We shall find that the love of music is aroused, and appreciation developed, in and through the three types of musical projects we have already mentioned—listening, performing, and creating. This leads to a very important inference, full of far-reaching practical consequences, which we state here: *Music appreciation is not a special type or department of music work; it penetrates every detail of music education; specifically it means far more than just listening.* Our third and last point will be a consideration of how appreciation leads to the effective development of the musical-mental abilities which constitute what we call musicianship.

## The Foundations of Music Appreciation

We have spoken of appreciation as that force in music education which evokes and develops the pupil's aesthetic enjoyment of music. So we must raise the question as to the sources of this enjoyment before seeing how these can be tapped. We have ample data bearing on this point. Studies listed in the bibliography at the close of this chapter by Beaunis, Downey, Gilman, Weld, Katz and Révécz, Belaiew-Exemplarsky, and Whitley all contribute to it, and the reader who wishes to go to these sources will find much of interest and value on which we have not time to comment here. As a result of these investigations, we are able to list the following sources of musical enjoyment.

1. **Direct sensory pleasure in tone.** The studies always report as one definite cause of musical enjoyment, pleasure in tone quality, in melodic curve, and in harmony. There is something deeper and, in a way, stranger here than many good music teachers seem to suspect. This is well illustrated

by the astonishing case of Sutermeister, reported by Katz and Révécz. Sutermeister was a music lover who was overtaken by complete deafness. In spite of this he discovered that it was possible for him to find the keenest and most sincere pleasure in musical performances, and particularly in orchestral performances, where there was a large tonal mass present. He did not derive this pleasure from touching any of the instruments while they were being played, or sensing the vibrations through the floor, as has been the case with other deaf persons. What seemed to take place was a direct induction, an immediate responsiveness of his whole body to tone. The psychologists who studied him report that he showed every sign of really intense musical feeling, and that his responses were entirely appropriate to the kind of music being played. This reminds us again of the finding by Miss Belaiew-Exemplarsky that children are naturally more responsive to pure tone than to any other one factor in music. And it shows us the extreme—almost the mystical—importance of good tone as a foundation for the love of music.

*We would conclude that in all appreciation work it is vital first to see that good tone is always used, and second to help the child to attend to it and enjoy it.* Reproducing instruments which deface the tonal beauty at once kill a major chance for building appreciation. In performance projects one of the essential points is always to insist upon clear and lovely tone. And no small part of the pleasure of musical creation is the discovery of an appealing tonal effect.

2. **Rhythmic response.** It very often happens in school music that the factor of rhythm is simply ignored. Even among professional musicians, rhythmic grasp is pitifully under-developed. We are reminded of an incident reported by Tobias Matthay. A group of piano teachers were invited

to criticize a pupil who was playing the Military Polonaise, and who was definitely blurring the rhythm of the second section. Not one of these presumably experienced people could pick out the error, though they were all vaguely aware of something wrong.

The psychological studies of musical enjoyment always report rhythmic response as one of its chief sources. So we are driven to conclude that a great deal of music education, both in the public schools and in conservatories of music, wholly ignores a most vital element in building love of music and comprehension of music. *We do not believe that appreciation can be properly taught at all unless the element of rhythm is properly handled in listening, performing, and creating.* We shall of course discuss these matters in detail in the chapter on rhythm, but for the sake of making our point concrete, one or two illustrations may be given here. In a great deal of listening, the pupil should be encouraged to respond to the rhythm in terms of free, large, bodily movement, stepping it out, skipping or dancing to it, or inventing a rhythm game. Again, in many listening projects and perhaps in almost all performance projects and creative projects, the rhythmic structure of the music should be brought effectively to the pupil's attention. By such means as this we release the rhythm of the music as a direct source of natural interest and make it one of the main foundations of our work in appreciation.

3. **Association and imagery.** If a composition has rich associations for a listener, if it is connected for him with a wide range of significant experience, the studies show that musical enjoyment is enhanced. Furthermore, the studies also show that imagery is frequently present in the listener, and that sometimes he builds up very elaborate castles in the air and sequences of ideas, which make the music mean more to

him. These are proper and legitimate sources of musical pleasure, and ought to be capitalized.

In this connection the following points should be noticed. (*a*) Whenever we present a composition either for listening or performance, we do well to capitalize all the life-giving associations naturally connected with it. This does not mean giving a lot of information about it. But it does mean showing that it arose out of a certain circumstance, that it is the expression of a certain mood, and that works of art in other fields—pictorial art and literature, for instance—have affinities with it. (*b*) The creative project perhaps best of all captures and utilizes the factor of association. We encourage the individual and the group to build a little poem about something that has interested them, and to work out a melody to it which all can sing. In this way we present music, not as a lonely art or an isolated stunt, but in terms of general culture and as a means of human self-expression. (*c*) While we may certainly utilize the factor of free imagination, there is a very essential caution to be observed here. *We should not let the child's imagination run away from the music.* It is possible to think up the wildest fantasies on a basis of musical suggestion, and these may have no reflex at all in terms of increased musical pleasure. For instance, one of Downey's subjects gave the following response to a composition: "First sensation that it was one of Mrs. Caudle's curtain lectures interspersed with soliloquies over her own hard lot. Later concluded it represented a tired father walking the floor at midnight with a cross, crying baby, and alternately singing Watts' 'Cradle Hymn' and scolding the baby." The composition, we may remark, was Chopin's Funeral March. Music educators do not want anything of this sort, and yet we may get it if we encourage the child always to look for a story or an idea back of the music, instead of helping him to concentrate with keener interest and richer understanding upon the tonal pattern itself. The management of imagination so that it helps, but does not introduce side issues, is a matter for very artistic tact on the part of the teacher. (*d*) Weld gives us a pregnant hint which may indicate the right way out of our difficulty. He says that in almost all the imaginings set off by listening to music, movement is an essential element. Thus we may perhaps capitalize the element of imagination while avoiding its dangers by asking the child what sort of movement he imagines in connection with music he hears—whether it marches, gallops, skips, or sways, etc.,—and then by having him actually demonstrate. In this way imagination and a feeling for rhythm are integrated.

4. **Grasp of musical structure and form.** Many intelligent people attend concerts, and come away largely unblessed because they have never been taught to hear the structure of music. To them this seems a very esoteric affair indeed. But it is not. It can be developed from the very beginning of music work in the schools. And it ought to be, because it is a prime factor in the instructed love of music.

We approach the problem of musical structure by teaching music phrase-wise from the first. Even in the first grade, the unit of attack is the meaningful phrase. In listening and performing the child is brought to a clearer and clearer apprehension of the phrase, and comes to see in every composition a sequence of phrases, some repeated, some contrasting, some involving variations. Later on, his sense of form in music is reinforced and extended by having him study songs, both as listening and performance projects, pointing out the structured phrase sequence of the poems, and the corresponding musical form. By such means we build up a direct sense of musical form, without any intellectualization, and thus capitalize this very important source of musical pleasure, and make it available for further growth in musical insight.

5. **Mental and emotional attitude.** This is the last of the sources of musical pleasure which we shall consider, for, although the studies mention several more, they seem to have considerably less practical relevance to the problem of teaching appreciation than those we have here discussed. As to the last mentioned, Beaunis in particular insists upon a prepared attitude on the part of the listener as essential for full musical enjoyment, and suggests that this accounts, at least in part, for such a profound musical effect as that produced by the Wagnerian Opera when performed at Bayreuth.

As an interesting and instructive contrast, we may consider the mental and emotional attitude common in connection with a radio concert.[1] Here we have an illustration of the stultifying and negative effect of attitudes that are casual, passive, merely tolerant, and lacking in expectation. Mr. Orton points out that American broadcasting practice tends to inculcate such attitudes on the part of the radio audience, and contrasts this sharply with the methods employed in Great Britain, where efforts are made to prepare the public for intelligent listening as a real source of enjoyment—where masterpieces are not ruthlessly cut on the assumption that the audience will not listen beyond a certain time limit—in itself a destructive notion of subtle yet pervasive force. Any lack of value for music education of which we may complain in connection with the radio, then, lies far less in the medium itself than in the mental and emotional attitudes produced in the listeners.

[1] This whole matter is very interestingly discussed in an article by William Orton, "The Level of Thirteen-Year-Olds," *Atlantic Monthly,* January, 1931, pp. 1-9.

We conclude, therefore, that everything possible should be done to have an expectant, receptive, interested attitude, if a musical project is to yield a tithe of its true educative value. The detailed method of presentation, and the whole physical setting, are very important. Where a room can definitely be assigned to music, as often happens in the platoon school or the departmentalized elementary school, it is found very helpful in producing the right atmosphere. We should remember that music education lives in terms of appreciation, and that false attitudes and bad emotional set can ruin appreciation.

One further and more general point from the studies demands a comment. It has been shown that there are wide individual variations in musical enjoyment. Weld recognizes three types of listeners—the motor type, characterized by strong physical reactions to music, such as beating time, singing, or whistling; the emotional type, which varies all the way from persons whose primary reaction is coolly critical to those who are dominated by a volatile and potent mood when listening; and the analytic or intellectual type. While we may not accept this classification as final, or as meaningful when applied to school children, yet it brings out a very important practical consideration. (*a*) Appreciation must help each individual to find his own typical sources of musical pleasure. Thus it must involve as varied a musical appeal as possible. (*b*) Music education should not try to destroy individuality of response in the interests of a supposed ideal which is uniformly desirable. It should build upon the tendency of the individual, both capitalizing and correcting it.

Evidently it takes more than a weekly "appreciation lesson" to capitalize all these sources of musical pleasure at all adequately. Assuredly it is absurd to straitjacket appreciation as a separate course and then forget all about it everywhere else.

Appreciation must permeate every part of music education. We are now to discuss more in detail how its sources may be tapped in three kinds of musical projects—listening, performing, and creating.

### Appreciation and Listening

Listening to music is the most characteristic medium of appreciation. So much is this the case that many people think of appreciation as exactly the same thing as listening. This is a very great mistake, as our definition of appreciation quite sufficiently shows. What we actually do is to use projects in listening as means to develop the understanding love of music. The psychology of this process has already been discussed. What we have to do is to handle the situation where the children listen to music in such a way that the various sources of musical pleasure are made effective. It is now our task to show in general how this can be done. We shall discuss three main points: the repertoire of music to be used, the types of response to be encouraged, and the types of procedure to be employed.

1. **Repertoire.** The following points are important in building up lists of compositions to be used for listening projects in appreciation. (*a*) A wide variety of styles, periods, and grades of music should be included. Enough of a range of music should be used *to make it possible for the pupils to discover for themselves their capacities for enjoyment.* In organizing the repertoire for presentation, a chronological order should not be followed. The same principles should control us here as control the arrangement of a well-balanced concert program. That is, music should be presented in a diversified manner, and in order of mood rather than of history. (*b*) Music involving special "program" interest, or as-

sociated with some story or idea may be particularly serviceable in capitalizing the tendency to build imaginative constructs and the natural values of association. Instances of such music are the Nutcracker Suite, which may be used as early as the third or fourth grade, The Peer Gynt Suite, which may have a place in the fourth or fifth grade, the Egmont Overture for the seventh grade, and the Eroica Symphony for high school groups with considerable musical background. The repertoire should include as much really great music as possible. Sometimes listening repertoires are open to criticism on the ground of poor quality. (*c*) In managing the selection of compositions, a primary aim should be to create for the pupil a core of familiar and well loved music. Gilliland and Moore compared very interestingly the "wearing" qualities of classical music and jazz, repeating some selections of each twenty-five times to the same listeners. They found that with repetition, good music is constantly more and more enjoyed. Thus we should return many times to compositions the children have already heard and enjoyed, and try to show them deeper meanings and richer beauties than they had previously perceived. Here is another instance of our principle of creative reviewing, which has such wide applications in music education. As a last suggestion, the work in listening can sometimes include a concert period, with a number of selections chosen by the class by vote.

2. **Types of response encouraged.** We must understand that listening is something far more than mere passive receptivity. It is a process of selection, of *noticing*. We capitalize the various sources of musical pleasure—tone, rhythm, associative and imaginal factors, musical structure—by directing the listener's attention to them, by having him listen to and for them, and think about them. More specifically, we

achieve this by encouraging him to respond to them in various ways. For it is a basic psychological principle that *we attend to those things to which we respond.* So let us consider the various types of response which should be sought and encouraged in connection with listening.

(*a*) First consider verbal responses, that is, responses in which the pupil is encouraged to say something or write something about the music he has heard. It is always tempting for the teacher to call for these, because they are so easily evoked and readily managed. But there are great dangers connected with their use. It is extremely easy to over-emphasize the intellectual elements as soon as we begin to talk or write about music. One should notice that among all the sources of musical pleasure listed above, knowledge about the music was not included. Yet there are schemes of so-called appreciation where the pupil is put through a perfect inquisition of questions about the music. He is required to underline the composer's name, the approximate date of the music, the musical style, and so on endlessly, on a formidable blank to be turned in later to the teacher. Procedures of this sort are hopeless from the standpoint of appreciation in general or music appreciation in particular. They represent the crudest applications of the idea that we learn by doing. The naïve inference is that so long as we get some sort of reaction from the pupil after he has listened to music, we have produced effective learning. This is even more stupid than thinking that the mere presence of any kind of interest proves that effective mental development is taking place. For the whole question is, what kind of reaction is being set up? *When we permit, nay encourage, or even require the pupil to produce verbal reactions chiefly involving intellectual analysis and knowledge, we actually work away from real appreciation and musical enjoyment.* We know certain schools where highly intellectualized appreciation work is carried on, in which the pupils speak of the periods devoted to it as "music depreciation"—and they are right.

Let us not be misunderstood: we must use and encourage verbal response. We must try in every way, however, to get the right kind of response, and avoid the wrong kind. The proper principle to keep in mind has never been stated better than by Hayward, in his excellent book, *The Lesson in Appreciation,* where he speaks of what he calls "aesthetic discussion." While the idea is specifically applied to literature, it also holds for music. Hayward finds that one essential part of the appreciation lesson must be a time when the pupils are encouraged to say frankly and freely what they have liked about the poem. The emphasis is not at all on content, meaning, or knowledge, but entirely on aesthetic appeal. This should be encouraged also in music appreciation. There can be no doubt that the ideal form for such expressions of feeling is actual speech. It makes for spontaneity and naturalness, and avoids laborious effort, and this is what we want. Moreover, it involves a sharing of impressions so that one pupil may stimulate others. So we would say that whenever and wherever possible, the children should be given the opportunity of expressing aesthetic reactions through speech. But with large groups this may need some supplementation in the shape of written expression. Here the use of cross-out, completion, or underlining blanks comes in. If these are to be used properly, their characteristics must be understood. Above all, we must consider the type of response we wish to produce. It is exceedingly easy, in using this powerful device, to fall into a double error. We may make out a long and elaborate form on which the pupil is to record his reaction, and produce a response which on the one hand is almost entirely in terms of knowledge and intellectual analysis, and on the other is far more like a characteristic test or examination response than a free reaction to beauty. This instantly kills appreciation. On the other hand, we may use completion blanks, blanks that call for underlining, and so on, to direct the pupil to the mood, meaning, and intimate structure of the music itself. The proper place for these devices is subsequent to the fullest and freest discussion on the aesthetic significance of the music. We must not use them as tests so much as agencies for directing response and attention into the desirable aesthetic channels. To summarize, the use of such devices involves the following advantages and limitations. (1) The form itself shapes and directs the pupil's response in a given direction. (2) His written response may be made far more rapidly and with less mechanical effort than by writing a short essay. (3) He has a written record, which can be used for several purposes later on. (4) The limitation of any such device flows from exactly the same source as its advantages, namely, its thoroughly and avowedly mechanical character, and its somewhat excessive control of the pupil's responses, which are necessarily limited to a few alternatives dictated in advance. It is far better than merely unguided response, or than no response at all. If used carefully, with sane principles of appreciation in mind, it can be beneficial. But it is always risky in inexpert hands, because one can so easily employ it to bring out responses in terms merely of knowledge. It is never an adequate substitute for free discussion through speech.

In the verbal responses which we encourage to music, we should try to get comment on tonal beauty, on rhythmic type, on structural characteristics, and on whatever associations and elements of imagination the music may involve. With the lower grades the teacher should always endeavor to have such comments originate from the class rather than from himself. Above all he should curb his natural tendency to hand out factual information about the music which is being played. We are averse to laying down iron-clad rules for the conduct of classes, but we would be inclined to say that a teacher in the lower grades should never introduce any composition with data about its composer, the date and period of its composition, etc., etc., but rather should announce it as a lovely piece of music and play it without further comment, after which the class may be invited to express themselves about it. Not until the junior high school level has been reached is factual comment really safe, and even then *it should be directly and immediately in the interest of a better and richer appreciation, not in that of information.* We cannot sufficiently insist on the importance of avoiding the transformation from aesthetic interest to factual interest that so readily takes place under a mistaken emphasis.

(*b*) Next we consider mimetic response. Pupils should be encouraged to express their feeling for music directly through physical action. That is, they should be allowed to step it out, marching, skipping, galloping, or swinging to it according to their decision as to its rhythmic demands. Furthermore, they should be trained to indicate the beginnings and ends of phrases while keeping time to the flow of the music. Or again, the class may be asked to listen, and indicate the entry of new subjects, or the return of old ones. Mimetic responses of various kinds can be very valuable indeed in concentrating attention upon rhythm, and upon musical structure. Such work has an indispensable place in a complete scheme of appreciation. It should not, however, be continued too long. For children above a certain age it becomes quite inappropriate and loses its value. If we want to carry mimetic activity beyond the lower grades, we have little option save to turn to Jaques-Dalcroze for advice.

(*c*) Inner response should be considered next. Davison very properly insists that there is a great value in simply listening in silence and without comment to great music. This is entirely true. We must not think that psychological principles always demand the establishing of large overt reactions, though of course if these are wholly lacking our work will be defective. Sometimes the children should have the experience of just silently listening, without comment or discussion of any kind before or after the music. Perhaps this may be specially practicable with compositions already familiar. In any case, there should be a minimum of introductory comment by the teacher. As we have seen, in grade school listening this should be cut to a vestigial limit, little more being done than to intimate to the children that something pleasant is going to happen. Above all, we must avoid smudging the musical horizon with the murk of fact. Along such lines we can build procedures which definitely capitalize mental adaptation, attitude, and mood. For great music is profoundly impressive, and should be left to tell its own tale and make its own effect as far as possible.

(*d*) Perhaps one of the very best of all responses to music that one hears, is the attempt to produce it for one's self. This should have a place in any really complete scheme of work in appreciation and listening. In the kindergarten, the child is encouraged to sing back spontaneously as the teacher sings. The same general idea can be followed right through to the twelfth grade. One great aim in listening should be the building up of what we may call a "passive repertoire," that is to say, a number of compositions which the pupils love, and which they hope one day to learn to perform.

3. **Special points of procedure.** (*a*) The phonograph is inevitably the mainstay of the listening program. It is important to have just as excellent an instrument as one possibly can, and thoroughly to routinize its use. (*b*) It is well not to rely wholly on the phonograph. A performance by the music teacher himself, by an outside artist, or even by a pupil, may often be helpful. It introduces a personal and intimate note which may be very valuable. (*c*) One cannot be too careful about every detail of the setting and presentation. As we have seen, a bad emotional atmosphere can ruin appreciation. (*d*) When a new composition is being introduced, say as little as possible. Never indulge in long historical, biographical, or technical disquisitions. Learn to say just enough to release the spirit and power of the music by creating the right mood of expectation. (*e*) It will sometimes be helpful to introduce a new composition by making the pupils acquainted with its chief motives or themes. After this introduction one should have the class listen for these themes as the composition is played through, and indicate in some way when they appear. (*f*) Interest in tone quality may often be capitalized and also built up by bringing into the class the various instruments of the orchestra, demonstrating their tone color, and then letting the class listen to compositions in which they are employed. As experience increases, the class may be asked to decide what instrument or combination of instruments they are listening to when a record is played. By such means they may be made timbre-conscious. (*g*) Routinize the detail of your procedure—the arrangement of the room, the seating of the class, the management of the instruments, etc. But never routinize the essence of what you do. Seek

new angles of approach. There are always plenty of them. Nowhere can the teacher be more creative than in handling listening projects. Develop above everything a varied program, appealing to the musical interests of the pupils from as many sides as possible. (*h*) Remember that listening is a *project*. That is, we want a definite purpose and a definite outcome. The suggestions already made are all along this line. We should bear in mind that one listens well only when one wants to. And one learns to want to listen by finding out what to listen for. (*i*) Encourage initiative and free responses from the pupils, both as individuals and as a group. Remember that they develop a love for music in terms of their own personal interest and will, rather than in terms of what the teacher wants them to do, or says or thinks they should do or say. The most hopeful thing in education is the child with an idea—even if the idea is wrong. (*j*) Retain the experimental attitude and the learner's spirit yourself. Remember that no one knows all, or nearly all, there is to know about appreciation and its development. And no one can be sufficiently skillful, or have enough transparent sincerity or childlikeness of heart, to foster with ideal sureness the love of music in little children.

Before wholly leaving this topic, something should be said about the development of children's concerts, which are such a notable feature of some of the very best American work in school music. The organization of sequences of such concerts can afford a very powerful musical appeal, and become a dynamic influence in favor of music, both in the schools and the community. Certain important points, however, must be taken care of. In the first place, a single concert a year is not very much good. The effect of concert attendance is cumulative. At first, orientation is required, and only if a series of such opportunities is afforded, will their full value be obtainable. Then, careful preparation in the schools should precede the concert so that the children will hear familiar music in the new surroundings. Classroom listening lessons ought to function both as general and specific preparation for the concert—general in the sense of giving an interest in music, and the right attitude towards it; specific, in presenting compositions which are included in the program itself. The choice of the program, or programs, again, is a very important point. They should be well diversified, and should be made up of music which combines high artistic excellence with interest and assimilability. It is desirable to have an atmosphere of intimacy in children's concerts; and to turn them into a musical spectacle, by using an enormous auditorium, is a mistake. Music should be made highly personal for the child. It is found, too, that the concerts are better appreciated, and mean more to the children if a small fee is charged. Moreover, if this fee covers a course of concerts, the children will be more likely to attend particular concerts from which they might otherwise stay away, but which they keenly enjoy when they actually hear them, such, for instance, as piano recitals. Last, but not least, every detail of the administration and management of these affairs must receive the most careful attention. Work along these lines has been carried on for some years in several cities with the most gratifying results.

### Appreciation and Performance

While listening is no doubt the most characteristic vehicle of appreciation, we have already seen that appreciation always means something more than listening, and demands other types of approach. We are now to see how the understanding love of music can be developed through projects along the line of musical performance.

By a performance project we mean a song that the children learn to sing, whether from the score or by rote, or a piece that they learn to play. Musical performance should be regarded as an agency for building appreciation. This is a point which many music teachers, in the schools and elsewhere, completely miss. They make performance an end in itself, instead of a means of creating a deeper love for, and a more precise understanding of, music. This at once has two unfortunate educational consequences. (*a*) It leads to quite a false emphasis upon technique, for, if children learn songs and pieces simply in order to sing or play them, rather than to discover musical values through them, music education instantly tends in the direction of elocution. (*b*) It devitalizes appreciation by limiting it to listening. But clearly, appreciation, as we have defined it, transcends listening, and is built up in and through actual music making, as one of its natural agencies. Experience in performing music makes us better listeners, and also wiser music lovers. For these reasons we insist that the performance project should be thought of in close connection with appreciation. Let us see what this implies.

1. Every new composition, whether vocal or instrumental, should be presented as an aesthetic project. This means that it should stand as an opportunity for the creation of beauty. Thus a new song or piece should not just be assigned in a routine manner. Every effort should be made to interest the pupils in it beforehand, and to give their interest proper direction. This may be done in a variety of ways, among which the following procedure may be specified for the sake of illustration. After a brief announcement that a delightful new

song is to be learned, we sing it to the class. If it is an instrumental composition, we play it to them or let them hear it on the phonograph. We then draw from the pupils comments and responses to the music, particularly stressing its beauty and appeal. If it is a song, we may call attention to the words, and their significance and relation to the music. The title may be utilized as a source of interest, particularly *after* free comment by the class. Whatever we do, our vital aim is not to present a new composition as a mass of notes to be mastered, but as a thing of beauty, the creative realization of which will be a delight. Here again, we should be on our guard against a factual emphasis, particularly in introducing the music before it has been heard and enjoyed. We wish always to set up an aesthetic impulse, a will to realize and enjoy beauty.

2. The cultural and emotional setting of the new composition should be developed. This should be done freely and spontaneously, and not by means of a lecture on the composer, the period, and so forth. With younger children this may mean little more than asking them what the song is about, and bringing out, by question and suggestion, the emotional tone involved in the topic. With children somewhat older, this element in discussion and development may have a wider scope, and it may interest them to compare the song with music to which they have listened, and by such a means their attack on learning to sing it may be made better and more meaningful. Factual data should never be introduced as fact for its own sake. This means that we never introduce mere information until the pupil is mature enough for this to function in terms of mood. But always we want to connect the performance project broadly with the pupil's cultural and emotional life. For we lose the valuable factor of asso-

ciation if we treat music as impersonal and anonymous—as a sort of natural phenomenon with no individual meaning about it.

3. Coming now to the actual business of learning to play or sing the composition, the study phase of the learning should bring out and emphasize only those factors in it which we found to be basic for musical enjoyment. That is, the attention of the class should be focused upon the tonal problems (which include tone quality, melodic curve, and for older groups harmony), upon the element of rhythm, and upon the phrase structure of the music. It is from these that pleasure is to be derived, and these are the factors on which good performance depends. The teaching of a song or an instrumental composition should not be done note by note. The units of effort and attention should be elements of musical meaning—melody, phrase, and rhythm.

4. The special element of technique should always be developed in terms of musical and aesthetic values. That is, when a technical difficulty exists, it should always be presented as a difficulty in producing a musical result or effect that is desired. As we shall see, technique for its own sake is almost a self-contradictory idea. We develop technique for the sake of music.

5. Finally, throughout all the learning, right up to the very end, the pupil should be definitely encouraged to criticize his own efforts, and given every chance to show initiative. The teacher should stimulate him to ask and answer such questions as these: Is the song or piece becoming more beautiful and effective as we work analytically at its various elements, aiming now at phrase analysis, now at tone quality, now at rhythmic grasp and precision? How does it compare with expert performances? Is there anything we can do, or any

element in it on which we can concentrate to make it sound better?

Two points should be made in closing this section. (*a*) Everything we have said implies that the compositions, whether vocal or instrumental, that are given to children, have enough musical quality and are well enough adapted to the child mind for them to serve as aesthetic projects. If this is not done, all the above suggestions collapse. For instance, a great deal of the so-called "music" used in elementary instrumental work clearly has no musical value. It is directed merely at the building of mechanical technique. Later on we shall argue that it is poorly adapted even for that. (*b*) *Performance projects properly handled from the standpoint of developing appreciation are also properly handled for performance itself.* The suggestions given above for capitalizing the appreciation value of songs to be sung and pieces to be played are almost identical with those we would give for teaching the child to sing or play them, leaving appreciation entirely out of account. Here we see once more how deeply appreciation penetrates the entire scheme of progressive music education.

### Appreciation and Creation

There are three types of creative projects in music which have a definite bearing on appreciation. These are musical composition, toy orchestra work, and the making and playing of musical instruments. In our judgment this represents their true rank in value. Some people feel that the last named project plays an important part in creative education, but too often it becomes a period in manual training.

1. **Original musical composition.** The fundamental principle underlying the management of such work in the

schools is strikingly stated by Ogden (*Hearing*). He insists that music education has placed far too much emphasis on technique, and that music, poetry, representative art, and the dramatic dance ought to be fused together. He goes on to say that one should give the child an idea, or better, get him to suggest one—for instance, a star, a tree, or a flower—and encourage creative response to it through words, gestures, colors, lines, the use of solids, and the use of tones and rhythms. This goes rather further than even very expert music teachers might care to venture. But the essential idea can assuredly be applied. This idea has been successfully put into practice in the schools of Kansas City, with very encouraging results. (For details refer to Miss Glenn's paper on Creative Song, listed in the bibliography at the close of the chapter.) By the third grade the children have been given a wealth of directed musical experience, through spontaneity and emphasis of self-expression. They are then encouraged to create short poems, and to develop music to which these can be sung. One such poem and song, *á propos* of the visit of the "Los Angeles" to the city, is cited below. Much of the work with the musical score is developed out of such creative projects. We will return to consider this later. But for the moment our interest is in the appreciation value of such work. Whether it could be undertaken earlier than the third grade is a question. Perhaps this would be possible for the exceptional child who has favorable home contacts with music. But the invention of musical ideas demands at least a moderate background of musical experience, or else the whole project fails. In any case this work represents an extraordinarily interesting educational enterprise. Incidentally we should say that to handle it properly demands considerable expertness and delicate aesthetic feeling on the part of the teacher.

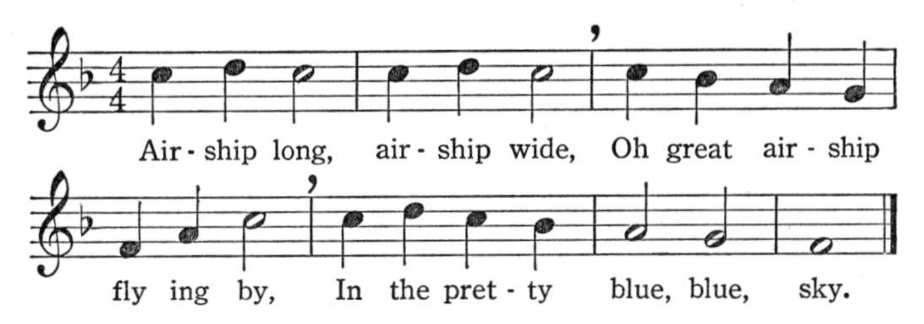
Air - ship long, air - ship wide, Oh great air - ship
fly ing by, In the pret - ty blue, blue, sky.

FIGURE 1. Song created by third grade children in the Kansas City schools.

2. **Toy orchestra work.** Within the last few years this type of work has greatly increased, and there are now repertoires of compositions for the use of the toy orchestra. Some supervisors may feel inclined to challenge it on the ground that it detracts from serious musical interest. But it certainly can be handled in such a way that this fault is not present. The great thing in approaching it is not just to put it into a system because it is new and seems fashionable in influential quarters, but really to understand its aim and value. *The toy orchestra is an agency for helping the child to think and feel musically. It has no direct relationship with instrumental work proper.* For this reason we are inclined to believe that while it has a real place, it is not a very large one. It may perhaps be introduced as part of the work of the primary grades, preferably in the second or early third grade. When it is used, the outline procedure is as follows. A suitable composition is chosen and played to the children on the phonograph, its phrase structure and rhythm being analyzed by them. The children can readily be familiarized with the

simple techniques of their instruments. So the chief project is for them to decide on appropriate orchestration. A great deal of the value of such work lies in letting them arrive at their own choices in this matter. Obviously the point is not to produce an artistic ensemble. When this is made the aim, and the teacher dictates the orchestration to be followed, and drills the children as if they were a little symphony aggregation, the whole thing becomes simply silly, and loses its educational value. The point of letting the children make the decisions is that this leads them to attend carefully to the music and thus understand it better. Then, when the choices have been made, the composition is played through with the orchestra carrying a sort of elaborate obbligato to the phonograph record. To the grown-up person the result may be rather humorous. As soon as we evaluate it from the standpoint of a finished artistic performance, we reduce it to an absurdity. But it has a real educational value *as a creative project,* because it demands concentration on and decision about a musical structure.

3. **The making and playing of musical instruments.** This idea has been worked out elaborately by Mrs. Coleman, and the reader interested in details of procedure is referred to her book. The essential procedure is to have the children make for themselves simple and crude musical instruments of various kinds, and on them produce music, either in solo or ensemble. There is an excellent opportunity for such work particularly in the lower grades. Undoubtedly it can broaden the child's musical horizons. It gives him first-hand experience with music making by other than vocal means. And it can evoke interest in and response to tone color and quality. But there are two dangers which seem to be involved. (*a*) Projects of this kind may readily turn into manual arts work

instead of music work. The mechanical difficulties of making an instrument which is at all effective may be so great that the child's whole mind is given to overcoming them. In such cases we pass out of the field of music education altogether. (*b*) We cannot agree that such work should be continued far into the grades. After all, toy instruments and homemade instruments have exceedingly limited musical possibilities. The mere fact that a hand-work project is going on is no more a sign that good education is going on than is the mere presence of interest. Most certainly work of this kind should have yielded all its values at an early age level, and its continuance late into the grades is likely to be an obstacle to musical progress partly because it takes up time that might be better spent, and partly because children always resent projects that seem to them unduly juvenile.

### Appreciation and Development of the Musical-Mental Abilities

We now come to the third and last topic of this chapter, the relationship of appreciation to the development of the musical-mental abilities which constitute what we speak of as musicianship. This discussion will lead us directly into the second main division of the book as a whole.

1. **Appreciation and ear training.** The proper beginning of ear training is not at all formal drill with abstract material, but actual synthetic functioning experience of musical beauty and meaning. *The beginning and the end of ear training is the ability to hear music more precisely.* So we would start off with actual compositions, presented primarily either in terms of listening or performing, and always handled as aesthetic projects—that is, as meaningful experiences which the pupil enjoys. The basic aim here is to lead the pupil to

love a piece of music and desire to hear it more perfectly so that he may love and enjoy it better. With this in mind we pass on to the study phase of our learning, in which we analyze various tonal elements for special study. For instance, we may pick out tone quality and phrase structure. On these the pupil concentrates his attention, so that he comes to recognize them more clearly and to grasp their effect more fully. Then a new and better synthesis is achieved, in which the pupil is able to hear the composition better than he could before. This is our schematic conception of ear training, details of which will be considered later. And its relationship to appreciation, in general at least, is clear.

2. **Appreciation and rhythm.** Training in rhythm, as we shall see later, is not best or most fundamentally carried on by means of drill in time values, counting or beating time, or studying the meaning of time signatures, etc. Rhythmic training demands first and foundationally large, free, and untrammeled bodily response to music. This in itself is an extraordinary liberation and intensification of musical pleasure. So by proper rhythmic training, our love for music becomes quite definitely increased. Two general points should here be noted. (*a*) Rhythmic training through physical activity should always be in the spirit of delightful play. (*b*) It must always be a response to the mood of meaningful and delightful music, whose delightfulness becomes enhanced by adequate emphasis upon the factor of rhythm. Thus again we approach rhythm not by way of formal drill, but through actual music whose aesthetic interest and appeal is the main motive for the activity.

3. **Appreciation and mastery of the score.** When the reading mastery of the score is taught as a hard and painful drill akin to mathematics, it is incorrectly taught. Reading music should mean the perception of aesthetic significance

and possibility in the score. Hence, we should move from actual rote music making directly to a more and more expert ability to recognize beauty in the symbolism of the notation. How this may be undertaken will be discussed later. Here we make three general points only. (*a*) We should give the child worth while music to read, so that his mastery of the score means at the same time a mastery of good music. (*b*) We should make each new reading problem a project in the recognition and the creation of beauty, not a quasi-mathematical affair. (*c*) We should organize the whole reading program as one of musical-mental development, not one of mastering an arbitrary and baffling symbolism.

In general, our position is that appreciation is the central motive force and the true aim of all music education. Children are led to wish to improve musically because of the proper management of appreciation. As they improve musically, the vital thing in their development is a deeper and more effective love for music.

### Summary: Outcomes of this Chapter

1. Appreciation has been defined as the whole set of influences in music education which lead to an increased and more intelligent love of music.

2. Our whole account of learning as a creative rather than a mechanical process indicates that appreciation is the heart of music education. Where we do not have it, musical development and learning do not take place.

3. The enjoyment of music depends on certain definite psychological processes. Thus appreciation means the stimulation of these processes in the child.

4. The mental processes on which appreciation depends must be stimulated and capitalized by means of musical projects along the lines of listening, performing, and creating.

5. While it is of course both necessary and valuable to have carefully organized sequences of material for listening projects, yet we should not think of appreciation as confined to a definite course or lesson and excluded everywhere else.

6. The skills of hearing and rhythmic grasp, and the apprehension of the musical score must be taught with appreciation as a motive and as a goal.

7. We should capitalize the natural affinities of music with other cultural fields for the purpose of giving a broad associative basis for music study. These correlations should not be made in terms of chronology, or on a factual basis. The point is not that a piece of literature, or an instance of painting or architecture belongs to the same period as a composition with which we propose to associate them in the minds of the children. What we want are instances of art and literature that show an identity of mood, and the use of historical, geographical, and personal backgrounds for the sake of making the mood and meaning of the music more significant and real. Correlation of this kind vitalizes both the work in music, and the work in other fields as well. Such correlation is now a well recognized educational principle in fields other than music.

8. Only a teacher who is genuinely musically-minded, and whose musical feeling is integrated with a broad and human culture can develop appreciation along the lines we have indicated.

### Questions for Discussion.

1. Can you formulate any definition of appreciation other than that here offered? Have you ever seen it otherwise defined?

2. Do you recognize in your own musical experience the sources of musical pleasure here listed? Would you add any not here considered?

3. Have you ever encountered or known of any scheme of music teaching in school which completely ignored and made no attempt to develop one or more of the sources of musical pleasure here considered? What is your reaction to it?

4. Would you agree with Weld's classification of musical listeners? Does your experience with children suggest any other classification?

5. Suggest ways and means of adequately recognizing and caring for individual differences in types of musical enjoyment.

6. Why do we call listening a project?

7. In what way does listening differ from passive hearing?

8. Give some concrete examples from school music of the stimulation of reactions to music which seem to you *(a)* bad and inadvisable; *(b)* good and advisable.

9. What would be your opinion *(a)* of having pupils write essays on music they had heard; *(b)* of having them indicate composer, approximate date, style, etc., by underlining the appropriate words on a printed form?

10. Why can we not confine appreciation work to listening?

11. Do you think that toy orchestra work, or work in making toy instruments could fulfill any aims other than those we have suggested? Would this imply a different and perhaps a wider use of these methods? For what other aims, if any, could toy orchestra work be used?

12. What do you think about the practical limitations of the use of creative projects generally?

13. Select a few grade school songs, and work out possible lines for correlating them with other fields of culture. What would be the value for musical education of doing this with children?

14. Show why appreciation should not be limited to a definite course or sequence of lessons. Would this mean that we ought not to organize a sequence of material for listening projects?

BIBLIOGRAPHY.

1. BEATTIE, JOHN W., MCCONATHY, OSBOURNE, and MORGAN, RUSSELL V., *Music in the Junior High School,* Silver, Burdett and Company, 1930, ch. 12.

2. BEAUNIS, H., L'emotion musicale, *Revue Philosophique,* 1918, vol. 86, pp. 353-369.

3. BELAIEW-EXEMPLARSKY, SOPHIE, Op. cit. *v.* ch. 2.

4. COLEMAN, SATIS N., *Creative Music for Children,* G. P. Putnam's Sons, 1922.

5. DAVISON, ARCHIBALD T., *Music Education in America,* Harper and Brothers, 1926.

6. DICKINSON, EDWARD, *The Education of a Music Lover,* Charles Scribner's Sons, 1911.

7. DISERENS, CHARLES, M., *The Influence of Music on Behavior,* Princeton University Press, 1926.

8. DISERENS, CHARLES, M., Reactions to Musical Stimuli, *Psychological Bulletin,* 1923, vol. 20, pp. 173-199.

9. DOWNEY, JUNE, A Musical Experiment, *American Journal of Psychology,* 1897, vol. 9, pp. 63-69.

10. GALE, HARLOW, Op. cit. *v.* ch. 4.

11. GATEWOOD, ESTHER L., An Experiment in the Use of Music in an Architectural Drafting Room, *Journal of Applied Psychology,* 1921, vol. 5, pp. 350-358.

12. GILLILAND, A. R., and MOORE, H. T., The Immediate and Long Time Effects of Classical and Popular Phonograph Selections, *Journal of Applied Psychology,* 1924, vol. 8, pp. 309-323.

13. GILMAN, BENJAMIN, Report of an Experimental Test of Musical Expressiveness, *American Journal of Psychology,* 1892, vol. 4, pp. 558-576; 1893, vol. 5, pp. 42-73.

14. GLENN, MABELLE, Creative Song, *Childhood Education,* 1929, vol. 5, p. 324.

15. GLENN, MABELLE, DEFOREST, MARGARET, and LOWRY, MARGARET, *Music Appreciation for Every Child: Teacher's Manual for Primary Grades, Teacher's Manual for Intermediate Grades, Music Notes One, Two, and Three; Music Appreciation for the Junior High School; Teacher's Manual, Music Notes Four and Five,* Silver Burdett and Co., 1925-1930.

16. Hayward, Frank H., *The Lesson in Appreciation: An Essay in the Pedagogics of Beauty,* The Macmillan Company, 1917.
17. Katz, D., and Révécz, Geza, Musikgenuss bei Gehöhrlosen, *Für die gesammte Psychologie,* 1917-18, vol. 37, pp. 283-299.
18. McConathy, Osbourne, Miessner, W. O., Birge, E. B., and Bray, Mabel E., *The Music Hour in the Kindergarten and First Grade* (1929), *The Music Hour, Elementary Teacher's Book* (1929), *Intermediate Teacher's Book* (1931), and *Teacher's Guide for the Fifth Book* (1931), Silver, Burdett and Company.
19. McKenzie, Duncan, *Music in the Junior School,* Oxford University Press, 1929.
20. Mursell, James L., *Principles of Musical Education,* The Macmillan Company, 1927, ch. 7.
21. Ogden, Robert Morris, *Hearing,* Harcourt, Brace and Company, 1924, ch. 13.
22. Schoen, Max, The Aesthetic Attitude in Music, *Psychological Monographs,* 1928, vol. 39, No. 2, Whole No. 178, pp. 162-183.
23. Schoen, Max, (ed.) *The Effects of Music,* Harcourt, Brace and Company, 1927.
24. Sherman, Mandel, Emotional Characteristics of the Singing Voice, *Journal of Experimental Psychology,* 1928, vol. 11, pp. 495-497.
25. Stone, Kathryn E., *Music Appreciation Taught by Means of the Talking Machine,* Scott, Foresman and Company, 1922.
26. Victor Company, *Music Appreciation for the Elementary Grades,* R. C. A. Victor Co., Inc., 1930.
27. Weld, Henry Porter, An Experimental Study of Musical Enjoyment, *American Journal of Psychology,* 1912, vol. 23, pp. 245-308.
28. Whitley, Mary T., Music from the Standpoint of the General Educator, *Teachers College Record,* 1927, vol. 28, pp. 675-678.
29. Wright, Frances, *Monographs on School Music, Elementary Grades Series,* Los Angeles, Wolfer Printing Company, 1929.

# PART TWO

# *Factors in Musical Mindedness and How They May Be Developed in School Music*

## Chapter Six

# *Ear Training*

### The Nature and Controlling Principles of Ear Training

Ear training is that phase of music education which aims to develop a precise and sensitive perception of and response to the tonal elements in musical beauty. Clearly this is of immense importance. We have abundant evidence that even presumably well-trained musicians often fail to hear with any precision music to which they are listening. This is strikingly illustrated in a study made by Whipple, using the reproducing piano. He played to a number of musicians two renderings of the same brief phrase from a Liszt Rhapsody, one by Paderewski, the other by Friedmann. A careful scrutiny of the two rolls showed a really immense difference in treatment, the two pianists handling time values, pedaling, etc., very differently indeed. And of course it was easy enough to see just where the differences lay. But not one of the trained listeners was able to analyze them by ear, though they recognized that different effects were produced. If this is true of musicians, what must be the status of the layman? We may be quite sure that to a great many people music is simply a moving blur of sound. And it is hopeless to expect people so situated to love music, just as it would be hopeless to expect a man who knew no Greek to admire the beauty of Homer read in the original. If school music is to justify its existence, if it is to give boys and girls a living, growing, musical insight and experience which will have for them a continuing meaning when they are men and women, it is bound to help them to hear music aright. *Ear training is a vital, an indispensable factor in a democratic scheme of music education.*

Before turning to questions of practical detail, it will be instructive to state the general principles underlying ear training, and controlling its procedures.

1. *The ability to hear music aright is something that can be developed by training.* If a person who knew no Greek heard the Iliad read aloud, there would be a sound in his ears. But he would not really hear the language. He would need a process of arduous training before he could perceive its subtle and noble sonorities and majestic cadences. And certainly we would not think for a moment that anyone who could so hear the verse of Homer had the ability as a sort of miraculous gift from on high. Yet we often encounter just this idea in connection with music. Of course it is absurd. The ability to hear music is exactly like the ability to hear language. Both come by training.

It is interesting at this point briefly to compare the sort of ear training demanded by our Western music with other sorts of hearing ability, particularly those developed in exotic music, in the tuner, and in the research worker in acoustics. Various types of Eastern music have no system of tonality such as we employ, and no harmonic system proper. And we often find under these circumstances that a power which always seems to us very impressive and extraordinary is possessed by almost everybody. This is the power of absolute pitch, which our music does not greatly favor, but which is brought out far more in many other kinds of music. Again, a piano tuner hears music so very differently from a musician that it is said that musicians often find it very hard to become good tuners. When a perfect fifth is struck, the musician notices a particular chordal quality; but the tuner notices the beats. And here again we have an illustration of contrasts in ear training.

Or lastly, a research worker dealing with certain types of problems in acoustics or the psychology of sound, will become exceedingly skillful in picking out the fundamental and overtones whenever a note is sounded. But musicians tend merely to notice the timbre which is the result of the particular combination of overtones that happens to be sounding. All these points illustrate once again the fact that the capacity to hear music in a particular way is produced by training.

2. *Ear training must be functional.* That is to say, it must actually produce the ability to hear music better. For instance, it should enable a person to go to a concert and enjoy it far better than he otherwise would, simply because he hears far more than he otherwise could. Much work in ear training is formal rather than functional. That is, it consists of drill in recognizing various intervals, chords, etc. When the pupil has been hurried through it all, he is not much nearer a working capacity to hear *music* than he was when he began. So we would insist that ear training must not be carried on by using skips, intervals, scales, arpeggios of various chords, and so forth. This involves us again in the theory of learning as habit formation. And it is always very doubtful if the child will find himself able to apply what he has learned in the drill to the actual hearing of music. *Thus ear training must be carried on in and through the three kinds of musical projects, —listening, performing, and creating.* There is not a single thing that can be set up in drill form that cannot be better learned in an actual musical context and as part of a musically-meaningful undertaking. Ear training, to be precise, represents one angle of the analytic or study phase of musical learning. We take a musical composition and call the child's attention to its tonal elements, so that he comes to perceive them better and more clearly. This in a sentence sums up our conception of how such work should be done.

3. *We develop the ability to hear aright by helping the pupil to react aright to the music.* Ear training has been already defined as the development of perception, and perception depends upon action. The geologist, the botanist, the military strategist, and the mountaineer will notice quite different things in the same landscape, because they have developed different sets of reactions to it. So always we build up in the child the power to hear what is in the music by having him do something about what is in the music.

4. *We should use the various musical media with an eye to their value for ear training.* Let us briefly consider a few of the ways of making music from the standpoint of their possibilities and limitations for ear training. (*a*) The voice is unquestionably the best of all musical media for developing a refined capacity for hearing music. This is because with the voice the factors of pitch, quality, intensity, and expression generally are so directly under control, and above all because their control is so largely *mental* rather than mechanical. Of course many singers never do develop a fine skill in hearing, but this is because they are content to be vocalists rather than musicians. "*Vox et praeterea nihil.*" (*b*) The various string and wind instruments rank next in ear-training value. Indeed the violin demands a keener sense of pitch than does the voice. But the trouble here is the presence of a difficult mechanical technique, which makes a direct mental control such as we have in singing impossible. (*c*) Probably the piano has less definite and inevitable ear-training value than any other musical medium. This is because we can get tone precise in pitch and fixed in quality without thinking about it, by the mere actuation of a lever. Thus, much pianistic education is really training in a variety of typewriting. The great value of the piano for ear training lies in the fact that its keyboard

is the most direct symbolic representation we have of the tempered scale and the phenomenon of tonality. This is something that school music is just beginning to recognize and capitalize.

5. *Ear training must be associated vitally with appreciation.* This is our last general point. It means this. *Ear training must always be for the pupil an adventure in the discovery of beauty.* It may involve hard work. This is all right so long as the hard work is not formal work. The whole meaning of ear training is that it transforms a piece of music from a jumble of sound into an ordered system of lovely tone. As soon as ear training loses contact with the thrill, the delight, the fun of music making through one or all of the three kinds of musical projects, it loses touch with value and reality.

To avoid a possible confusion in the mind of the reader we should add one more comment by way of footnote and warning. Ear training and rhythmic training are very closely associated. The very same procedure may develop abilities along both lines. The working teacher must not think that now he will give a little bit of ear training, and now switch over to rhythmic training. Both flow forward together in music education. Nevertheless, it helps our exposition a great deal to draw a distinction here, and in a sense a real one exists. Ear training, as we use the term, applies particularly to the tonal as distinct more or less from the rhythmic element in music. But ear training and rhythmic training constitute a functional unit in educational practice.

### I. The Apprehension of Phrase and Melody

Music no more consists of notes than a poem consists of letters. We would never dream of trying to teach children the meaning and beauty of a poem by having them spell through the letters it contains. No more must we dream of trying to teach the child the meaning of a piece of music by having him attend to and spell out the notes it contains. Both the poem and the music are structures of meaningful phrases. *And so the most foundational thing in enabling the child to hear the music properly is to teach him to grasp its phrases and its melody.* This is the first and also the most important of all those tonal elements in musical beauty on which ear training must concentrate. In dealing with this topic we shall first discuss the psychology of melody and its application to teaching; then we shall consider the reasons for our claim that developing melodic grasp is the most important thing in ear training; and lastly we shall make some general comments.

1. *The psychology of melody and its applications to teaching.* A great deal of attention has been given to the psychological analysis of our experience of melody. Out of this, three main points have arisen which have very direct practical significance for music education.

(*a*) First of all it has been shown that the essence of a melody or a phrase is its unity. Humphrey carried on an experiment in which he trained his subjects to give a determinate automatic reaction to a certain tone. This means that after sufficient practice they always responded when, let us say, middle C was sounded alone, but not to any other tone sounded alone. But he found that these very subjects hardly ever gave the response when middle C was played as one of a sequence of tones. That is to say, a tone produces one psychological effect when it exists all by itself, but quite a different one when it is part of a phrase. Again, Heinlein showed that our feeling for tones depends largely on the presence of what he called a "melodic configuration," that is, on the relationship of the tones to one another in a complete musical phrase. Ortmann, in his elaborate monograph, brings out the same point in another way. He insists that the melodic unity, as it were, permeates every tone in the melody, so that if one tone only is changed, the meaning and the value of all the others is changed also. The most extensive and scientifically adequate piece of work along this line has been done by Bingham. He again emphasizes the reality and essential importance of the melodic unity. And he calls attention to another matter which is of vital practical interest. He had his subjects listen to sequences of tones while freely moving the index finger of one hand up and down. A device made a permanent graphic record of the movement. And it was found that whenever a sequence of tones (or as we may roughly call it, a tonal phrase) began and ended, there was an appreciable change in the movement. From this he drew the significant conclusion that the melodic unity is a *unity of response*. That is, we feel the phrase as a unit when, if, and because, we respond to it with a unitary reaction. Thus we would claim that a phrase is not to be thought of as just so many notes, but as a unity in its own right. If the reader feels at all puzzled over this idea of the phrase rather than the note being the unit—and it is too important an idea to be left in a fog—a simple illustration may help. Let him listen to anyone talking and try to count the words. He will find this is impossible. And the reason is that he hears not words but meaningful phrases. In just that very way music is made up of unitary phrases.

(*b*) The second point about melody that emerges for us from the studies is the explanation of our sense of pitch as "high" or "low," and of the movement of pitch in melody as "up" or "down." After all, in sound, *per se,* there is no such thing as highness or lowness, or up-ness or down-ness. All we have here are vibrations of different frequencies. Thurstone has argued that we contribute the feeling of up and down from our bodily reactions, our responses to sound. In speaking of singing a high note he says "the whole bodily attitude is one of climbing." For instance, even a trained singer will show a tendency to raise his eyebrows in singing a top note. When a low note is sung, the characteristic pose is one with the head drawn down and the chin lowered. Of course expert singers learn to inhibit the obvious, breathless scrambling up or down after notes of extreme range, but if we watch them carefully, it is evident enough that their bodies are really performing just such antics on a small scale. Again, Thurstone points out that if we sing the sequence C-E in time to the step, it is natural to sing the low tone on the down step, and very awkward to do the reverse. So for him the up and down of pitch which constitutes the melodic curve is due to physical response. It is the feeling of this response, correlated with the sound, that gives us our sense of tonal direction. And he says that this largely accounts for the aesthetic power of melody, because we do not merely hear the melody with our ears. We sense it with our whole body.

(*c*) The third point to be mentioned is that every phrase has a rhythmic structure which is independent of its melodic direction but which is an essential component of its unity. This can easily be illustrated. If we tap for every note of a phrase, or if we take a step for every note of a phrase, we have tapped or stepped the rhythmic structure of the phrase.

Thus we learn from psychological research that in teaching phrase properly *we must emphasize its unity and do this through response; we must emphasize its up and down, or melody curve, and do this through response; and we must emphasize its rhythmic structure.* Let us see how these ideas may be applied in school music, and more specifically, through the three kinds of musical projects,—listening, performing, and creating.

(1) The beginning of the whole process is the rote song taught phrase-wise. In outline the procedure is as follows. The teacher sings the song through to the class. It is important that this be done as beautifully and expressively as possible, because the aim is to set up a preliminary synthesis, a sense of the project. Some comment on the meaning and beauty of the song is valuable for the same purpose. Then the class sings the first phrase. When they have mastered this, they go on to the second phrase. When this is mastered, they sing the first two consecutively. The learning is pushed on in this sequence until the song can be sung as a whole. This is known to psychologists as the "repetitive part method" of learning, and it is recognized as perhaps the most effective that can be used. Thinking back to the psychology of melody and phrase we see that its value lies in the fact that we teach the phrase as the unit, and we do it by having the pupils respond to the song phrase-wise,—that is, the phrase unity is made the basis of response. If note errors occur, the singing should not be stopped till the end of the phrase. Anything that breaks up the phrase-wise response is bad. We do not want to set up a note-wise response or an anxiety about notes.

(2) The next step forward to be undertaken in the first grade, and even more thoroughly in the second, is to give the pupil experience in recognizing and picking out identical phrase patterns in songs he is learning to sing. When we speak of identical phrase patterns, we mean phrases which are exactly alike in melody, rhythm, and absolute pitch placement. An instance of a song which lends itself to such treatment is presented below. In order that the pupil may not get cues from

the language, it is desirable to have him sing with a neutral syllable while this kind of analysis is going on. He should learn to pick out identical phrases in rote songs which bring in varied phrase types,—those based on the tonic chord, on neighboring notes, on diatonic progressions, and on other intervals.

## The Postman

Abbie Farwell Brown
German Folk Song
1. Post-man! Post-man! Why is he late a-gain?
2. Post-man! Post-man! Have I a let-ter, Sir?
Post-man! Post-man! Where can he be?
Post-man! Post-man! Hur-ry and see!
Here he comes hur-ry-ing, Here he comes scur-ry-ing.
Why are you lin-ger-ing? What are you fin-ger-ing?
Lis-ten! Lis-ten! Yes, it is he!
Yes, Sir! Yes, Sir! That is for me!

FIGURE 2. Rote song for recognition of identical phrases. (From *The Progressive Music Series*, Book One, p. 8, by permission of the publishers.)

Various devices and types of response may be used to have the pupils indicate their recognition of the identical phrases. This work involves a more elaborate and analytical response to phrase elements, and so carries the development of phrase apprehension and the sense of phrase unity further than the mere phrase-wise learning of the song. This type of ear training is absolutely essential and fundamental in the development of the child's musicality.

(3) Yet another type of experience is that of responding to the beginnings and ends of phrases. This may be carried on in connection either with performance projects, *i.e.,* songs that the pupils are learning to sing, or with listening projects, where the music is suitable. The children close their eyes and make free movements with both arms in time to the music, bringing their hands together at rest for a moment at the end of each phrase, and commencing the movement with the new phrase. Jaques-Dalcroze works for virtually the same result by having pupils step in time to the notes, coming to a halt at the end of each phrase and beginning the new phrase with the same foot as that with which they ended the preceding one. This is a good deal more difficult, and for many reasons may not be so practical. Other forms of reaction could obviously be invented. The essential thing is to have the children sense physically the beginning, the rise and fall, and the close of the phrases.

(4) The physical sensing of pitch again can be taught in the first and second grades by having the pupils move their hands in the air as the melodic curve rises or falls. Where a diatonic progression is involved, the movement may be by steps. Where larger intervals occur, the movement may be by skips. It would seem advisable to work for a continuous rather than a discontinuous movement, however, as what we

The Clown
Nellie Poorman
French Folk Song
Jol - ly and gay is the fun - ny old clown,
Mer - ri - est fel - low that comes to our town;
Ev - 'ry - one laugh-ing wher - ev - er he goes,
Tumbling a - bout in his com - i - cal clothes.
When I am old e-nough I'll be a clown.

FIGURE 3a. "The Clown" (from *The Progressive Music Series,* Book One, p. 30) with the same rhythmic figure throughout. Used by permission of the publishers.

want is a continuous pitch-curve, rather than note-wise jerks.

(5) In the second and third grades experience in responding to the rhythmic structure of the phrase may be introduced. While we shall return to this in our chapter on rhythm, it seems well to discuss it here for the sake of clarity. The point

## Twinkling Fireflies

Anna M. Pratt — Alfred G. Wathall

3
4
Fire - flies shi - ning in the night,
Twin - kling like the stars so bright;
Here and there, In the air,
Oh, you are a pret - ty sight!

FIGURE 3b. "Twinkling Fireflies" (from *The Progressive Music Series,* Book One, p. 11) with the same rhythmic pattern in three out of four phrases. Used by permission of the publishers.

here is to take the song phrase-wise, and have the pupils perceive (and this means respond to) the identity or difference of the rhythms of the phrases. Two song illustrations are given above, one in which the rhythm pattern is the same throughout, the other where an identical rhythm pattern is used in three out of the four phrases. Other instances are the song "Bubbles" (*The Progressive Music Series,* Book One,

p. 9), where one rhythmic phrase pattern is used, the song "Whippoorwill" (*ibid.* p. 16), where the rhythmic pattern of the first phrase is used four times, and the song "Little Sister's Lullaby" (*ibid.* p. 31), where there is one slight variation in the rhythmic phrase pattern. These rhythms should be clapped out or stepped out, with a clap or step for each separate note in the phrase, *not for each beat of the measure.* Tapping is to be discouraged, for it is too small a movement. *We want to set up the feel for the rhythmic swing of the phrase, and in this way build up phrase-grasp in terms of response to the essential, meaningful unity.*

(*d*) The creative projects in the third grade come as a sort of climactic development of all this work, carry it further, and confirm its results. With the kind of experience we have described behind him, the child should be able to develop significant musical ideas of his own. Here is a very fine type of response to the phrase unity. He is now actually thinking in phrases as units, having an up-and-down contour and rhythmic pattern. Moreover, when a tune is suggested in class, its phrase interest may be made the center of the teacher's criticism and discussion. That is, the children may be led to recognize the aesthetic superiority of certain types of phrase-endings, and thus their grasp of phrase is definitely increased.

(*e*) Such work as this with phrase and melody leads naturally and directly into the mastery of the score. In the creative project the pupil learns how to write music. It is probable that for some time before this he has been singing with the book before him, and that his attention has been called to the symbolism of the musical notation in ways that will be described in Chapter Eight. As his mastery of the score increases, we can use it as a device for phrase recognition, writing the song on the board and having the pupil encircle identical phrases with his hands, indicate beginnings and endings, and so on. In general, the increasing power to visualize music gives many opportunities for types of response which lead reciprocally to a more discriminating and precise hearing of the music.

2. *Why melodic grasp is the most important aim in ear training.* It will be remembered that we made the statement that building up a keen appreciation of phrase and melody was the most important thing that ear training had to do. Of course this is what justifies the length of our discussion of the psychological basis of melody and its educational applications. But some readers may feel inclined to challenge such a claim. Certainly the conventional, formalized schemes of ear training that have been used in the past, and indeed are still widely employed, seem to work in very different directions. So we must give reasons for the position we take.

(*a*) In the first place, training in response to phrase is important because it is the bridge between the tonal and the rhythmic elements in music. We have already indicated, and shall later confirm the view that much rhythmic training consists essentially in calling attention to the rhythm pattern of the phrase. Hence, to develop a feeling for phrase unity and melodic direction is to work towards both tonal and rhythmic grasp at the same time. (*b*) The phrase is the unit of musical structure. No one can really come to a perception of the form of a composition unless he grasps it in terms of phrase. Therefore, work with the phrase is the basis of our developed sense of musical form. (*c*) When we come to discuss reading in particular, and mastery of the score in general, we shall find once more that the natural approach is through the phrase. The pupil is taught to perceive the meaningful phrase structure in the notation, rather than to spell out the separate notes. And the proper approach to this is obviously to build up a preliminary apprehension of phrase by ear. When the score comes to be used, it constitutes a device which carries skill in hearing further and makes it more precise. And particularly it enables the pupil to perceive the involutions and relationships of the phrases better than before. (*d*) Any creative work in the way of actual composition is essentially a creation of phrases. A note-wise approach to such work, an attempt to have the pupil build his tune by deciding painfully what the next note ought to be, would inevitably fail. What little we know of the psychology of musical composition clearly shows that it is not a matter of building musical structures note by note, but of conceiving phrases and groups of phrases as units. (*e*) We shall find later on that the real approach to the problem of technique is through grasp of phrase. Technique is not a matter of mechanics or acrobatic agility, but of music making. What we need to work for in trying to build up a facility is to make the phrase not only the unit of musical meaning, but also the unit of motor effort. In this way we transform technique from an obstacle into a means of musical development. And the foundational training looking towards technique will be in responsiveness to phrase. (*f*) Lastly, we shall find that most of what we call expression in music,—the management of tone color, tempo, and dynamics—aims essentially at bringing out the phrase unities, and is demanded by the phrase. So once again we see that training in apprehension of phrase is a primary element in musical development.

There are two elements in ear training that have nothing directly to do with melodic apprehension. These are the development of the feeling for harmony and for tonality or key.

But even here we shall find that our best approach is in and through melodic experience.

3. *General comments.* A few comments of a general nature remain to be made before we pass on from this topic. (*a*) Melodic apprehension is taught ideally through the medium of the voice. By no other means can we so clearly and directly sense the curve and sweep of the melody and the beginning and ending of the phrases. It should perhaps be said here that all the methods suggested for producing a feeling for up and down and for phrase endings, need to be built into vocal experience. When we clearly feel the melody with the voice, we feel it best of all. The technique of the voice depends with surprising directness upon the structure of the music. Thus, when we teach the children to apprehend a rote song phrase-wise, we indirectly yet effectively teach them breath control. On the one hand, breath control is vital for voice production; on the other hand, we naturally sense the phrase on the breath. (*b*) Developing melodic apprehension absolutely requires the use of good melodic material. Once more we must not be bound down by any alleged law of proceeding from simple to complex. Experience with melodic material of high value is essential at all costs. Much of the material used in school music will not measure up to this demand. Too often it is "sight reading" music, designed for mere drill purposes (learn-to-do-by-doing) rather than beautiful music which expresses the impulse of an artistic spirit. (*c*) Instrumental work properly conducted can greatly extend the pupil's conception of and feeling for melody and phrase. It is perfectly true that no musical medium carries the phrase so naturally as the voice. But the mere fact that, with an instrument one has to work at and overcome motor problems

in order to make the phrase intelligible, calls for a degree of attention to phrasing which is valuable in itself.

## II. Apprehension of Harmony

The second function of ear training which we will discuss is the development of a feeling for harmony in music. This is one of the points on which psychological findings can be extremely useful guides to the music teacher, showing what sort of procedures are hopeless, and along what lines to work for a constructive result. The literature on the nature of the harmonic experience is very extensive. Much of it is highly technical and contentious, and there are a great many clashing theories. The reader who is interested in the various questions involved is advised to study the contributions by Watt and Ogden listed at the close of this chapter. What seems most useful to do here is to proceed much as we did in the case of phrase and melody, that is, to sum up the most important findings relevant to music education, and then to show their practical bearing.

1. *The psychology of the harmonic element in music.* We shall do no more than state conclusions rather dogmatically, for a complete theoretical justification of the positions we take would call for a long and intricate discussion.

(*a*) *The place of harmony in music.* Ogden has insisted that all music,—and this includes musical systems quite different from our own—has been controlled by two distinct principles, the principle of melody and the principle of harmony. Practically all music except our own Western system has been developed on the basis of melody. That is, it is purely melodic music, and when harmonic effects have occurred, as of course they have whenever more than one voice is used or any sort of accompaniment is introduced, they have been incidental and have never been capitalized. Western music alone has come to recognize and make much of the possibility of harmony. It is both interesting and instructive to see how this has come about. Before the day of the composer and theorist Rameau, there was an extensive development of polyphony, both in sacred and secular music. Rameau was the first to perceive that a new principle, a new type of musical effect was really involved—the principle of harmony—for the earlier polyphonic music simply put the various voices together without paying much attention to the chord effects produced and without working for harmonic beauty or interest. While he did not himself develop a new style of music in his own compositions, he formulated the laws of the later musical development in his recognition of the significance of the tonic, dominant, and subdominant chords, and of chord sequence. Since his day many musicians have greatly exaggerated the rôle of harmony, and have treated music as consisting of blocks of chords built up from the bass. This has been responsible, as Cecil Gray puts it, for "some of the worst music ever written." Some very modern music, which wholly ignores melody, and works for effects of cloudy harmonic sequence, well represents another kind of exaggeration of the harmonic element. All this simply means one-sided music, exactly as purely melodic music is one-sided music. Obviously the ideal music will be that which achieves a balance between all possible elements of tonal beauty.

So much for theory. Out of it we glean a practical conclusion of much value. *Harmony should not be taught or sensed as blocks of chords, but as that shifting sequence of beautiful qualities which arise when several melodic lines are sounding together.* This indicates at once that the proper beginning for harmonic training is in ensemble, and particularly vocal ensemble. So school music offers just the opportunity we want in this direction. The fact that a great many school music teachers almost completely fail to build up any feeling for harmony in their pupils is due, not at all to the impossibility of doing it in their situation, but to not knowing how to go about it.

(*b*) *The nature of chords.* We must remember that a chord, psychologically speaking, is always a quality. This idea is brought out strikingly in the work of Edmonds and Smith, and Moran and Pratt, listed at the close of the chapter. Edmonds and Smith asked their subjects to give free and direct descriptions of two-tone clangs (octave, third, fifth, etc.). Now it might be thought that different people would feel these two-tone chords very differently. But the surprising thing in the study was precisely the high agreement among the listeners. Thus the octave was very commonly characterized as "smooth," the seventh as "astringent," the sixth as "luscious," the fourth and second as "rough," the third as "mellow," etc. Of course the same word was not always used, but the same idea was forthcoming with unexpected regularity. Moran and Pratt carried these findings a step further by showing that various two-tone chords retain their identity even when slightly mistuned, so that a third still seems like a third, and a sixth still seems like a sixth even when the vibration ratios are wrong. This is the basis for our claim that a chord is essentially, in experience, a qualitative identity. And the practical meaning of the point for music education is that in developing the harmonic sense *we need to have the children make friends with chords and recognize their quality rather than analyze them.* Chord analysis has no value at all except in so far as it helps the direct synthetic grasp of the identity of the tonal combination as a quality or a color.

2. *The practical issues of these psychological results.* It is quite clear that what is required is the introduction into the school music program of material with genuine harmonic interest, and the teaching of the child to recognize the harmonic content that is given. It is often said that the proper way into harmony is through polyphony. The point in fact is strongly urged by Davison. This is quite true, but it is only a half truth. In the evolution of music, polyphony was familiar for centuries before it was recognized at all that harmonic possibilities existed. It is not only possible, it is very easy, for a child to carry a part in ensemble singing without any particular awareness of the harmonic effects being produced. The real point of insisting on the polyphonic approach is seen in the case of the child whose whole contact with music has been through private lessons in piano. Unless he has been most skillfully taught, he is almost certain to think of and feel harmony as blocks of chords rather than as a beautiful shifting of colors as different parts come into juxtaposition. But the child in public school music gets the melodic approach anyhow. The danger is that he will never be made effectively aware of harmony. For this reason we feel that much of the part-song work used in the grades is altogether too polyphonic and not sufficiently harmonic in its interest. We question, for instance, whether the ideal approach to part-singing is through the extensive, almost exclusive use of rounds, though this is extremely common. The important thing is to be clear as to what we are aiming at; to see just what mental processes we wish to arouse. The child who is singing in a round has essentially the problem of sticking to his part, and of course this means that his attention is riveted to that one part and very little else. He has little encouragement, and indeed little chance, to feel himself contributing to a total harmonic, quali-

tative effect. It may be said that this cannot be avoided, and that if we are to have parts, those who sing them must give their primary attention to them. But this is not quite true. It all depends on the type of music we use. There is a real difference in terms of musical experience between singing the tenor part in a hymn tune and the tenor part in a four-part canon. In the one case we have part-singing that is primarily harmonic. In the other we have part-singing that is primarily melodic. It is our decided opinion that the balance between melody and harmony has not been well maintained in our grade school singing, and that music teachers in their enthusiasm for melody have tended unduly to ignore harmony. This is always apt to show up when instrumental ensemble work begins, for here a sense of the harmonic effect of the whole aggregation is an important guide for the individual.

Specifically then, we would recommend beginning part-singing by building up chords with the class, and by reversing the parts in chords, so that the firsts transfer to the seconds, and *vice versa.* As a very important element in this process, the holding of chord tones and interchange of parts gives the class a chance to listen to their intonation. Listening to each other improves tone quality, balance, and "in-tuneness." We believe that more part-song work of definite harmonic interest should be used, and that devices to call the child's attention to the total harmonic effect are very valuable. With the older children hymn tunes make admirable material of the kind indicated. The analysis of chords into their component notes may be a desirable aid in some cases, but always its aim should be the creation and reinforcement of a sense of the chord as a qualitative unity. We have seen children who had much trouble in singing the dominant seventh arpeggio, obviously because it was just a sequence of notes in which they had no feeling for the identity of the chord. *The reader should notice that we do not argue for the complete avoidance of polyphonic part-singing. But we do feel that the tendency to over-emphasize this needs a rather drastic corrective in order to secure a more balanced program.*

## III. The Apprehension of Key or Tonality

The third main aim of ear training is the building of an apprehension of tonality. This word is used in a number of different senses both by musicians and psychologists. We shall employ it to mean the feeling for key.

1. *The nature of tonality.* The evolution of our modern feeling for tonality, and of the various musical scales is another long and complicated story into whose details we shall not enter here, though the reader will find them discussed in the literature mentioned in the bibliography. But some very enlightening and important points arise, which we now consider.

(*a*) Bingham has pointed out that tonality is essentially a *system of expectations.* That is, when we have music in a certain key, the presence of any given tone leads us to expect certain sequential tones. If these expectations are violated, an unpleasant effect is produced. We are set to go in a certain direction, and meet with frustration. Many textbooks on harmony make considerable use of this idea by pointing out in various ways the tendential effect of the tones of the scale, —the leading note, the dominant, the mediant, and so on. Frances Wright, in her monograph, has called this "tonal magnetism," and suggests teaching the child to recognize certain tones as "magnet tones." Duncan McKenzie is speaking of the same thing when he writes about the "mental effect" of the *Tonic Sol-fa* system as largely used in Canada and Great Britain. *In building a feeling for tonality the aim is to create in the child the proper system of expectations regarding the component tones of the key.*

(*b*) The scale does not produce tonality. Tonality produces the scale. We may regard this as a well-established and authoritative result of psychological investigation. Some years ago the psychology of music was largely dominated by what Max Meyer has called the "diatonic fallacy," which is the idea that all music depends upon the diatonic scale. Even so great a scientist as Helmholtz was guilty of this mistake, so that it was even possible for him to try to read chromatics and accidentals out of the musical system, and to speak of them as "akin to howling." As a matter of fact, the selection of certain tones to constitute a scale has been largely a matter of practical and social convenience. In music education, too, the fallacious notion of the primacy of the scale has had enormous influence. But we now see clearly that *the proper approach to tonality is not through the scale.* We build a feeling for tonality by taking actual melodies, and calling attention to the tendential values of the various notes. In this way we create a system of expectations which is precisely what we mean by a sense of key.

2. *Devices for teaching tonality.* Any and every teaching device by which we try to develop tonality must work in just this direction. It must be a means of directing the child's attention to the tendential effects of melodies he is singing, playing, or hearing. So we see once more that working towards a grasp of key is an analytic phase of musical learning.

(*a*) By far the commonest device for emphasizing tendential effects and building a system of tonal expectation is the application of the *so-fa* syllables. In England the system is known as the *"Tonic Sol-fa,"* a teaching device which involves, among other things, a notation of its own. In America, school music teachers use the *so-fa* syllables, largely without the rest of the system, because they are easily applied and so far represent the simplest device for practical application. Their use is now conventional and most teachers do not think the system through to its psychological meaning and value. Our position is that *the value of the "so-fa" system lies in its power of defining and bringing before the learner the tonality element in music.* Everything we have to say about it flows from this idea.

First, we should see from all that has been said that it is quite needless to teach the *so-fa* system as a whole, that there is no need to drill the children directly on memory-knowledge of the seven syllables and their chromatic variants. Indeed it is dangerous to do this, because unless we are careful we are back to the point of approaching tonality through the scale. Rather we should begin with the stage of rote song, and teach the syllables (instead of words) as one verse of the song. In this way the tonality effect of the melody is brought into prominence.

Secondly, we should understand that the *so-fa* system is not capitalized to its full value unless the so-called tendential effect —the tonality effect proper—of the various tones is made explicit. This is not done in America as it might be, largely because our teachers use a part of the system only, as a mere convenience, and without understanding its psychological significance. We have said that elementary textbooks on harmony call attention in one way or another to the tendential effect of the various tones of the scale. And the music teacher whose musical apprehensions have been properly developed should himself be keenly conscious of these effects. Of course the idea is not to impart them to the children in any such generalized, technical manner as may be appropriate at the level of the conservatory student. But there is no good reason why they should not be made progressively aware of the reposeful effect of *do, mi,* and *so,* and of the tendential quality of *re, fa, la,* and *ti* in the major tonality, and of the characteristic alterations in effect that occur in the minor tonality. The indicated procedure would be to have the tones sung slowly and attentively, and thought and imaged carefully, noticing the tendential and reposeful effects produced. Another device would be to associate the tones sung with the syllables with the system of hand signs worked out in connection with the *Tonic Sol-fa* system. These hand signs have fallen into some disrepute among American school music teachers, because they have seemed somewhat artificial and mechanical. But after all, the same objections apply to the syllables themselves. And the hand signs ingeniously suggest the tonality effects which we wish to emphasize. The whole topic is explained in detail in Duncan McKenzie's excellent book, *Music in the Junior School,* to which the reader is referred for further information.

Thirdly, we may refer to the old debate as to whether to use the fixed or the movable *do.* We must bear in mind that what we want is not the development of the scale but the building of tonality. With the fixed *do* system the emphasis is at once on the intervals of the scale. Hence we feel strongly that for the kind of work we have in mind, the use of the movable *do* is definitely preferable. Our aim, it should always be remembered, is to teach *relationship within the key.*

Fourthly, let us consider the criticism that is sometimes leveled at the use of the *so-fa* system by school music teachers. Sometimes it is said that the whole thing is quite artificial; that other methods and devices can be satisfactorily used; and that we ought to get rid of the syllables. Our reply is very simple. Until an adequate substitute is found, we must continue to use the *so-fa* system. If we let it go, we must put something else in its place, or wholly give up the teaching of tonality. Some alternatives are in use, and no doubt they have their good points. Our interest is not so much in the *so-fa* system as such, but in setting up some practical and effective device for developing a keen feeling for key.

(*b*) There is one other device for bringing out tonality relationships on which something ought to be said. This is the use of the piano keyboard. The one outstanding value of the piano in ear training is that its keyboard is a direct graphic representation of the relationships among tones. There can be no question that if a scheme can be devised for bringing rote songs into early and intimate relationship with the piano, we shall have something decisively better than our present approach through *so-fa*. The advantages of the pianistic approach are these. The keyboard is a complete graphic representation of tonal relationships, including accidentals. It represents everything directly, where the *so-fa* and kindred systems represent tone only conventionally. Its use directly enlarges the pupil's musical experience through music making in another medium. All in all, there can be little question that the piano is the best available medium for the teaching of key. The problem is to make it usable in school music situations.

3. *Special problems in teaching tonality.*

(*a*) First we have the problem of modulation. As soon as we come to modulated music we become aware of the limits of the *so-fa* system with movable *do*. Indeed, with highly chromatic music, passing rapidly from one key to another, the system simply breaks down, and becomes an added problem rather than a help. In simple modulations, such as we have in the usual grade singing materials, the procedure may be to isolate and recognize the "bridge tone" between the two keys, and then to help the child to apprehend the shift of expectations produced by the new key.

(*b*) Then there is the problem of the minor mode. The two methods of dealing with this question constitute the approach, first through the relative minor, and second through the tonic minor. We must remember again that we are interested in tonality rather than scale. This interest indicates the approach through the relative minor rather than through the tonic. The minor tonality involves a shift of expectations rather than a new set of scale relationships, and this situation is what we ought to emphasize. The transformation of a major scale into its tonic minor is just the problem in which we are not primarily interested. Incidentally we may say that there is convincing evidence showing that sadness is not the essential characteristic of the minor mode. The point is discussed at length by Heinlein, who summarizes most of the literature, and insists that the sadness we often find in the minor is really read into it, and that the essence of the mode is the different distribution of tonal relationships as compared with the major.

(*c*) It may be asked just how much formal drill we would recommend in building a grasp of tonality. Our reply is, as little as possible, and that little in close and definite conjunction with musical situations. For instance, where we have a phrase involving a tonic chord sequence (*do-mi-so*), or a leading tone-tonic sequence (*ti-do*), it may sometimes be useful to drill a little on these sequences in general. But formal drill work apart from illustrating an actual musical problem is just what we do not want. Our sense of tonality is wholly built up by the analytic study of the tone relationships of melodies that are heard, sung, or performed.

(*d*) The creative project may be of particular value in building a definite sense of tonality. In an article on "Creative Music" in *Childhood Education,* to which reference is made in the bibliography, it is explained how the third grade children come to decide that their melodies sound better if they "come home," *i.e.,* return to the tonic. This, of course, is definitely a tonality effect, which is thus discovered through creative work, and could hardly be demonstrated so effectively by any other approach.

(*e*) Lastly, a word should be said about the relationship of the feeling for tonality and the symbolism for key as given in the musical notation. Here as elsewhere, we build towards a grasp of the significance of the symbols through rich experience of the thing symbolized. As the symbols themselves come to be more and more meaningful, they have a reciprocal effect in the way of clearing up, defining, and generally clinching the background experience.

## IV. The Development of Auditory Imagery

Building up the power to image and think in tone is the last of the functions of ear training with which we shall deal. Miss Agnew's work shows its great importance. She found that musicians always report the use of tonal imagery, and that the great composers constantly emphasize it in their accounts of their own creative processes, and in their advice concerning musical training. The developed use of auditory imagery is one of the very best means of helping to make a pupil's work really musical rather than mechanical, because a great deal of playing and singing goes on without any keen attention to the effect desired, and so without any keen critical discrimination as to the effects actually produced. Kovácz in his paper on musical memory, the main outcomes of which were described in the chapter on musical learning, says that one reason why it proves better for students to learn a composition from the score without playing it, is that it remains flexible longer, and does not stiffen prematurely into a definite mold which is hard to break. Of course his procedures with advanced and well-trained piano pupils cannot be duplicated in school music. But the underlying principle of the use of musical imagery most assuredly can and should find an application in our field.

Thus we would say that a regular aim of grade school work in music should be to give the children opportunities to think music before they sing or play it. The teacher sings a phrase, and gives the class a moment or two to think it through before they try to sing it. When mistakes are made, the teacher may re-sing the phrase, and then ask the class to think it through and try to see where it was different from their own performance. Again the monotone can often be greatly helped by being led to think or image pitch, for his trouble may lie, as we have seen, in improperly directed attention. As preparation for reading a song at sight, the class should observe the notation throughout, noting and *thinking* the familiar phrase types, and the less familiar motives and figures,—all before actually singing. When the score has been mastered, it should always be used for more than merely reading. It may be used as a means of cultivating musical imagery by having the class go over a song or piece in notation and then listen to it as sung, to decide whether it sounded as they thought it would. These are but a few illustrations of how musical imagery may be developed and encouraged in school music. There are really no particular psychological problems, and no great dangers to guard against. The teacher who recognizes the very great importance of this type of ear training will readily find other opportunities of developing musical imagery in connection with the carrying through of the three classes of musical projects.

### Ear Training in Relation to Theory and Harmony

The work in ear training that we have been describing is the natural foundation for the formal course in harmony. Indeed, such training is the only way to make the study of harmony really functional and vital. Unless the student comes into the harmony course already keenly responsive to melody, harmony, and tonality, and able to think effectively in terms of tonal imagery, there is no way at all to avoid making the subject a drill on the application of deductive rules, and so much more akin to mathematics than to music. The proper degree of ear-mindedness cannot possibly be developed in a semester or a year. It is necessarily the outcome of many years of carefully directed experience. The inadequate sections on "ear training" that we find in so many elementary harmony textbooks are positively pathetic. They can no more rescue the subject from formalism than a candle can warm a railroad station. But they are witnesses to a very real need. When school music does not furnish the student with enough skill in hearing and thinking tone to render possible a vital harmony course in senior year in high school, the program stands condemned on a most serious count. The sort of harmony course which is clearly indicated is by no means the conventional affair where rules are learned from a textbook and applied in formal exercises which may appear "interesting" to the technically-trained teacher, but which are meaningless musically to the pupils. Rather it should be closely associated with listening, performing, and creating. It should involve an analysis of the basis of fine musical effects produced by great composers. It should aim consciously at the creation of more and more interesting music, using the various effects and laws to enrich and give broader scope to the pupil's musical ideas. Finally, it should produce playable and singable music, which should be performed in class and subjected to constructive criticism.

### Summary: Outcomes of This Chapter

1. Ear training is training in the power to perceive the tonal elements in musical beauty. It always involves setting up the right kind of responses to music. It should not proceed in terms of formal drill, but as an analysis associated with the three types of musical projects.

2. While the use of the voice offers the best all-round opportunity for effective ear training, yet every musical medium has its unique possibilities and limitations in this regard, which ought to be understood if that medium is to be used with maximum educative effect.

3. We have discussed ear training from the viewpoint of developing a grasp of phrase and melody, of harmony, and of tonality. There are other possible directions which ear training could certainly take. For instance, one might undertake to teach absolute pitch, something that could be done successfully, as the studies on this topic in the bibliography show. But the three types of ear training work discussed seem the foundational ones from a practical point of view.

4. Developing melodic grasp depends on responsiveness to melodic unity, to melodic curve, and to the pattern of the phrase rhythm. For many reasons this appears to be the most important factor in ear training.

5. Developing a sense of harmony means building up a

feeling for chords as qualitative effects produced by the juxtaposition of voices in polyphony. But mere polyphony will not guarantee an adequate harmonic consciousness. We need music definitely harmonic in interest, and a direction of attention towards the total ensemble effect.

6. Developing a sense of tonality means building up a proper system of expectations. Tonality does not depend on the scale, but *vice versa.* Hence we approach tonality through analyzing the element of tonal relationship in actual music.

7. No scheme of ear training can be considered adequate which does not make constant provision for developing musical imagery.

8. High school harmony should be regarded as the natural culmination of the ear training phase of school music work.

9. The relationship of this chapter to the rest of the book calls for a word of comment. It is more or less an arbitrary matter whether to discuss certain topics in a chapter formally devoted to ear training, or to treat them elsewhere. For instance, we deal with tone quality and musical structure in connection with appreciation, and with dynamics in the chapter on expression. But they have an obvious relationship to ear training. As a matter of fact, they belong in both places, and our classification is to a large extent based on convenience and ordinary convention. Furthermore, the treatment of rhythm is very closely associated with ear training; and we regard reading as essentially an extension and particularization of aural and rhythmic grasp through the use of a visual symbolism. So the chapter on ear training has vital and functional relationships with most of the other topics of the book, and this should not be a source of confusion.

10. Finally, we wish to point out that ear training, as we conceive it, is essentially associated with appreciation. We use actual music, along the lines of listening, performing, or cre-

ating. We study its tonal beauties. In this way we build up a better and more intelligent appreciation of it. Thus we find appreciation as both the motive and the goal of ear training as we conceive it.

QUESTIONS FOR DISCUSSION.

1. Could we say that ear training is the center of music education? Why?

2. Have you ever known of processes and methods in music education which took no account of ear training?

3. Assemble from this chapter illustrations of the claim made in the first section that perception depends on response.

4. What are the objections to the use of formal drill in ear training? Mention and discuss some formal drill processes in ear training.

5. Can you think of any ways of teaching a song that involve a note-wise rather than a phrase-wise approach?

6. What are the three psychological characteristics of melody which must be remembered when we try to teach melodic grasp? Can you think of any applications of these ideas in addition to those suggested in this chapter?

7. What is the essential value of the *so-fa* system? Suggest ways of using it *(a)* which capitalize this value; *(b)* which fail to capitalize it.

8. Do you know any substitutes for the *so-fa* system?

9. What would be the practical advantages of the pianistic approach to tonality?

10. Why do we argue against beginning part-singing entirely with rounds?

11. What instances do you know of the exaggeration or overvaluation of the harmonic element in music?

12. Discuss the importance of musical imagery, and suggest methods for developing it.

13. What criticisms would you make of the conventional course in harmony, either in high school or in a school of music?

14. Show how a developed feeling for melody, for harmony, and for tonality will deepen our appreciation of music.

BIBLIOGRAPHY.


1. AGNEW, MARIE, A Comparison of Auditory Images of Musicians, Psychologists, and Children, *Psychological Monographs,* 1922, vol. 31, No. 1, Whole No. 140, pp. 268-278.
2. AGNEW, MARIE, The Auditory Imagery of Great Composers, *Psychological Monographs,* 1922, vol. 31, No. 1, Whole No. 140, pp. 279-287.
3. BAIRD, J. W., Memory for Absolute Pitch, *Studies in Psychology, Titchener Commemorative Volume,* 1917, pp. 43-78.
4. BINGHAM, W. VANDYKE, Studies in Melody, *Psychological Monographs,* 1910, vol. 12, No. 3, Whole No. 50.
5. BOGGS, LUCINDA PEARL, Studies in Absolute Pitch, *American Journal of Psychology,* 1907, vol. 18, pp. 194-205.
6. EDMONDS, E. M., and SMITH, M. E., The Phenomenological Description of Musical Intervals, *American Journal of Psychology,* 1923, vol. 34, pp. 287-291.
7. GOUGH, EVELYN, The Effects of Practice on Judgments of Absolute Pitch, *Archives of Psychology,* 1922, No. 47.
8. HEINLEIN, CHRISTIAN PAUL, A Brief Discussion of the Nature and Function of Melodic Configuration in Tonal Memory, with Critical Reference to the Seashore Tonal Memory Test, *Pedagogical Seminary and Journal of Genetic Psychology,* 1928, vol. 35, pp. 45-61.
9. HEINLEIN, CHRISTIAN PAUL, The Affective Characters of the Major and Minor Modes in Music, *Journal of Comparative Psychology,* 1928, vol. 8, pp. 101-142.
10. HUMPHREY, GEORGE, The Effect of Sequence of Indifferent Stimuli on a Response of the Conditioned Reflex Type, *Journal of Abnormal Psychology,* 1927, vol. 22, pp. 194-212.
11. JAQUES-DALCROZE, EMIL, *Rhythm, Music, and Education,* tr. Harold F. Rubinstein, G. P. Putnam's Sons, 1921.

12. McConathy, Osbourne, Embs, Anton H., Fouser, C. E., and Howes, Maude M., *An Approach to Harmony,* Silver, Burdett and Company, 1927, pp. ix-xii, 166-170.

13. McKenzie, Duncan, *Music in the Junior School,* Oxford University Press, 1929, ch. 2.

14. Moore, Henry Thomas, The Genetic Aspect of Consonance and Dissonance, *Psychological Monographs,* 1914, vol. 17, No. 2, Whole No. 73.

15. Moran, Helen, and Pratt, Carroll C., Variability of Judgment on Musical Intervals, *Journal of Experimental Psychology,* 1926, vol. 9, pp. 492-500.

16. Mull, Helen K., The Acquisition of Absolute Pitch, *American Journal of Psychology,* 1925, vol. 36, pp. 469-493.

17. Ogden, R. M., *Hearing,* Harcourt, Brace and Company, 1924, ch. 13.

18. Ogden, R. M., The Tonal Manifold, *Psychological Review,* 1920, vol. 27, pp. 136-146.

19. Ortmann, Otto, On the Melodic Relativity of Tones, *Psychological Monographs,* 1926, vol. 35, No. 1, Whole No. 162.

20. Pear, T. H., The Experimental Examination of Some Differences between the Major and the Minor Chord, *British Journal of Psychology,* 1911, vol. 4, pp. 56-88.

21. Seashore, Carl Emil, *The Psychology of Musical Talent,* Silver, Burdett and Company, 1919.

22. Smith, Franklyn Orion, The Effect of Training in Pitch Discrimination, *Psychological Monographs,* 1914, vol. 17, No. 3, Whole No. 69, pp. 67-103.

23. Thurstone, L. L., The Problem of Melody, *Musical Quarterly,* 1920, vol. 6, pp. 426-429.

24. Watt, Henry J., *The Foundations of Music,* Cambridge University Press, 1919, chs. 2 and 8.

25. Wright, Frances, *Monographs on School Music, Elementary Grades Series, Number One*, Los Angeles, Wolfer Printing Co., 1929.

Chapter Seven

# Rhythmic Training

## The General Problem of Rhythmic Training

The general problem of rhythmic training is closely similar to that of ear training. We must separate, emphasize, and bring to the consciousness of the learner the rhythmic element in music he is hearing, performing, or creating. This is the essence of the undertaking. There are a few preliminary points which call for comment.

1. We have here yet another type of learning by analysis and synthesis. Beginning with a total, synthetic, functional, musical experience, we call attention to one of the factors involved in it. As this is mastered, we return once again to a better synthesis, a completer experience.

2. Rhythmic training should never be of the type of mechanical drill. It should always be motivated by appreciation and should have appreciation for its goal. This means that we take actual music which yields immediate pleasure to the child, treat it in such a way that a fine response to its rhythmic elements is set up, and in this way leads to a discovery of new beauty and fresh sources of pleasure. Rhythmic training, in fact, is yet another phase of music education carried on in and through the three types of musical projects.

3. We shall see that just as with ear training, rhythmic training is ideally begun in the field of song, and that instrumental experience can carry rhythmic experience and development further in certain directions.

## The Nature of Musical Rhythm

One great reason why rhythm is often taught in quite impossible ways, or perhaps even not taught at all, is simply that the teacher himself has no clear and definite notion of what rhythm in music actually is. So long as ignorance of this sort remains, it is hopeless to expect any intelligent approach to the problem of rhythmic training. That this should be the case,—that many teachers simply do not know what rhythm is and fail to recognize it when they encounter it—is certainly strange in view of the general lip service to rhythm in music education. But we have abundant evidence of the reality of the situation. Therefore we must embark on a rather elaborate exposition of the nature of musical rhythm.

1. *The general rhythmic character of Occidental music.* The great and unique rhythmic characteristic of our Occidental music is that it always involves a phrase rhythm superimposed upon a beat or *Takt*. In other types of music this is quite often not found. For instance, in much Oriental music we have a perfectly free play of phrase rhythm, without any organizing and restricting beat at all. Such music has a rhythm like that of free verse or of prose, at once simpler and more untrammeled than the rhythm of our music. This of course explains at once why Western musicians, listening to exotic music of this type, find it almost impossible to grasp its rhythmic contours. In this connection an experience reported by Myers in listening to a Malu bell orchestra is very instructive. He says that the average Occidental listener simply has no notion why some of the bells in the ensemble are struck just when they are, as there is not any rhythmic demand that he can catch. However, if an inexpert player takes the place of an expert, the Malu audience is instantly aware that errors are being made. Moreover, the difference between our music and other musical sys-

tems in this respect explains why so many Occidental musicians have an idea that exotic rhythms are very complicated. In a sense they are. But the really important thing to see is that this complication comes precisely from freeing them from a regularly recurring beat and so, paradoxically, from a certain simplification.

Now it may be asked, why has our music developed the device of a recurrent beat or *Takt,* which is something that has happened in almost no other musical system? The answer is that we have gone much further in the direction of polyphonic effect than is the case in any system of exotic music. We have already seen that one of the consequences of this is the liberation of harmony as one of the chief constituent elements of musical beauty, and so the invention of a whole range of unique effects. But also it has had a definite result in rhythmic development. For as soon as we begin to have a number of parts all moving together, it becomes essential to have some means of organizing them and holding them in fixed relationships to one another. This is the essential function of the *Takt* or bar-beat. The Elizabethan madrigal music is a half-way step between the earlier music which had neither the bar line as a notational symbol, nor the rhythmic feel for which the bar line stands, and our modern music, in which a recurrent beat is felt even when the score is written without bar lines. Madrigal music used the leading voice as the means of holding together the whole ensemble, and, moreover, it made a good deal more of the direct rhythm of the words than is the case with modern art song. But as soon as we began to have still more elaborate ensemble effects, involving instruments, and stressing the musical rather than the language rhythm, a more potent regulative device was demanded. This could only be supplied by the bar line and the time signature in the score, symbolizing and corresponding to the feel of a regular pulsation under-running the free phrase rhythm, and organizing the entire pattern. This at once meant a loss of rhythmic freedom, and here as a matter of fact we have one of the most notable contrasts between our music and that of other races. On the other hand it has meant an enormous gain. We have sacrificed absolute freedom of rhythm for the sake of our polyphonic and harmonic system, and so in foregoing one opportunity for beauty, we have created others.

Thus the foundation of rhythmic training is the clear recognition by the teacher of these two elements in musical rhythm, —phrase rhythm and *Takt,* or beat. Just as soon as we emphasize one and ignore the other, our scheme of rhythmic education fails. The most common error is to ignore the phrase rhythm and work only in terms of the beat; and this makes rhythmic training quite impossible. But the opposite mistake is sometimes made,—often inadvertently indeed—and the phrase rhythm is taught just as if there were no such thing as an underlying organizing beat. *The aim of rhythmic training must be to do equal justice to the two elements in musical rhythm.*

2. *The phrase rhythm.* Let us now see how the two elements just discussed may be singled out and handled in music education. We begin with the phrase rhythm.

(*a*) The first thing to do is to make quite sure that the reader clearly understands the meaning of this term. It may be illustrated concretely in the following way. Take a musical phrase, preferably a simple one, such as occurs in songs for children in the lower grades. First sing or play it through. Then clap for each note in it, keeping the time values just as they were when you sang it. The sequence of claps will be the structure of the phrase rhythm. Or again this same structure can be laid out in a written symbolism just as we can scan a phrase in a poem, or for that matter in a piece of prose, by using the conventional symbols for strong and weak syllables. This is exactly what we had in mind in speaking of the rhythmic analysis of phrases in the preceding chapter. When we talk of teaching phrase rhythm, we mean giving the pupil an intimate and direct grasp of this structure.

(*b*) Having reached this point, there is a crucial question now facing us. How must the child sense and feel this phrase rhythm structure if he is to have what we have called a grasp of it? *He must feel it in terms of action.* When one has "scanned" a musical phrase, so that one can see its rhythmic skeleton, one has made a chart of its motor swing. In order to apprehend its rhythm, one must feel in one's muscles the pattern that lies before one's eyes. It is not enough to understand it. One must also directly sense it. Here is a place where perhaps a very intelligent child will fail and disappoint us. He is able to see at a glance what we mean when we scan the music on the board. The symbols are all as clear as daylight to him. But when he tries to clap out the rhythm, and still more when he tries to sing it, his grasp weakens and we get a nerveless, formless, indefinite reaction. A rhythmic response is always a structured response, and the structure may be intellectually represented in a scheme of scansion, but this alone will not set up the response. Thus we clearly see our problem in dealing with phrase rhythm, and one of the main topics of this chapter will be to show how one may help all children to a direct muscular sensing of rhythmic structures.

(*c*) A phrase rhythm can always be sensed in many other media than music. This is directly involved in what we have been saying and in the illustrations we have given. But it is important enough to call for separate notice. One can have exactly the same rhythmic structure in a sequence of words, in a dance, or in a visual sequence. Jaques-Dalcroze has spoken of the rhythmic factor in music as a transposition of rhythm into tone. It has been pointed out by Stetson that rhythm, of all elements in the musical complex, is that one which can most easily be separated and treated and studied in isolation, in the abstract as it were, and on its own account. Of course this is what opens up the really great possibilities for teaching rhythm. Whenever we have a factor that can be easily analyzed and made an object of attention all by itself, we have something that is easy to teach. The whole notable success of such a system as Dalcroze Eurythmics depends precisely on the possibility of isolating the rhythmic element in music, and thus building a very great rhythmic skill. When school music teachers simply ignore rhythm, and make no organized effort at all to deal with it, they are turning their backs on an open gateway leading straight towards musical development. For the opportunity literally cries aloud to be taken.

(*d*) We should understand that in music there are two kinds of rhythmic emphasis,—intensity, and duration. That is, a strong rhythmic pulse may be strong in the sense of having more intensity, or in the sense of being longer than those preceding and following it. Of course this is true also of language rhythm, but in language the two factors of intensity and duration are not quite so explicitly marked off as in music. This means that the ordinary symbols used for scansion, where one sort of mark is used for a strong pulse, and another for a weak one, will be inadequate, because there are two kinds of strength. The vital thing to remember is that *rhythmic strength means and must be sensed as emphasis in response.* A strong response will tend to produce a louder tone. Also it will tend to take a longer time, and so produce a longer tone, than a weak response. This is why a strong rhythmic pulsation may appear in either or both of two guises, —intensity and duration. It also shows once more why we must sense rhythm, not primarily as an affair of differences in intensity or duration, *but primarily as an affair of response or motor feel,* for this is the source of the differences in duration and intensity.

3. *The beat.* Here we have the regulative principle which underlies the phrase rhythm.

(*a*) *The relation of the beat to the phrase rhythm.* Sometimes at sea we become aware of a vast, massive, and regular swell coming from some distant storm, with an intricate and shifting pattern of lesser waves over-running it. This precisely illustrates the relationship of the beat to the phrase rhythm. We find exactly the same thing in poetry, where the phrases twine and intertwine about the meter, and thus constitute a major element in the beauty of the poem. In fact, the beat or *Takt* is often spoken of as the meter. We do not quite like this term, however, because it suggests something mathematical when really we are in the presence of something rhythmic, something which must be sensed not in terms of durations but of muscular effort and release, if it is to be grasped at all.

In most of the songs used with grade school children there is an exact correspondence between the strong elements of the beat and the phrase. That is to say, the phrase demands accentuation just at the points where the beat also calls for accentuation. But this by no means always happens in music. What we call syncopation is a precise reversal of this relationship. A weak element in the phrase rhythm comes on a strong beat, and *vice versa.* For instance, a note may be held over the strong beat of the bar, or a rest may occur on the strong beat of the bar. In these cases we have an antagonism between phrase rhythm and *Takt. Syncopation is impossible unless we have two rhythms running together, and we cannot feel syncopation properly or play it aright unless we have a balanced feeling for the two lines of rhythm.* There are still more complex and subtle antagonisms between phrase and beat to be found in music. Of all composers Schumann was fondest of devising interesting rhythmic effects by pulling the phrase emphasis away from the emphasis of the beat, and then working back again. Thus we see that the complex structure of musical rhythm, as involving both beat and phrase, becomes a great source of beautiful and interesting musical effects in the hands of a master. Moreover, in polyphonic music, and even in music where a melody is accompanied harmonically, we may have several simultaneous lines of phrase rhythms, overlapping and reinforcing one another in endless complexities. When our musical system abandoned the free rhythm and beatless structure of the exotic systems, it gained a factor of rhythmic interest which could not otherwise be achieved.

(*b*) *How we sense the beat.* We feel and sense the *Takt* or bar-beat rhythm in music just as we sense the phrase rhythm,—in terms of muscular pulsation and bodily swing. Counting and tapping are always make-shift devices, which may be necessary, but which do not in themselves exemplify the essence of the rhythmic experience. *The child does not sense the beat by attending to the arithmetical number of pulses in a bar, but by catching the swing.* A sailor walking the deck of a ship will not steady himself by counting the waves, but by catching the sense of the pulse and surge of the sea, and molding his muscular responses to it. This is what we must aim at in trying to give the child a feeling for the beat.

All music swings in two's, three's, or four's. Indeed some authorities would say that all music swings in two's or three's, and that a fourfold swing is apprehended in fact as two two-fold swings. Here time signatures are quite deceiving. For instance, rapid music in 12/8 time[1] is really apprehended as a four-fold swing; 5/4 time is apprehended either as a three followed by a two or a two followed by a three, and its peculiar effect is due to this odd alternation of swing; 6/8 time is apprehended as two three-fold swings. *Always the important thing is the sense of the muscular swing rather than the arithmetic of the time signature and the bar.* So in teaching the beat, the thing to do is to have the pupil swing or beat in a special pattern.

4. *Sources of error in teaching rhythm.*

(*a*) One great source of error in building the apprehension of rhythm is the fallacious notion that rhythm essentially involves repetition and regularity. How absurd this is we may see at once by remembering that prose has a perfectly definite rhythm, but without a recurring pattern. When a music teacher thinks and works in terms of this idea, it means at once that he absolutely ignores the phrase rhythm, and does not teach it at all. Of course there are such things as regular and recurrent rhythms. This is usually true of the beat. We find such rhythms in the tom-tom accompaniment to the dances of primitive peoples. (In such instances the figures of the dance will correspond to the phrase rhythm in Occidental music.) Moreover, these repetitive and recurrent rhythms have a sort of hypnotic power, precisely because they

[1]The first movement of the Sonata Appassionata is an instance of this time structure.

so potently impose a fixed and definite order of response. *But the truth is that any structured response is rhythmical, whether we have recurrence or not.*

(*b*) A second, and extremely fatal source of error in dealing with rhythm is to try to approach it through time. The relationship of time to rhythm is extremely obvious, though one would never guess it from the jumbled thinking and writing emanating from some writers who deal with the point. By the time values of a phrase we simply mean the mathematical durations of its notes. If we wanted to do so, we could express the whole thing in terms of thousandths of a second. However, in music we use far larger subdivisions of time, and work in terms of whole notes, half notes, quarter notes, etc.

A great many school music teachers think they are getting at rhythm when they drive the pupil's attention down upon the duration values of the notes. This is one of the completest and most fatal mistakes that could be made. *Rhythm does not come from time; time comes from rhythm.* When a composer creates a beautiful phrase, he does not first think it all out as a succession of half notes, quarter notes, etc. He feels it first of all as a total rhythmic and tonal entity with a certain swing and bodily feel which is the foundation of its appeal. When he writes it out he has to use the conventional time values symbolized in the score, but even these may do some violence to the detail and *finesse* of his feeling for it. To approach rhythm through time instead of through muscular response is a tragic absurdity. As we shall see later, it is a symptom of a still more serious error,—the error of approaching music through the score instead of approaching the score through music.

(*c*) The last source of error in dealing with rhythm is one that we have already touched upon, but which we must mention more formally here. It is the error of slighting either the phrase rhythm or the beat. By far the most common mistake is to slight the phrase rhythm because many teachers have only a vague notion that there is such a thing. In such cases, if the pupil is asked to indicate the rhythm of the phrase he will indicate the beat. But we sometimes see the opposite error. If we then call upon the pupil to indicate the beat, he gives the phrase rhythm,—that is, he indicates the individual notes rather than the underlying pulsation. In either case he is failing to achieve the sense of total musical rhythm which he needs.

### Rhythmic Training Through Muscular Response

It is generally recognized that when we experience rhythm we experience muscular response. That is to say, the rhythm does not exist in the stimuli,—either in the tones or in the words. It exists in us, and we read it into the stimuli. So, clearly, if we wish to give the pupils a keen feeling for the rhythm of a song, we must produce a situation in which that rhythm will live and work potently in their bodies. Hence rhythmic training must be carried on by producing and guiding the right kind of muscular response.

The motor responses indicated as desirable for the teaching of rhythm have three characteristics. (*a*) They should be large muscular responses. Tapping with the finger, for instance, is open to criticism because of the smallness, the puniness of the reaction. It is impossible to feel the sweep and swing of the rhythm in the small directive muscles of the finger. The large muscles of the legs, arms, and trunk should be used. (*b*) They should be free muscular responses. The pupil should be able to make a free, unimpeded, sweeping movement, such as is seen in the best orchestral conducting. It is well known that an orchestra will have much more difficulty in following a director who makes jerky movements, stopping at the end of each swing, than one whose movements constitute a continuous free curve. This is another reason why tapping is not a good medium through which to sense rhythm. Clapping may be better than tapping if the pupils are encouraged to clap vigorously and freely, with plenty of arm and body motions. (*c*) They should be highly coördinated movements rather than movements involving only one limb or one set of muscles. One senses rhythm in terms of total bodily coördination, not in and through the swing of a single limb, or the tensions and relaxations of a single muscle set.

To repeat, rhythm must be taught through muscular response. *Unless this is done, it can never be taught properly.*

1. We begin work of this kind in connection with grade school singing and listening. We take a suitable song that the children have already learned to sing with enjoyment, a song that is in process of being learned, or a composition set up for a listening project. Then we proceed to emphasize and play up its rhythmic structure, for the immediate purpose of increasing enjoyment in and mastery of the particular composition in question, and with the remoter aim of developing general rhythmic grasp and insight.

2. We have the children respond to it along lines of rhythmic play. The activities we set up and encourage should have the following characteristics. (*a*) They should be total bodily activities, large rather than small, sweeping rather than disjointed, coördinated rather than simple. Such movements as swaying, marching, skipping, galloping, etc., are indicated. (*b*) They should be "realizations" of the rhythm rather than

activities of the old "action song" type. That is, the children should embody directly in their movements the rhythmic structure of the music. The purpose of this work is to transpose the rhythmic demands of the tone into action, and then transpose the rhythm sensed in terms of large movement back again into the tone. (*c*) They should involve responses both to the *Takt* and to the phrase rhythm. In the first case the children swing to the beat or "meter." In the second, they make a movement for each note, sensing the sweep of the phrase as a totality in the coördination of many movements, *e.g.*, by walking or running forward with a step to each note, and indicating the end of the phrase by a change in the flow of movement. It may be well to set up movement types which embody and represent both phrase rhythm and *Takt* simultaneously. For instance, in rhythmic dancing, each step-unit may correspond to a measure or bar, and each figure of the dance to a phrase. (*d*) Such rhythmic activities should always be made as spontaneous as possible. It is well to ask the children to decide upon the sort of movement the music demands. Such a procedure works towards rhythmic discoveries on the part of the pupils themselves. (*e*) The movement set up should always be expressive of the spirit and mood of the composition. Remember that rhythm is one of the most potent sources of musical enjoyment, and that a rhythmic structure is by no means a mere mathematical affair. It is instinct with life, feeling, and meaning. Encourage the children to react to the feeling of the music and to try to express it in movement. (*f*) Remember that you are not trying to train a troupe of aesthetic dancers. So do not insist on grace and elegance of action. Rather urge the child to listen to the music, to live for the time being in the music, and to let the music itself carry him about the room and tell him what to do. (*g*) Banish inhibitions, shyness, and self-consciousness by every possible means. This is another reason for not criticizing the pupils from the standpoint of the gracefulness of the movements they make, though as a matter of fact the children who most intimately sense the music will often achieve a surprisingly graceful and natural result. Inhibitions upon free motor self-expression are perhaps the greatest of all impediments to a really full feeling for rhythm in music. The aim should be to have the children feel the sweep of the music in some such way as the great conductor does. Eminent conductors are not notable for their inhibited physical responses to rhythm. One great trouble with us musically is our stodgy anti-musical conventionality.

Work of this kind directly capitalizes one of the chief sources of musical pleasure. It helps the child, as nothing else can do, to sense the inwardness of musical effects. Its meaning has been admirably expressed by Matthay who says, in effect, that if we hum the Beethoven themes as we wander through the woods, they become extraordinarily vivid; for many of them, as we know, were conceived in similar surroundings and to the rhythm of a healthy walking stride.[1]

One remarkable fallacy about this kind of work is seen in the occasional comment that it belongs rather to physical education than to musical education. This is entirely incorrect and involves a deep misunderstanding of the purposes of the procedures we have described. The explicit aim is not to build up physical health and strength, or to promote grace of action. We base ourselves on the admitted fact that rhythm is a motor experience. Once this is allowed, it is hard to deny that the best way to sense and feel rhythm is to set up large motor

[1]*Musical Interpretation,* 3rd Ed., Boston Music Co., 1913, p. 32.

responses. To be sure there is a *correlation* here between physical education and musical education, just as music education makes contacts with all sorts of subjects in the school curriculum. The distinction should always be drawn in terms of aim and purpose. When we employ large physical movement to build grace and skill of body, we are in one field. When we employ large physical movement to help the pupil sense and feel the rhythmic structure of music, we are in another.

3. Rhythmic experience in terms of free motor response is the best possible training for rhythmic grasp where such free response is impossible. There are many musical situations where large and free movement is ruled out. Instances are those of listening at a concert, playing an instrument, singing in an ensemble group, or scanning the phrase rhythm of a song. If a person makes such situations as these his primary approaches to the teaching of rhythm, he places himself at a grave disadvantage. Indeed it is doubtful whether the fullest success in building rhythmic grasp is ever possible under such limitations. The most talented pupils get less than they might, and those with little natural feeling for rhythm get practically nothing at all.

The proper psychological sequence is always from the large, obvious, "explicit" movement, to the small, relatively hidden, "implicit" movement. For instance, the child learns to talk by talking aloud, and only little by little comes to a command of inner speech, by means of which so much adult thinking is done. So also with rhythm, if the experience of large, free movement is never given, rhythm is always apt to remain more or less mathematical and intellectual, and its full power and assurance is never felt. Furthermore, the well-known fact that the child first gains control of the "fundamental" or larger muscles and only later on reaches full mastery with the smaller or "accessory" muscles, is an added reason for rhythmatizing him through the large muscles, and through generalized responses, in the lower and intermediate grades.

4. A comment may be made here as to the relation between rhythmic training and instrumental music. Certainly no instrumental medium can be considered ideal for the first contact with rhythm. The ideal medium is song, because mechanical difficulties are slight, and because free physical movement is possible during the act of singing. A mechanical instrument, however, is by no means a barrier to rhythmic action. If it were so, if making music on it demanded absolutely no rhythmic response, then so far as the operator was concerned it would not be a musical instrument at all. Street organs, musical boxes, reproducing pianos, and phonographs belong to this class of music-making devices. But every instrument through which a musical personality can directly express a musical thought requires rhythmic action in its operation. Only the rhythmic action is no longer free. The rhythmic pulsation, the tension and relaxation of the action, must be carried on in terms of just the sort of activities demanded by the instrument. Instead of creating rhythm with the body as a whole, instead of perfectly free movement, we have rhythm sensed in a bowing arm, in fingers and wrists, and so forth. Instrumental technique is really rhythmic action limited to certain kinds of movement determined by the mechanics of the instrument. Hence we should not expect to teach rhythm in terms of action that must by definition be limited. The proper approach to instrumental technique is through a sensing of phrase rhythm and *Takt* in terms of large physical movements.

### RHYTHM AND TIME

We have already touched on this question, and have explained that by time in music we simply understand the problem of the duration values of the notes and rests. But the topic is so important that a separate section must be devoted to it.

1. Time patterns in music always depend on rhythm. *A rhythmic idea creates a certain time pattern.* The logical and psychological order is never from time to rhythm. If the pupil is given a keen feeling for the phrase rhythm superimposed upon the onflowing beat, the chief problem of teaching time, which is to give a feeling for the proper holding of notes and rests, will be overcome. Moreover, we cannot properly reverse this order, for it is quite unnatural to try to build up a sense of a unitary phrase rhythm through detailed notewise attention to the lengths of the constituent notes. Therefore we unqualifiedly hold that it is wrong to begin with a study of note lengths early in the grades, and to try to make pupils observe that one note is twice as long as another, and so forth, as a step towards rhythmic grasp. We begin with the rote song taught phrase-wise, with just as little emphasis as we can upon the specific mathematical lengths of the notes. We isolate the rhythmic structure in terms of muscular action, with long and short notes appearing perhaps as slow and rapid steps, but always directing attention towards the feel of the total action pattern rather than towards the detailed unitary constituent elements.

2. As rhythmic grasp grows better and firmer, and, above all, as the child begins to read the score, with its refining and defining influence on all the musical-mental processes, the time problems become more and more definite and sharply

outlined. Hence, they can be attacked more and more directly. We introduce a song in which an especially difficult or awkward time problem appears, as, for instance, that of the dotted quarter note followed by an eighth note. We review a familiar song containing the problem. We then isolate such problem, make it the object of definite analytical study, and organize it back into the synthetic experience of singing the song in question, and of reading other songs with the problem in new contexts. Furthermore, we may treat such problems not primarily as time problems at all, but as rhythm problems, by devising physical activities which will give the pupils the motor feel of the time patterns. In this way playing and singing in accurate time is developed as a particularization and refinement of rhythmic grasp.

3. Instrumental music will often be found to give valuable added experience in building up a good sense of time as a particularization of rhythmic grasp. In particular it has been claimed that the strings make uniquely exacting demands in the matter of precise and accurate timing, in connection with attack, release, and duration. Here once more we see the process of making general rhythmic grasp and feeling quite precise and definite as it comes to expression in a distinct and accurate time pattern.

4. The music teacher is urged to pay special attention to rests. Often a rest is treated as a mere pause or break in the music. This is wrong. Rests should always be sensed as factors in the rhythmic flow, and as deriving their musical and aesthetic meaning from this fact. They should not be attacked mathematically, but muscularly. That is, they should be felt properly before they are counted properly. Or at least, counting should not be the basis of a correct treatment of rests, but a means of building a proper feeling for them.

5. It should be understood that rhythmic performance always involves a certain subtle departure from the strict time values indicated in the score. The tendency always is to dwell on the strong pulse and to shorten the weak one. Now this is not really an error at all, because the score, with its mathematical time values, is nothing more than an approximate indication of the musical pattern. Again and again we find the great composers saying in effect that they could not exactly indicate their musical and rhythmic conceptions in the medium of the score. Always there is room and need for "interpretation," for a reading between the lines, and for the introduction of light and shade to make the real meaning clear. We have excellent scientific evidence for the statement that rhythm nearly always involves some distortion of the exact time. Stetson and Tuthill had several accomplished musicians, including one ensemble player of really superior ability, tap out certain rhythmic patterns, one of which was a series of simple triplets. It was found that this seemingly easy task could never be done in perfectly strict time, and that there was always a prolongation of the strong beat and an abbreviation of the weak ones. We can notice exactly the same thing when we hear a congregation sing the Doxology. Nearly always there is a hold at the end of each line, which is probably not indicated in the score; and if the organist deliberately pushes through in strict time, the people at once feel that there is something wrong. In this they are perfectly right, because the natural motor feeling for the rhythm, which demands time out for a strong pulsation, is broken up and antagonized. Rhythm is sacrificed for the sake of time, and the result is uneasiness and annoyance. Incidentally it is just these temporal distortions for the sake of rhythmic ease that are the foundation of what is known as *tempo rubato,* and

we shall return to the topic in our chapter on expression. For the present, however, this shows us once more how impossible it is to build from time to rhythm, and also how impossible it is to go from the note-wise study of the score to a true and full feeling for the beauty of the music, which is resident in the phrase as a tonal-rhythmic unity.

### Some Devices Used in the Teaching of Rhythm

In the light of our analysis we now seek to evaluate some of the devices commonly used in teaching rhythm.

1. **Counting.** This is sometimes used in connection with motor activities in which rhythm is expressed, and also, of course, in connection with singing and playing. One should not take an extreme attitude either for or against it. The excellence of educational procedures does not depend on the devices that are used, but on the intelligence with which these devices are applied. So it is important to understand both the values and the limitations of counting. Obviously its value is that it very clearly outlines the beat. But its great danger is that it emphasizes the mathematical rather than the rhythmic aspect of the beat. What we want the pupil to become aware of is not that bar lines following a certain kind of time signature contain two, three, or four beats, but that a certain kind of swing or sway must permeate the music. So we would say that counting must always be used as a means, never as an end. It can help to set up the form of response, the muscular feel that we want. But it actually impedes rhythmic development when the child is led to think of certain notes coming on certain counted beats rather than on a certain pulse of effort. One suggestion here may be of some practical value, particularly in instrumental music. We may use the ability to count as an index of precise grasp of

the *Takt.* While counting will not necessarily transfer to a real sensing of the beat, the inability to count as one plays is a sure sign that the beat is not being properly sensed.

2. **Tapping the beat.** Many of these comments apply also to tapping the beat. This has two advantages over counting. It involves more extensive muscular action, and it does not emphasize arithmetic. If it is used, one would urge that it should never be feeble, flabby tapping with the smallest available muscles. We can think of just about one poorer way to mark rhythm than by weak finger tapping, and that would be by winking one eye. In any case it is no adequate substitute for larger free coördinations, and if an approach has been made through these, the formal employment of tapping ought hardly to be necessary.

3. **The metronome.** The metronome has a two-fold value. It can be used to set tempi; and it can be used to discipline and check runaway tendencies better than almost anything else. But it has two great limitations. It is entirely external as a criterion, whereas we want to establish an inner feeling for rhythm in terms of response. Its very regularity is unrhythmic, for, as we have seen, the presence of rhythm positively demands some modifications of strict time. Once more the metronome, like counting, can be used as a test. If a person has a good grasp of *Takt,* he ought to be able to follow the beat of the metronome if he wishes to do so.

4. **Tapping the phrase rhythm.** This device has its place in rhythmic analysis of the phrase. But it has the typical objections which are urged against any kind of tapping movement. It is no kind of substitute for large, free, coördinated movements.

5. **The use of words.** One of the very best ways of giving a grasp of a musical rhythm is by connecting it with

words. This is far better than counting, because words have a natural rhythm of their own, while the number series does not. So we can choose words which fit into the phrase rhythm. Thus we also see the value of song experience in building a grasp of rhythm, looked at from yet another angle. The words of a song are always a teaching opportunity in many ways. Their rhythm can be used to give the child a sense of the rhythm of the phrase to which they are fitted. Thus it is recommended that the words of songs that are being learned should be scanned so that the class may have the experience of reading them through with special attention to the rhythmic pattern of the song. The connection of words with music may also be used in instrumental music, by devising language phrases with a rhythm identical with that of the musical phrases. Much work along this line has been done by Wedge, whose book will be found suggestive, particularly by teachers of instrumental music.

6. **Ensemble.** Ensemble experience is full of value for the development of rhythmic grasp. When one plays or sings in a group, one must be carried along largely by the group rhythm. Attack and release become matters of paramount importance, as they do not in solo work, or in unison singing. Thus we create a situation where rhythmic precision is at a premium. In organizing work both in vocal and instrumental ensemble, its value in building up the rhythmic sense should always be kept in mind.

7. **Conducting.** Lastly we should mention conducting. The good conductor "realizes" the musical rhythm in leading the group of performers. Thus experience along this line is very valuable for developing and refining the sense of rhythm. We should do what we can to permit children themselves to have the experience of directing ensemble. For in-

stance, in toy orchestra work, pupils should be selected to lead the group. Every school music teacher should have some specific training in the art of the baton, which means so much more than beating time. Such training means far more than developing an external knowledge of how to convey one's wishes to a group of performers. It sharpens the whole feeling for rhythm. This applies both to the phrase rhythm and the beat. The good conductor feels the pulse of the music moving steadily along, and even the hold is sensed as an essential element in the rhythmic flow. One criticism often made of American conductors is that they are so interested in producing effects that they fail to feel and to indicate properly the sequence of the organizing beat. The aim, in training the school music teacher in conducting, should not be to help him to develop a repertoire of dramatic tricks (which are not properly part of conducting at all), but to lead him, first, to sense the rhythm keenly, and, secondly, to exteriorize it with compelling effect.

## Summary: Outcomes of this Chapter

1. The problem of teaching rhythm is another instance of the proper management of the analytic or study phase of learning. We must isolate the factor of rhythm in actual musical situations, and bring it to the learner's attention.

2. Due to the character of Occidental music, we must recognize and deal with both phrase rhythm and beat. The phrase rhythm is a free rhythm which is superimposed upon the regular, recurrent rhythm of the beat. The pupil must arrive at a balanced perception of both these elements if his grasp of musical rhythm is to be adequate.

3. The foundation of all rhythmic training is large, free, coördinated, muscular response. Both phrase rhythm and

beat should be taught by this means. Work of this kind should be made spontaneous, and should be an expression of the spirit and meaning of the music. It is entirely different from the action song which dramatized the music rather than realized it.

4. The proper approach to time problems is through rhythm. As the perception of rhythm grows clearer, the feeling for time values will become more precise and refined. The impossibility of moving from time to rhythm is seen in the fact that rhythm actually involves distortions of the time.

5. Lastly a word should be said about the most elaborate of all systems of teaching rhythm,—Dalcroze Eurythmics. It is not part of the program of this book to characterize in detail highly-developed special methods, particularly when these are readily accessible elsewhere. The eurythmics system, however, is the completest realization in terms of educational method of the psychological principles of rhythmic apprehension. Every teacher of school music should make it a point to familiarize himself with it, in the writings of Jaques-Dalcroze and others associated with him. Much experimentation and some excellent results have already been achieved by able American music educators in applying Dalcroze principles to rhythm study in the restricted area of the elementary grade class room.

### Questions for Discussion.

1. Just what is meant by saying that rhythmic training must be motivated by appreciation and aim at appreciation?

2. Discuss any procedures of a drill type that you have ever known to be tried out in teaching rhythm.

3. In what way is the rhythm of Occidental music more restricted than that of Oriental music? What special rhythmic

opportunity do we find in Occidental music which does not exist in other systems?

4. Discuss some ways in which a school music teacher might easily be apt to ignore (*a*) phrase rhythm (*b*) beat.

5. Discuss our criticism of the use of the word "meter."

6. What practical difficulties are there in the way of teaching rhythm through free physical response?

7. Take a poem in blank verse and analyze it to show that it has the same structure as music, *i. e.,* a sequence of free phrase rhythms over-running a regular beat.

8. Discuss the idea that all music swings in two's or three's.

9. What reasons are there for denying that time rather than rhythm is primary? What sort of teaching procedures do you know that tend to work from time to rhythm?

10. In connection with the various devices for teaching rhythm do you find (*a*) any values (*b*) any limitations, which we have not mentioned?

11. Do you know any other devices for teaching rhythm? If so, discuss them.

12. Make a written report on Dalcroze Eurythmics.

BIBLIOGRAPHY.

1. BUECHER, KARL, *Arbeit und Rhythmus,* 5th ed. Leipzig, 1919.
2. DALCROZE Explains His Method, *Literary Digest,* September 1, 1923, vol. 78, pp. 31-32.
3. FINDLAY, J. J., Rhythm and Education, *School and Society,* 1923, vol. 17, pp. 8-10.
4. GEHRKENS, KARL W., *Essentials in Conducting,* C. C. Birchard and Company, 1919.
5. HALLOCK, M., Pulse and Rhythm, *Popular Science Monthly,* 1903, vol. 63, pp. 425-431.
6. JAQUES-DALCROZE, EMIL, *Rhythm, Music, and Education,* Tr. Harold F. Rubinstein, G. P. Putnam's Sons, 1921.

7. Jaques-Dalcroze, Emil, Technique of Moving Plastic, *Musical Quarterly,* 1924, vol. 10, pp. 21-38.
8. Kendrie, Frank E., *Conducting and Orchestral Routine,* H. W. Gray Company, 1930.
9. Morton, W. B., Some Measurements of the Accuracy of the Time-Intervals in Playing a Keyed Instrument, *British Journal of Psychology,* 1919-1920, vol. 10, pp. 194-198.
10. Mursell, James L., *Principles of Musical Education,* The Macmillan Company, 1927, ch. 3.
11. Myers, Charles S., A Study of Rhythm in Primitive Music, *British Journal of Psychology,* 1904-1905, vol. 1, pp. 397-406.
12. *Newer Practices and Tendencies in Music Education,* Music Supervisors' National Conference, Research Bulletin, No. 13, 1930.
13. *Premier Congrès du Rhythme, Compte Rendu,* Geneva, Institut Jaques-Dalcroze, 1926.
14. Ruckmick, Christian A., A Bibliography of Rhythm, *American Journal of Psychology,* 1913, vol. 24, pp. 508-519.
15. Ruckmick, Christian A., A Bibliography of Rhythm (Supplementary List), *American Journal of Psychology,* 1915, vol. 26, pp. 457-459.
16. Ruckmick, Christian A., A Bibliography of Rhythm (Second Supplementary List), *American Journal of Psychology,* 1918, vol. 29, pp. 214-218.
17. Ruckmick, Christian A., A Bibliography of Rhythm (Third Supplementary List), *American Journal of Psychology,* 1924, vol. 35, pp. 407-413.
18. Sears, Charles H., A Contribution to the Psychology of Rhythm, *American Journal of Psychology,* 1902, vol. 13, pp. 28-61.
19. Stetson, Raymond H., A Motor Theory of Rhythm and Dis-

crete Sensation, *Psychological Review,* 1905, vol. 12, pp. 250-270, 293-350.

20. Stetson, Raymond H., Rhythm and Rhyme, *Psychological Monographs,* 1903, vol. 4, No. 1, Whole No. 17.
21. Stetson, Raymond H., Teaching of Rhythm, *Musical Quarterly,* 1923, vol. 9, pp. 181-190.
22. Stetson, Raymond H., and Tuthill, T. E., Measurements of Rhythmic Unit-Groups at Different Tempos, *Psychological Monographs,* 1923, vol. 32, No. 3, Whole No. 145, pp. 41-51.
23. Stoessel, Albert, *The Technic of the Baton,* Carl Fischer, Inc., 1920.
24. Wedge, George H., *Rhythm in Music; A Text Book,* G. Schirmer, Inc., 1927.

CHAPTER EIGHT

# *Mastery of the Score*

## THE SCORE AS AN AGENCY FOR MUSIC EDUCATION

The aim of this chapter is to show how the teaching of the score may be made an agency for musical development. We should say at the outset that we think of mastery of the score in wider terms than merely as the teaching of reading. Essentially the score is a system of symbolism that has been evolved to represent musical ideas, and its mastery, which involves its use both in reading and in expressing original musical thoughts, consists in the ability to grasp these ideas symbolically represented.

1. **Educational values in the mastery of the score.** Let us begin by raising the question as to why the score should be taught in school music work. In general there are two reasons. The score is an indispensable musical tool; and when properly taught it is an agency for developing musical mindedness.

(*a*) We need not say a great deal about the value of the score as a tool. Unless grade school pupils achieve some sort of mastery of it, the work in secondary school music will be very greatly impeded. There is also no doubt that after he leaves school, the person who is able to deal with and understand music notation is definitely placed in a favorable position to continue work with music, and to broaden his musical interests. Points of this kind are self-evident, and they are the reasons which the teacher ordinarily has in mind whenever he thinks about the wider problems and meanings involved in teaching the score. But in our opinion these are not the decisive reasons for its use in grade school music. There is quite another way of looking at the whole matter, and to this we now turn.

(*b*) What seems to us the most fundamental reason for emphasizing musical notation in the grades is that, when this is properly done, it leads to a development of musical mindedness. So long as we think of the score as a mere tool, its mastery may appear to us in the nature of a more or less artificial accomplishment. But is this actually the case? In many of the biographical accounts of great musicians, the point is brought out that they acquired a mastery of the score and an ability to read and write music at an astonishingly early age. Clearly this capacity was an essential element in their musicality, and when we learn of a man like Liszt performing absolute miracles of reading, we are not in the presence of some artificial trick, but of the application of a profound and expert musicianship to the interpretation of musical symbols. Furthermore, careful attention to the scoring in a first rate modern edition of some classical composer ought to suggest, at least, that reading and musicianship are closely allied. For modern editing does really wonderful things in the way of indicating musical meanings on the printed page, so that the notation actually *looks* musical and strongly suggests musical ideas and musical effects.

*So our main emphasis ought to be mastery of the score as a means of organizing musical experience.* We should use it to clinch and carry further all those abilities which we considered in connection with ear training and rhythm. The study of the notation should give the pupil a better and more accurate grasp of melody and phrase, of harmony, of tonality, and of rhythm, and should provide an opportunity for further work in musical imagery and the thinking of music.

2. **The proper approach to the mastery of the score.** All this implies that the proper approach to the mastery of the score must not be by formal drill or a quasi-mathematical study of the notation, but through music. To be specific, we believe that the score should be introduced and taught in connection with projects in creation and performance. We shall show just what sort of procedures this implies later on, but for the moment we will make two points.

(*a*) The ideal first approach to the score is through song. The reason is that here we have the mechanical problems of music making reduced to a minimum, and a very direct contact with musical meanings. The sequence we have in mind should be one where musical experience built up in rote song is made more definite, by the gradual introduction of the score as a symbolism for the various elements which the pupils have been trained to recognize by ear, and by motor rhythmic activity.

(*b*) The child who must approach the score through instrumental music of any kind is always at some disadvantage. In an ideal situation he would already have had some musical comprehension of the score before beginning instrumental work, both because it is a valuable tool, and because he needs the type of precise musical development which early work with the notation can afford. No instrumental means can equal the voice as a medium for apprehending the notation, because of the exigency of mechanical problems, which are apt to absorb a great deal of the learner's attention to the detriment of anything else.

3. **The proper place of reading in music education.** All this helps to orient us in the debate about the proper place

of reading in music education. This is quite a contentious subject, about which we find two types of extreme views, neither of which seems justifiable.

(*a*) We have the position of those who begin with note and staff drills in the second grade, and make these the center and the most absorbing concern of the grade school music program. Our criticisms of these procedures, and of the educational views on which they depend are as follows. First, they emphasize notational detail rather than musical values in the symbolism, taking up such points as note names, the lines and spaces of the staff, note lengths, etc., etc., for direct learning at an early stage. It is all too easy to build up in the pupils an adequate, intellectualized, *memoriter* knowledge of these factors without really developing any true musical mastery of the score. Secondly, these procedures call for so much time spent on drill in notational detail, which the children find somewhat difficult and boresome, that no time is left for the many other really motivating factors in the program of music education, which cannot be set aside without disastrous results. The plea that children can be interested in the problematic study of the notation carries no weight at all, because as we have insisted, it is not the *presence* but the *direction* of interest that is the important thing.

(*b*) Then we have the position of those who hold that reading and the score should be considerably postponed and minimized, perhaps being held off until the fifth or sixth grade. It is argued sometimes that all early work in the grades should be in the way of rote singing, and sometimes that it should consist entirely of "appreciation." Again we make two criticisms. First, the postponement of the score in order to give more time to "appreciation" involves a very inadequate notion of what appreciation really is. Appreciation must include not only listening projects, but also projects in performance and creation; and if we build up the pupil's mastery of the score in and through such projects, his appreciative understanding of music and his ability to use the notation will advance hand in hand. Secondly, we should easily see that the postponement of the score till very late in the grades implies the idea that its mastery is in the nature of a mechanical stunt, whereas, in our view, it is an essential element in developing musical mindedness.

### The Phrase-Wise Teaching of the Score

If we wish to use the score as a means of refining and developing the pupil's grasp of musical meanings, it is essential that when we first present it to him, his attention be concentrated not on the separate notes, but on the symbolization of the musically-meaningful phrases. This is what we mean by the phrase-wise approach to the score. Let us see on what sort of evidence this proposition depends.

1. **Evidence from research in the reading of language.** Recently the reading of the score has been compared to the reading of language, and much of the extensive research material in that field, together with many of the practical conclusions derived from it, have been thought to apply to music. While no doubt there is much truth in this, a note of warning should still be sounded. For though there may be, and almost certainly are, extensive similarities, there are also likely to be important differences. Thus it is a mistake to press the analogy between reading music and reading language too closely, as some enthusiastic persons have undoubtedly done. For instance, attempts are made to find in music precise equivalents to the letters of the alphabet, syllables, phonics, etc., etc. How far we can go in these direc-

tions will not be known until a great deal of laborious research in reading music has been done. For the time being it is well to remember that while in a general way the psychology of mastery in one symbolism is the same as that in another, yet there are real and striking differences between musical notation and written language.

Still there is one general point which emerges, and which undoubtedly will apply to our field. *Expert mastery of a symbolism always depends on the ability to apprehend a great many separate elements at a single glance.* This may be illustrated from the study of the telegraphic language by Bryan and Harter, to which we have already referred. These men showed that as operators increase in expertness, they pass from the first stage, where they must attend to each individual letter, to the second, where words become units, and so on to a higher stage, where whole phrases are apprehended at once. The same thing is seen in typewriting, where increase in mastery and speed does not depend so much on speeding up the individual strokes, as in being able to react instantly on the keyboard to words and phrases without any thought for the position of their component letters. It is shown most strikingly of all in the research material on the reading of language. A technique has been developed for photographing the eye movements made by readers as they go through written material. It is found that whenever reading is at all fluent, whenever meaning is being steadily absorbed, the reader may pause perhaps only three times on each line. Because he sees clearly only during the pauses in his eye movements, it is evident that what he actually and literally perceives is only a comparatively small portion of the printed surface. The truth of this may be made more apparent when we remember how easy it is to read along and entirely miss typographical errors. The reason is that we are not reading letters; we are not even reading words; we are reading groups of words or phrases. If we take the eye movement of a pupil dealing with something that is very hard for him, for instance, a page of Latin—we find that he fumbles about with his eyes, and looks again and again at each small detail of every word. It is exactly in this letter-wise attack that his difficulty lies. As the language becomes more meaningful to him, this instantly shows through in his ability to catch the shape of phrases and the structure of sentences at a glance or two. And finally we reach the enormous reading speeds of those who, like Macaulay, could take in a whole page in the time an ordinary person would need to read a sentence. Moreover, we should notice that this fast reading is not careless reading, except from the standpoint of correcting proof. *The very same factor that produces speed means also the ability definitely to apprehend meanings, because it is a response to the meaningful elements of language rather than to its mechanical constituents.*

The clear implication for the music teacher is that he should call the child's attention from the first to the meaningful elements in the score,—that is, to the phrases which carry the musical thought. This principle has already revolutionized elementary language reading. It is well tried and recognized. And it should be, and is, applied to music. A slightly different angle on the same idea is suggested by two very interesting papers by Thorndike in which he compared reading to reasoning. To sum up his position in a very general way (and to do this indicates a considerable lack of justice to the subtlety and significance of the argument), when one reads well and succeeds in getting accurate meanings, one is reacting to thought units embodied in and qualified through language. *Hence, when we argue for the phrase-wise approach to the score, we mean that the child should be taught to respond to the musical thought elements, and not to the separate notes.*

2. **Evidence from the nature of musical symbolism.** Most music teachers do not take the trouble really to think out the way in which the score symbolizes music. But to do so is a profitable exercise, for the score is one of the most ingenious of all creations. If we understand its principles explicitly, we gain much insight on how to deal with it.

Music notation is essentially a scheme for indicating pitch relationships and time relationships. (Incidentally, we may note that this means that it cannot directly symbolize rhythm.) It has the following peculiarities. (*a*) It may indicate precisely the same time pattern in several quite different ways. This is clearly seen in the illustrations below, where the music sounds precisely the same, in spite of the marked differences in notation. (*b*) Two sets of notational symbols may look

FIGURE 4. Two identical time patterns indicated differently in the notation.

very much alike, and yet give us music which sounds very different. This again is illustrated in figure 5. (*c*) Two phrases which look exactly alike on the staff may be totally different because they are in different keys. (*d*) Two phrases which look very different in that they are laid out on different lines and spaces in the staff may be very similar, because they have the same internal key relationships. To sum up the point, a quarter note does not always mean the same thing in time value or bear the same relationships to other notes, and a note on the third line of the treble staff does

FIGURE 5. Figures which look very similar but have different time and rhythm values.

not always mean the same thing tonally. In other words, we have exactly the same sort of problem that makes algebra baffling to the child's intelligence—the problem of variability —the problem of a symbol which may mean many different things.

We believe that what might be called a grammatical attack on a symbolism of this kind is entirely wrong. By this we mean taking up the various elements in the notation—lines and spaces, note symbols, note lengths, key signatures, time signatures, and all the rest of the symbolic apparatus—and dealing with them one by one in a logical order, until, as a final revelation, the child begins to see that they mean something musically and aesthetically. It has so often been found that this is the wrong and wasteful way that we have no confidence in it. Such a procedure will work where we have a very intelligent child, and a teaching situation such that we can keep his nose to the grindstone long enough. But we can get just as good results very much more quickly by reversing our approach. We should begin with actual musical meanings, *i.e.,* actual phrases that the child sings, show how these are directly represented in the score, and build towards a mastery of the complex variable symbols as the child feels the need for them and as his musical intelligence comes to be able to use them. In this way his mastery of the score comes to be a concomitant of his mastery of music and his expanding musical experience.

### Mastery of the Score Through the Creative Project

Probably the best possible way to approach the score is through the creative project. This means a highly informal and spontaneous procedure, with the central emphasis on musical meaning and musical pleasure.

1. **Background.** The creative project is impossible unless the pupil has a background of ordered musical experience. It is obviously hopeless to expect him to make music unless he already has a pretty precise feeling for what music really is. For this reason its placement in the third grade is recommended. If we attempt it earlier, the pupil will not have made the musical-mental development that is demanded for such an undertaking. If we place it later, other approaches will have been initiated and a different and perhaps more or less antagonistic orientation to the score will have been set up. Specifically the pupil must have built up a feeling for phrase and melody, and for the tonality relationships and rhythmic contours of phrases. This is achieved through projects in listening and performance, as has been described. We cannot hope for any sort of adequate melodic creation from pupils whose melodic experience is limited, who have no apprehension of the musical phrase. And if we attempt it without the proper foundations, we lose its very great educational value. The creative project in the third grade provides

an opportunity for carrying further, refining, and clinching the whole course of previous musical-mental development by definitely connecting the child's experience with phrase, tonality, and rhythm, with the score.

2. **Procedure.** In explaining the procedure of the creative project, we should understand that the first and fundamental thing is to encourage the child to express something. He brings in some idea that has interested him, some significant experience, and he makes a short poem about it. This is the preliminary step. In describing what follows, we quote from an account of the management of this type of work in the Kansas City schools.

> 1. The poem was written under a staff on the blackboard.
> 2. Measure bars were placed before the accented words by the children.
> 3. The poem was read again and the words or portion of the words which were to receive more time were underlined.
> 4. The rhythm pattern was examined to see whether or not there were the same number of measures in each phrase.
> 5. Several children suggested a tune for the first phrase and the class voted on the tune it preferred. (In this work the teacher must be able to jot down on a piece of paper the tune in syllables or numbers so that he can sing or play each tune for the class several times.)
> 6. The class sang the proper *so-fa* syllables in the first phrase and some child put it on the staff.
> 7. In a similar way the second phrase was developed. The children discovered that in most cases they did not care to have the second phrase end on the "home" tone.
> 8. By observation of many songs they discovered that very often they liked to have the third phrase similar to the first phrase.
> 9. Unless the last phrase was a question the children decided that they preferred having the last phrase of the song end on *do*.

10. The children usually chose their own *do,* the teacher telling them where their *do* was located on the staff. They very soon began to want to put in their key signatures. Therefore they began remembering that if *do* was on the first space, there was a flat on the *fa* line, and if *do* was on the second line, there was a sharp on the *ti* line.

11. They were able to add the time signature after they had written their first phrase, having learned through experience that every song swings in two's or three's or four's.

(Quoted from *Childhood Education, Op. cit,* by permission.)

Often the child who thought of the song would be allowed to copy it on a big sheet of paper. In any case all the children copied the song, or the teacher had mimeograph copies made, so that each child might have one to add to his creative music book. Emphasis throughout was on "pretty tunes and poetic expression."

Evidently some of these procedural details might be modified, and class motivation might be aroused in a variety of ways. But the essential thing is that here we have the teacher guiding a learning process by helping the children to create something of their very own, and to express it in the symbolism of the score.

3. **Educational values.** It is quite apparent that this procedure involves far-reaching and rich educational values. It involves an approach to the score entirely through music making. The score evidently becomes a means of clearing up and recording musical conceptions, but it is handled incidentally to the musical project itself. We have here the sharpest possible contrast to music writing as so often undertaken. When children are required to write out a song from a printed page—and often the music writing stops with this activity—we are dealing with copy-book drill work of the most objectionable kind. Attention is at once diverted from

musical meanings, and concentrated—we almost said cramped—upon the slavish reproduction of notational detail. For this narrow experience we have nothing but condemnation. The first formal approach to the score through the creative project and the writing of music is probably better than that through the performance project and reading, because it means a more precise and also a less formalized attention to the score. At the same time it carries this procedure through with a powerful motivation derived primarily from a direct interest in musical beauty and expressiveness.

## Mastery of the Score Through the Performance Project

This activity means approaching the score by way of teaching pupils to read music which they sing. Creative work is usually undertaken by the third grade because, by this time, the children have acquired a musical vocabulary with which, under the teacher's guidance, they may express themselves. In such situations, the performance project may be postponed perhaps till the fourth grade. Naturally with a foundation of creative effort the reading of music will then go on very fast indeed. Where for any reason creative work cannot be undertaken to any extent, the formal connection of the score with the project in performance may well come in the second or third grade. Let us see just what this involves.

1. **Background.** Once more the type of musical background possessed by the pupil is of central importance. The pupil must have a grasp of phrase, and of tonality relations and rhythmic structure within the phrase. We deal with the score first and foremost as a means of symbolizing the phrase, and of indicating its tonal and rhythmic components. Evidently these things must have meaning to the pupil before he comes to the problem of their symbolic representation. To

try to set up a phrase-wise approach to the score with pupils who think music wholly in terms of notes, and to whom the very idea of a musical phrase is unknown, would be utterly absurd. We may remark that in their preliminary rote song experience pupils have often sung with books open, so that they are familiar with the look of the score, and through the early third grade have "read" songs in varying degrees of independence from help by the teacher. But here we deal with the first formal attack upon the notation whenever introduced.

2. **Procedure.** In describing the procedure demanded by the phrase-wise approach to the score, we may make our meaning clearest by working in terms of an actual illustration. Let us consider the method indicated for teaching the song "Feathers" given herewith.

(*a*) The first step is the teaching of this new song by rote, phrase-wise, in the way already described for presenting rote-songs. (*b*) Next we focus the attention of the children upon the phrase repetitions involved in the song, using a neutral syllable, and diagraming the four phrases by curves on the blackboard, one below the other. (See also phrase-wise notation of song on page 218.) This procedure isolates phrase elements, and leads to a firmer aural grasp of the phrase structure. The children find that the first and third phrases are identical, and the second and fourth are different. (*c*) The next step is the teaching of the *so-fa* syllables as an additional rote verse, in order to bring out tonality relations and further define the phrase structure. (*d*) The next step is connecting the song with the score symbolism. The teacher places the notation of the song on the board, a phrase to each line. The class sings it through with words and with a neutral syllable, while the teacher points phrase-wise to the score. The teacher then picks out particular phrases, and the class or individual child sings the phrase with the *so-fa* syllables. (*e*) Particular attention is called to the distinctive characteristic of the repeated phrase, namely the tonic chord figure. This is not done

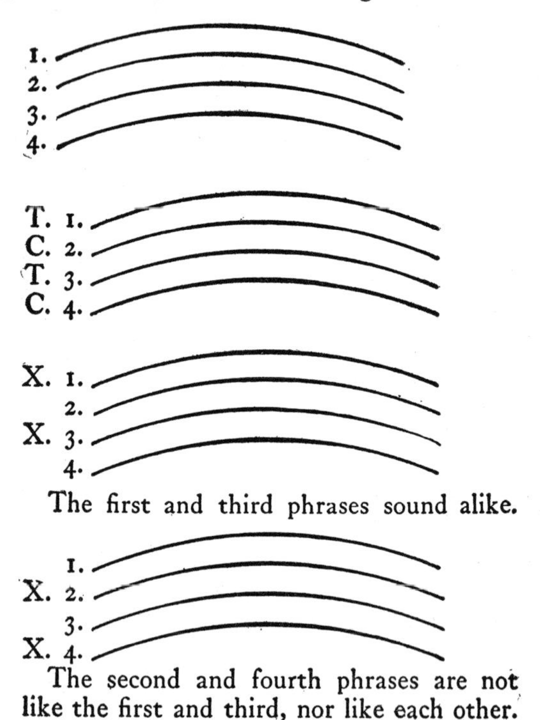


FIGURE 6. The song "Feathers" written phrase-wise.

by pointing it out note by note, but by bracketing the whole figure with the hands, and having the children sing it. (*f*) The last step is the singing of the song completely through with words, a neutral syllable, and the *so-fa* syllables directly from notation. Singing from a book is review and repetition of the lesson from the board. This is the first and crucial contact made between the performance project and the score. While the details of procedure may be considerably varied, the essential idea is the treatment of the score as a symbolic representation of musical meanings embodied in phrases. Furthermore, songs involving various types of figures are subsequently introduced into the program—that is, songs with

FIGURE 7. The song "Feathers" written phrase-wise, and corresponding with the diagrammatic representation of its four phrases as shown on page 218. (From *The Music Hour,* First Book, p. 8, by permission of the publishers.)

phrases containing tonic chord figures, diatonic figures, neighboring tone figures, and figures with intervals.

The psychological development beyond this point is clearly indicated. It involves the progressive introduction of songs learned more and more completely from the notes rather than by rote, and of song material which contains more and more intricate and unfamiliar combinations and variants of the fundamental figure patterns.

3. **Educational values.** It should be clearly stated here that we are not primarily interested in recommending a definite procedure which we think is ideal. Indeed, there is probably no such "best of all" procedure for teaching anything. What we are trying to do is to make clear by means of concrete illustrations the psychological principle of developing a mastery of the score as a representation of musical meanings. It may help in this direction if we discuss some of the educational and psychological advantages of the procedure just described. *Any variation from it must always retain these values, and a routine or stupid following of the indicated steps without any comprehension of their psychological purpose will dissipate them.*

(*a*) This procedure deals with the problem of the score in its proper setting of musical development rather than as a specialized stunt. We should notice particularly that the pupil is not at first taught the note names, and that his attention is not even called to the separate notes, but to the note patterns or phrases as totalities. In this way reading and the mastery of the score is placed in its proper psychological setting.

First, it is developed as a direct and natural evolution of rote singing. If we begin with drill on notational detail in the second grade, there is an abrupt transition from music making to something which for the child, at any rate, has nothing to do with music making. We instantly set up a task that is not a musical project, and so has no place in music education. The recommended procedure and its possible variants aim at helping the child to see the score as a picturization of musical experiences he has already come to enjoy.

Secondly, it sets up the various problems of the score as musical problems rather than as problems in the mastery of an abstract symbolism. The real functional problems cease to be those of knowing lines and spaces and note names and all the rest of it. They come to be those of recognizing in the score certain musically-meaningful ideas.

Thirdly, this procedure, with its constant emphasis on phrase and melody, means building musical training and training in the mastery of the score upon the natural aesthetic structure and meaning of music rather than on its theory.

(*b*) This procedure favors a correct internal sequence of development in reading ability. This it does because it definitely calls for a correct distribution of attention, and the sort of visual grasp of total meanings which we know to be the essence of reading skill and mastery of symbolisms.

First, the child is trained to respond to the score, to see it, to attend to it, and to think the score phrase-wise rather than note-wise. That is, mental and visual grasp from the very first is directed away from the note in isolation, and towards the unit of musical meaning.

Secondly, incidental learning is properly capitalized. We sometimes encounter statements to the effect that if the child is not trained to attend to lines and spaces, note names, etc., he will not "learn" them. This may be true if we mean that he will not be able to recite them from memory, or indicate them in a rapid fire speed drill. But it is entirely false if it means that he will not be able to use the symbolism properly.

He can learn to recognize the pattern of the score without any attention at all to its formal detail, and later on when attention is called to detail, he will find virtually that he already knows it. On the one hand, the learning of the score is not wholly unguided and informal, as Davison seems to recommend. On the other hand, attention is not directed towards detail but towards the representation of significant musical ideas, which is the essential thing.

Thirdly, we work towards the reading of music as contrasted with the spelling of notes. Some of the work in reading music in the grades would be much better adapted to create ability for proofreading than for musical expression. In reading, a total grasp of the phrase is essential, and the making of note errors is a secondary matter. A note error in early reading is important only in so far as it indicates a failure to grasp the total phrase. As a matter of fact the sort of reading which a choir director or a conservatory teacher would like to see possessed by his pupils, and which an accompanist needs, is one which involves rapid and sure grasp of the meaning and sweep of the phrase rather than a painful note-by-note accuracy. This phrase grasp is the essential mark of the really expert reader, who creates musical effects from the score rather than by spelling it out note by note.

(*c*) This procedure makes it possible for us to use good and interesting music in connection with the building of mastery of the score. If, however, our approach is by the study of notational detail and note-wise attack, then our music must be simple, *and simple from the standpoint of note spelling.* This probably involves a great deal of music in one or two keys, because we are interested in drilling on key signature and recognition. With the limited range of the child's voice, this means the exclusion of a great many songs. Furthermore, we may be reluctant to use sequences of different intervals, and tend to cling to uniform intervals. All this means that we have songs that are musically uninteresting, monotonously grouped to illustrate a point rather than to express an aesthetic idea. Here we see once more the danger of always working from simple to complex, rather than organizing our whole process so that we can plunge the pupils into genuine and interesting experiences. What we want in music education is the setting up of problems in making music rather than in musical theory.

(*d*) This procedure is an excellent illustration of a movement from preliminary synthesis through analysis to a final synthesis. The child begins with relatively unanalyzed experience in rote song. Little by little the phrase elements of the song emerge into prominence. These are progressively connected with the symbolism of the score, and this in itself defines them more impressively. Mastery of the score, which takes the form of the ability directly to recognize from notation the melodic curve and general musical meaning of an unfamiliar song, is thus brought about by a progressive analysis and synthesis in which phrases come to be more and more distinctly recognized.

### Mastery of the Symbolisms for Key and Time

While the proper attitude towards the symbols for key and for time has been suggested in what we have said, it may be well to bring up the matter for explicit comment.

1. **Key.** With regard to teaching the key symbolisms—key signature and accidentals—the essential point is that they must not be approached in terms of theory. By the time the child reaches the third grade he should have developed a considerable feeling for tonality through the use of *so-fa* or

some alternative system. As soon as he begins to make contact with the score, the problem of the proper representation of *do,* and the proper indication of sharps and flats begins to arise. These matters should be handled incidentally and inductively. That is, the child should not be taught all the key signatures *memoriter,* or drilled on some abstract rule for forming them and finding *do.* Rather the question should be attacked afresh with each song, until finally the pupil is able to write and recognize the key indications without help. In dealing with the creative project as a means of developing mastery of the score, we saw that the *teacher* should put the key signature on the board at first, and should help the children to find *do.* This is to avoid a direct and more or less mathematical approach, which would be inevitable if we set up for the pupil the problem of working out the proper key signature. We also saw that the pupil rapidly and with interest reaches the point where little help is required. In the approach to the score through the performance project, the same principle holds, though of course its application is different. We must not undertake formalized drill in connection with key signature. Rather we should develop it when necessary in connection with each new song. In the earlier stages of phrase-wise reading, nothing need be said about key. All we want is that the child may recognize the musical pattern. But little by little there emerges the fact that *do* lies in different places, and that figures with similar tonality fall differently upon the staff. Here is where key signatures begin to acquire a meaning in terms of the child's experience and necessity.

2. **Time.** Once again we would insist that the symbolism for time—time signature, bar lines, and note length—be handled incidentally and inductively. It is a capital fallacy to

think that we can go from the symbol to the experience. What sort of experience do we want in order to make the time symbols meaningful? *Always it is experience of rhythm.* Remember that it is not the three-ness or four-ness of a measure, or the quarter-ness or half-ness of a note that is the essence of the matter. *It is the rhythmic pattern that expresses itself in these time values and numbers, but that is essentially an experience of action which gives meaning to the time symbols.* The composer did not do a stunt of musical mathematics when he conceived and wrote down his piece of music. He created a rhythmic unity, which had to be expressed—and could be only approximately expressed—through sequences of indicated time relations. The task of understanding and using the score is in part a reconstruction of the rhythm from the time indications. This is why we would say that counting is at best a means rather than an end. It is also the reason why we would discourage any sort of emphasis on the mathematical relationships of note lengths at an early stage. All these things become meaningful when presented as outcomes of rhythm and rhythmic action.

## Some Devices Commonly Used in Teaching the Score

It may be helpful if we briefly discuss in the light of the ideas we have developed, a few of the devices which are commonly used in developing mastery of the score.

1. First of all we may mention the layout of the printed or written score. Here two points are to be made. (*a*) The score should be laid out phrase-wise, that is, a phrase to a line, for young children. This at once tends to bring the phrase structure to attention, even without directly teaching it. (*b*) It is perfectly allowable to introduce symbols, the meaning of which the child does not yet know, such as slurs,

for instance. We must abandon the prejudices which go with the dogma of simple-to-complex-known-to-unknown, together with the dogma itself. The more musical the scoring of children's songs can be, the richer are the teaching opportunities because the more dynamic and real is the situation. At the same time the presence of theoretical details often encourages the factually-minded teacher to emphasize them to the exclusion of music making.

2. The blackboard is one of the most commonly used educational devices, and we need do no more than just mention it. It may be used for picturizations of phrases and rhythms to be seen by the group and analyzed for the group by some individual. Obviously it is required in connection with creative projects.

3. Flash cards containing musical figures and phrases have a limited use in building up mastery of the score—in order to emphasize speed of recognition and response.

4. We would question the use of the empty score with a movable note on the ground that we do not want to call attention to the individual note, but to the whole phrase. We cannot see how it is possible to make much use of this device without working directly towards and almost certainly achieving, a note-wise rather than phrase-wise direction of attention.

5. We would question the device of having the children point at the notes of the score as they sing, from much the same angle. This is not so objectionable as the use of the detached note, for, after all, the phrase as a whole is there before the child, and his attention may readily be called back to it. However, it seems a device that ought to be used just as little as possible. To employ it for the teaching of rhythm is of course obviously absurd.

6. A chart with all the key signatures displayed is some-

times recommended. It is suggested that it may be kept permanently before the children and used for occasional reference in teaching key symbolisms. This is most practicable in platoon schools or departmentalized grade schools, where there is a regular room for music. Employed in the suggested way this device may help. But the danger is that with all the key signatures laid out, some teacher's formalizing tendencies will again get the better of him, and he will indulge in some nice lessons in mathematics instead of bothering with the trivialities of mere music.

7. We have already commented on the possibilities of a pianistic approach to tonality, and this would also mean a pianistic approach to the score. There is no doubt that the piano keyboard has educational possibilities that our schools have not yet realized. But one should remember that actual experimentation on a real instrument is enormously better in every way than problemizing with a keyboard diagram, which may be a geometrical rather than musical agency.

8. Lastly, we may call attention again to the system of outlining phrases by curves, as illustrated in figure 6, on page 218. The value of this is that it strongly emphasizes the unity and totality of the phrase, and also the sequential relationship of the phrase units to one another.

## Summary: Outcomes of This Chapter

1. Mastery of the score has an essential place in elementary music education. The score is both a musical tool, and an agency through which musical mindedness, and specifically the grasp of phrase, tonality, and rhythm may early be clinched and particularized.

2. Research on language reading indicates that mastery of any symbolism means ability to deal with it in large units.

Hence we conclude that the essential thing to emphasize in dealing with the score is its representation of total phrases rather than notes.

3. An analysis of the nature of the score as symbolism, with its peculiar variables, reinforces this idea.

4. The phrase-wise approach to the score may be made through creative projects or through performance projects.

5. The symbolisms for key and for time should be dealt with incidentally and inductively rather than formally, directly, and deductively.

6. The ideas here presented furnish a basis for the evaluation and criticism of devices proposed in connection with the teaching of the score.

### Questions for Discussion.

1. State as fully as you can just what complete "mastery of the score" means, and what abilities it involves.

2. Describe in detail some scheme known to you which to some extent represents a "quasi-mathematical" approach to the score.

3. To what extent should rote song work, listening, etc., be sacrificed from the third grade onward for work with the score?

4. What methods of approaching and dealing with the score, other than by calling primary attention to phrase, are possible?

5. Contrast the creative project as we have prescribed it with any plan of "music writing" you may have seen. What difference is there from the standpoint of educational values?

6. Which do you think is the better way of introducing the score for the first time, the creative project method which involves writing it, or the performance project which involves reading it?

7. Which of the educational values we discussed in connection with the performance project as an approach to the score would apply to the approach by the creative project? Which would not?

8. In the light of our discussions of the educational values of

these two approaches, evaluate any other methods of dealing with the score that you may know.

9. Explain in detail what is meant by approaching key and time symbolisms inductively and incidentally. What would be the opposite kind of approach?

10. In the light of the principles of this chapter, evaluate any devices for dealing with the score other than those we have discussed.

BIBLIOGRAPHY.

1. BAKER, EARL, and GIDDINGS, T. P., *High School Music Teaching,* George Banta Publishing Company, 1928.
2. BROOKS, FOWLER D., *The Applied Psychology of Reading,* D. Appleton and Company, 1926.
3. BUSWELL, GUY T., *Fundamental Reading Habits. A Study of Their Development,* University of Chicago Press, 1922.
4. DAVISON, ARCHIBALD T., *Music Education in America,* Harper and Brothers, 1926.
5. GLENN, MABELLE, Creative Song, *Childhood Education,* 1929, vol. 5, pp. 324-329.
6. GRAY, WILLIAM SCOTT, *Summary of Investigations Relating to Reading,* University of Chicago Press, 1925.
7. JAQUES-DALCROZE, EMIL, *Rhythm, Music, and Education,* Tr. Harold F. Rubinstein, G. P. Putnam's Sons, 1921.
8. MCCONATHY, OSBOURNE, MIESSNER, W. O., BIRGE, E. B., and BRAY, MABEL E., *The Music Hour, Elementary Teacher's Book,* Silver, Burdett and Company, 1929, pp. 38-43.
9. MURSELL, JAMES L., *Principles of Musical Education,* The Macmillan Company, 1927, ch. 8.
10. PARKER, HORATIO, MCCONATHY, OSBOURNE, BIRGE, E. B., and MIESSNER, W. O., *The Progressive Music Series, Teacher's Manual,* vol. 1, Silver, Burdett and Company, 1915, pp. 25, 39-42.

11. THORNDIKE, E. L., Reading as Reasoning: A Study of Mistakes in Paragraph Reading, *Journal of Educational Psychology,* 1917, vol. 8, pp. 323-332.

12. THORNDIKE, E. L., The Psychology of Thinking in the Case of Reading, *Psychological Review,* 1916, vol. 24, pp. 220-234.

# PART THREE

# Executant Factors in Music Education

# Chapter Nine

# *Technique*

## The Problem of Technique in Music Education

In John Bunyan's superb allegory of the Pilgrim's Progress we read how Christian and Faithful, in their journey towards the City, came to a place where they were met by two men fleeing back in pallid fear and exclaiming, "There is a lion in the way! There is a lion in the path!" In spite of this, though with some tremblings, Christian and Faithful pressed on. But when they came to the place where the lions were, they found that they were chained.

At this point in our exposition, as we definitely approach the executant problems of music education, we too find that there is a lion in the path. Its name is technique, and it has badly scared many music teachers, who have felt themselves powerless before it, and have never achieved what might have been. We shall see that when boldly faced, its threat simply ceases to exist. But many have been deceived into two responses that are wholly disastrous,—surrender and flight. Let us for a moment consider them, one by one.

1. Those who surrender to technique are they who think it is so difficult and so exigent that it must necessarily dominate the whole of music education, and that if anyone wishes to become a musician, he must cultivate technique as an end in itself. This is the view often adopted, sometimes unconsciously, though sometimes quite deliberately and explicitly, by a great many studio teachers, and by not a few instru-

mental supervisors and school music teachers. Inevitably it colors their whole attitude towards the type of progressive music education which we have been trying to describe and defend. It makes them skeptics in regard to it. They think that to make music education center about appreciation and the development of a musical mentality is just to succumb to a debauch of fine words, to ignore unpleasant facts and genuine difficulties, to side-step the necessity for the hard grind at technique, and to slump hopelessly and spinelessly into "soft pedagogy." But as soon as they come to this they stultify themselves, and for two reasons. First, they destroy the real educative value of their own work, and become trainers and teachers of tricks, rather than missionary servants of the beauty and power of music. Secondly, they fail to bring about even technical advancement, because they throw away all chance of effective motivation, and propose to deal with technique by way of habit building rather than by creation and development. Such music teachers are devoured by the lion to which they have made surrender.

2. Those who flee from technique are they who try to pretend that technique has no place at all in genuine music education, that really it does not matter, and that there is no room for it, at least in school music. But to take such an attitude is to ignore rather than to solve the problem. The necessity for technique as a requirement for real effectiveness in music making is indisputable, and to say that we can do without it is like denying that a stone wall towards which we are driving a car, really exists. Again this means disaster. Music teachers who think along such lines flee from the lion.

3. The viewpoint and approach we wish to suggest, defend, and explain is that technique really furnishes an opportunity for musical development, and that the notions of learning and

musical growth we have enunciated are involved in a unique and intimate manner in building technique. Once more we shall hope to show convincingly that the proper way to attack the whole business of technique is with appreciation as a motive and appreciation as a goal, and that the outcome of increasing technical proficiency is really a deeper musical-mental proficiency, which of course means a deeper and more understanding love for music. *For us the educational problem of technique is essentially the problem of spiritualizing the motor side of music making.* We must insist that this is a problem which cannot for a moment be shelved by any conscientious music teacher who wishes to deal effectively with the realities of his work. This we believe to be the constructive and intelligent attitude. We go one better than Christian and Faithful. We get on the lion's back and ride him away.

### The Nature of Technique and the General Requirements for Developing It

The first thing we need is a general point of view on the whole question of technique. Many music teachers have either never thought much about this, or else, knowing nothing of the psychology of human skill, have arrived at entirely indefensible notions. Let us try then to show what technique really means and implies.

1. Technique may be defined as the ability to produce musical results in a given medium,—voice, piano, violin, etc. We absolutely refuse to think of it in terms of formal vocal or digital agility, acrobatics, speed, endurance, and so forth, or of mastery of such formal motor problems as the trill, the scale, etc. These are the incidents rather than the essence of technique, and should, we believe, be approached incidentally

rather than directly in music education. Amy Fay, in her very interesting book *Music Studies in Germany,* describes the first lesson she took with Kullak. Her teacher abruptly asked, "What do you know of double thirds?" and incontinently thereupon rushed up and down the keyboard in double thirds, to the obfuscation of his poor pupil. This is exactly what we do not mean by technique. Technique is not "knowledge of double thirds," or anything like it. It is the ability to make beautiful music. Christiani[1] has said, "Discrimination of touch is the intellectual, the internal part of technique; finger velocity, only the mechanical, the external portion." Matthay[2] again has given as his opinion that not even a child beginner should be allowed to sound any succession of sounds without being made to understand that even in the simplest attempts, there must be shape or progression. Now it is just this ability to "sound a succession of sounds" in such a way that their musical "shape" becomes apparent, that constitutes the very essence of music making, and also the very essence of technique. These statements were made on behalf of teachers and relatively advanced students of piano, yet they have a meaning on which every school music teacher may well ponder. So we define technique in terms of music making—that is, we give it a purely *functional definition.*

2. We make a distinction, to be stressed more later, between technique and mechanics. Our distinction here is not quite that ordinarily made. By mechanics we mean those purely physical conditions which must be maintained in order to actuate the instrument adequately,—such things as the proper

[1] CHRISTIANI, ADOLPH F., *The Principles of Expression in Pianoforte Playing,* Harper and Brothers, 1885, p. 68.

[2] MATTHAY, TOBIAS, *Musical Interpretation,* 3rd. Ed., Boston Music Company, 1913, p. 45.

holding of the violin and grasp of the bow, *embouchure,* placement on the piano keyboard, breath support, etc. These are the conditions without which the instrument can never be made to sound as it should, for purely physical reasons. To put it in another way, the instrumental performer and the instrument together constitute a physical unit for the production of music. This unit has one set of motions inevitably prescribed if the violin is involved, another if the clarinet is involved, another if the piano is involved. It is this determinate type of motions prescribed by the instrument (including here the vocal instrument) that we understand by mechanics. Technique on the other hand is the actual movement pattern set up within the limitations of mechanics. We shall find that the very essence of this movement pattern is its musical significance,—its correspondence with the musical structure. There is no essential musical meaning in a certain way of holding the violin and bow. That is determined by the acoustic and other physical properties of the instrument, and it belongs to what we call mechanics. But there is a great deal of musical meaning in the bowing movement itself. This belongs to technique proper. The free, eurythmic dancer "realizes" music in a sequence of absolutely unimpeded movements, the only limitations upon which are the natural limitations of the human body. The executant musician also "realizes" the music in a series of movements which constitute his technique. But they are no longer entirely free. They are limited not only by the movement capacities of the body, but by the exigencies of the instrument. One further comment should be made here. While we speak of the pattern of motion imposed by the physics of the instrument as "mechanics," this does not mean that we acquire it by a mechanical process of learning. It is unfortunate to have to use two such similar words in senses so different, and the reader should be guarded against the possible confusion that may result.

3. We claim that the primary approach to all technique should be through the voice. Many reasons for this will emerge later. But here we state the chief one. It is that in singing we have a means of making music in which mechanics are limited to an absolute minimum, and in which technique is almost exactly the same thing as direct musical feeling. Thus we believe that one way to conquer the technical problem that we find in instrumental music, and even to capitalize it as a means of musical advance, is to begin building the motor feeling for and apprehension of music through song. In this way the child comes to experience what music making actually is before he has to tackle the job in a forbidding medium.

4. We shall find that in establishing the motor control we call technique, our primary reliance must be upon the factors of ear training and rhythmic grasp which we have discussed so fully. We work for motor control through hearing music as it actually is, feeling its rhythmic structure, and imaging the effects that ought to be produced. Technical development depends upon the application of musical mindedness to motor control in the production of music, and thus it yields two kinds of fruit; first, a finer and better musical mindedness, and, second, a more thoroughly musical system of motor response. As a corollary we shall find once again that the phrase-wise approach is essential because the phrase, as the unit of musical meaning, also becomes the unit of motor control.

5. We shall find a very intimate connection between technique and expression. In the next chapter we shall see that

really when we work for technical control in a composition, we are working for refinement of musical expression, and the controlled creation of musical beauty.

### The Establishment of Motor Control

So far the discussion has been general only. We make it concrete, and give it a relationship to educational practice, by bringing it down to the detailed conditions under which human skill is created, and human motor control is established. We shall find that motor skill is not set up through a mechanical process of habit building, but that it depends upon purpose and intelligence. *The way to deal with technique in music education is not by the application of hard mechanical drill, but by the use of intelligence and purpose.* If great skill were a result of habit building, then clearly musical technique would become a bag of tricks. But this is not the case. Great motor skill is intelligence working in terms of physical action. And technique is musical intelligence working in terms of physical action. This is the vital point we wish to explain and establish, for it is the key to the whole problem of technique in music education.

In certain respects, all techniques are the same. Physical skill has the same general conditions whether it takes the form of using a golf club, a tennis racket, a billiard cue, a typewriter, a piano, a violin, a flute, a drum, or a set of vocal chords. Always it is *motor intelligence* rather than a habit structure. And the conditions of its acquisition and maintenance are the same. In discussing these conditions it will be instructive to use many illustrations from realms other than those of musical skill, just because of the identity of all great skills.

1. **Organizing the movement cycle.** The basis of every technique is the organization of a movement cycle. To take

a non-musical instance, skill at golf depends on the organizing and unifying of the swing, and progress is blocked until this complex coördination runs off as a single pulse of voluntary effort. Note that the swing is not compounded of a number of constituents, such as movement of the legs, back swing, straightening the left elbow, keeping the eye on the ball, etc. It must be built as a unit and must function as a unity. Analytic practice of course may be necessary, but always the vital thing is the growing functioning synthesis. We are dealing not with a mechanical sum of subsidiary movements to be learned one by one and then put together, but with a unit of response, to be learned by analysis and synthesis. And we should notice that the response is always geared to, and unified by, a goal. The good golfer is not the person who runs off a sequence of subsidiary habits in a certain order, but he who can hit his ball where he wants it to go. Golfing intelligence expresses itself in the fine adjustment of the swing—the movement cycle—to the end to be achieved. This well illustrates what we mean by a motor skill or technique being intelligence and purpose expressed in terms of physical action. All this is exactly true of the various musical techniques. There are more types of swing in music than in golf, and they often have to be made at awkward angles and from difficult stances. But the essence of the affair is always the same. Just as the golfer's movement cycle is determined by golf meaning,—that is, by the wish to get the ball to a certain place—so in music the movement cycle is always determined by the unit of musical meaning to be made over into sound, that is, upon the phrase with its tonal and rhythmic constituents. Thus the proper technical approach to either a song or an instrumental composition is always in terms of giving out each musical unit on a distinct, unified, finely graded and adjusted pulse of effort. So once more we see the vital importance of the phrase-wise approach in music education. We can understand why Jaques-Dalcroze insists that those who have a fine rhythmic grasp find technical problems astonishingly easy. The reason, of course, is that such people already have the proper motor feeling for the music well established, and all they have to do is to transpose it as required by the mechanics of the medium they are to use.

2. **Economy of control.** The second general condition of motor skill is economy of motor control. The control of movement is established by a discharge along the motor nerves. Now this discharge is not continuous, but alternating, at a rate that varies with different persons, but probably never goes much above 10 per second. Suppose that we have an individual whose motor nerves send down discharges to the muscles which intermit ten times per second. It is very clear that if he moves his arm in a horizontal direction, and takes one second to do it, the movement comes under the control of the nerves ten times in its course. But if he makes the same movement much more quickly, taking now only one-tenth of a second, it is again clear that the reaction is under control once only instead of ten times during its course. Or again, this person may start a movement off, and then, as it were, switch off the control, and let it run free, just as if he had thrown his hand, or arm, or leg in some direction. This is pretty much what the snake does when it strikes, or what the golfer does when he swings. The complex coördination is prepared. The movement is pushed off. And it swings through. *Evidently we have here a bare minimum of nervous control.*

This minimizing of nervous control by reaching a point where one can set the coördination almost in the way a combination lock is set, and then shoot it through on one pulse of nervous effort, is part of the basis of all great skill. It yields the following advantages. (*a*) It greatly decreases the likelihood of error. Every control point is a chance for a mistake. If a typist must anxiously direct his attention to every key he is to hit, and make a separate controlled effort in each case, there is a good chance for a mistake every time. But if he has reached the point where he can set beforehand the coördination required to write out a whole phrase, and then shoot it off on a single pulse, it is evident that his chances to make mistakes are enormously diminished. He may botch the whole phrase, but once it is well started he is not likely to make errors unless the coördination falls to pieces. This is the reason why speed and accuracy in nearly all skills go together. Their basic conditions are the same. Both depend on economy of control. (*b*) The next great advantage of economical control is that it makes for the highest possible pitch of intelligibility and fine grading in the reaction. A delicate billiard shot or putt is not brought off by elaborate agonizing over detailed motor control, but by very clearly apprehending the goal, setting the coördination that such a goal demands, and running off the whole movement with a free, facile, and confident attack. So in music, beautiful expression is not produced by hard-working attention to each note, but by delicate phrase-wise coördination and impulsion. This is the reason why the child with the improperly placed voice cannot sing expressively. The effort and extensive control required merely to sing the approximate tones is so great that we simply have no free, phrase-wise coördination or attack at all. (*c*) A movement cycle given with a minimum of control along its course makes transition to the next "swing" much easier. It takes a golfer with a very facile and economical control indeed to swing two and fro half a dozen times without pausing, and drive that number of balls effectively, one after the other. In exactly the same way a musician who makes heavy weather of one phrase is sure to be badly placed for the next. The proper situation is one where the coördination for the phrase is set, and the whole movement cycle run off freely, with an impulse of nervous direction to start it, but little along its course, and then everything cleared for the next attack.

3. **Relaxation.** We often hear of the "gospel of relaxation" in music, but few music teachers really understand it. In technique it means two rather different but still closely related things.

(*a*) Relaxation means the freeing of the positive movement from the pull of antagonistic muscle groups. We must never forget that every movement we make is not only a swing but also a letting go. When we flex the arm, the flexor muscles pull. But also the extensor muscles relax. If they did not, we would have a condition of rigidity, of tetany. So a relaxed movement is one in which the pull of antagonistic or irrelevant muscles is reduced to a minimum necessary for guidance. One very interesting study indicates that this is one of the chief things that happen as skill increases. Men were set to pedal on a bicycle crank, against a certain fixed braking resistance. It was found that the actual amount of effort put forth by the body (measured by metabolism) steadily increased as the work continued. In other words, the subjects worked *harder* per unit of time the longer they went on. The reason was this. At first only the positive muscles were used, and everything else was relaxed. Before long, however, other muscles began to stiffen up. The antagonistic muscle groups were not properly "switched off." Irrelevant muscles began to come into play, so that the subjects worked not only with their legs, but with their whole bodies. But it was found, —and this for us is the interesting outcome—that persons who were specially trained were able to postpone the time when relaxation was lost, and a given number of revolutions on the crank began to cost more and more physical effort. Hence the reason why highly-skilled persons can go on far longer than those who are not skilled, is not at all that the former have stronger muscles, but that they put off the evil day of tenseness, the period when the body begins working against its own increasing, counteracting pulls, far longer than the latter. The way to work for relaxation as we have here described it, is to work for economical coördination in terms of the goal to be achieved. Each thrust of the crank becomes a unified, well-outlined, economical, and elegant pulse of effort. Or in music, each phrase is carried through with just the positive push that it needs, and subsidiary movement is cut out.

(*b*) In the second place, relaxation refers to the transition from one movement to the next. This is really only another aspect of the economically controlled movement cycle. We see it perhaps better in tennis than in golf, for in the former game one shot follows fast after another. If one shot is so difficult or so ill-controlled that the player cannot recover from it, his next effort is at once compromised. And in music, if a phrase cannot be carried through with a well-unified and facile pulse of effort, the attack on the next one is made weaker and less easy. The tense effort may carry one through the given phrase. But it is very likely to mean a breakdown immediately afterwards.

*So always in working for relaxation in musical technique, the essential thing is to have the pupil think and feel in terms of phrase units carried on a single pulse of effort. The phrase controls technique.* Particularly we should notice that relaxation is not an affair of the joints or the throat. It is not a static affair at all. It depends entirely on the type and control of movement. And it is established by infusing musical intelligence and a feeling for musical shape and structure into the movement complex required to actuate the instrument.

4. **Posture.** We make a distinction between posture and pose. Pose refers to the outward shape of a bodily position, and posture refers to its inward nervous and muscular control. Pose pertains to mechanics. Posture is the essential thing in technique. In order to actuate an instrument properly and to make it sound as it should, the player must take and hold a certain pose. But within the limitations of this pose, a system of skilled, rhythmic movement must be carried on. This is technique, and it depends on the postural aspect of the bodily position.

Posture is really a type of movement. When we actually move the arm through a curved course, various muscles are pulling and relaxing, one set overbalancing the rest. When we hold the arm stationary, straight out from the shoulder, the muscles are still pulling and relaxing, but they are so adjusted that they just balance one another. Thus precisely the same mechanism is operating as in the case of what is more ordinarily thought of as movement.

Now a posture may vary all the way from great freedom to extreme rigidity. In the former case, the antagonistic pull of the muscles is reduced to a minimum, and just enough tension is maintained to hold the limb against gravity. In the latter case, the limb is held not only against gravity, but also against the pull of various muscles. *Now what we want is postural freedom within any pose that may be demanded by the instrument.* Without postural freedom, high skill cannot be attained. One reason why so much technical drill is absolutely ineffective is that postural tension is permitted, and this will ruin any and every kind of fine, graded, or rapid response.

One great mistake made by music teachers, both in the studio and in the classroom, is to concentrate attention entirely on the shape of the pose, and to ignore wholly the freedom of the posture. It is a very dangerous thing to worship some pose as "correct," and think that this is the essential thing. This is done constantly in specialized methods in instrumental music. For instance, the air has resounded from time to time with debates as to whether one should have a high or a low wrist when playing the piano. While one cannot quite go so far as Rubinstein's advice to Hoffman, "Play it with your nose," and agree that pose simply does not matter, yet we are bound to insist that those who give all their attention to the shape of the pose and none to postural freedom, make the acquisition of technique a hopeless task, because they antagonize one of the main conditions for any sort of skill.

## Mechanics

The problem of mechanics is of special interest in connection with instrumental music, and we shall return to it when we come to discuss this. For the moment, however, there are a few general points that need to be made.

1. Mechanical demands should be rationalized. One of the curses of music education has been the stupid tradition of a right way to do certain things, which had no basis in reason, which would not stand critical examination, but which was maintained as a sort of religion. We would advise every instrumental instructor to try to list on paper the essential mechanical adjustments which his pupils *must* learn to make if

they are to get music out of their instruments. He will usually be surprised to find how few and how definite these are, and how readily they may be taught if only they are clearly recognized and intelligently attacked.

2. The mechanics of any instrument should be taught from the first, taught continuously, and taught incidentally to the making of music. A severe criticism of much instrumental work—and this applies conspicuously to much class instruction in piano—is that it consists in having the pupil try to play without any effort being made to show him what he must do to get effects out of the instrument. Undoubtedly many teachers make difficulties here where none exist. The mechanics of the various instruments are not dreadfully complicated or extremely hard to learn. The reason why so many people think it very difficult to play an instrument well is that no one showed them the A B C of dealing with it when they were children. Their music lesson simply consisted of having the teacher hear what they had done, and make a few more or less relevant comments. *It is a positive fact that the mechanical alphabet of any instrument is simple enough to be taught to a child from the very beginning, as an incident to genuine performance projects.*

3. Training in the mechanics of an instrument should always tend towards what is known as "feeling for the instrument" rather than the building of a set of habits. That is, our aim is to help the child to use his instrument as a means of producing a certain range of musical effects.

### Implications for the Pedagogy of Technique

This somewhat lengthy general discussion of the conditions and nature of human motor skill, which the reader may perhaps find a little trying and theoretical, is absolutely necessary as a background for an intelligent attack upon the educational problem of technique. We must go to the root of the matter, because the subject itself is not a simple one, and because it is little understood by the very people who most need a comprehension of it. *The great outcome, which we must constantly bear in mind as a guide to practice, is that motor skill is motor intelligence. A musical technique is musicianship working through the nerves and the muscles.* We build a skill not by adding habit to habit, but by creating free, facile, unified coördination in terms of a definite goal to be achieved. Let us now turn to the practical educational outcomes of our analysis.

1. The beginning of all technical development is the phrasewise learning, feeling, and singing of the rote song. In other words, technique has for its origin the intimate motor apprehension of the phrase structure of music. What we call "having a technique" means very largely possessing the combined mental and physical ability (and the two are intertwined) to deal with music in terms of its significant phrase units. This has two direct and immediate implications. (*a*) Singing is the natural foundation of executant work in music, because by no other means can we so intimately and directly sense its structure in the reactions of our bodies. (*b*) Proper work for technique really means working for musicianship and a feeling for the shape of music. It is not an affair of learning an instrument, but of learning to sense and release the musical meaning and structure under the conditions imposed by the instrument.

2. Technical difficulties should always be thought of as difficulties in establishing and carrying through phrases on a unified, free, easily controlled pulse of effort. They are difficulties in "realizing" the music in action, in the sense in which

Jaques-Dalcroze uses the word, under the limiting conditions imposed by the instrument. In general such difficulties are of two kinds. (*a*) Difficulties within the phrase, due to a stiffening, a failure of coördination and control, a breakdown of the movement pattern, so that the phrase-wise swing is lost. (*b*) Difficulties in carrying through a sequence of phrases, where the phrase-wise swing and attack breaks down because of what precedes or follows it. Wrong notes, or bad vocal tone, etc., are symptoms of these difficulties, and should always be thought of as due to failures in the movement cycle. Where mistakes, troubles, and difficulties of this sort occur, they obviously demand analytic practice,—that is, stopping and taking the movement cycle to pieces to find out what is wrong with it. But this should never become formal drill. It should never lose connection with actually felt problems in music making. There should be a constant swing back from the analytic work to the synthetic attempt, until the controlled movement cycle has established itself.

3. We have here an illuminating and decisive insight into the problems of speed and endurance, as well as accuracy. All these things depend on the same factor of free and facile motor placement. When the instrumental supervisor talks about giving the pupils a little "speed technique," he should have in mind something like this. He should take a musical phrase whose rendering demands some speed. He should have the pupils grasp it clearly and definitely, by listening to it, singing it, and thinking it. Then he should have them go over it carefully—and this means slowly—attending always to its total swing and feel, and concentrating on constituent notes only to build up the total, unified movement it requires. When the phrase has been grasped in terms of the movements called for by the instrument, and not before, the attempt

should be made to speed it up. For a time this will not work well. But at last speed will come, and it will come as a consequence of the consolidation and perfection of the movement cycle as a whole. The one thing he should not do is to operate in terms of formal exercises. Let us recall what was said in this connection in the chapter on learning. It is not the slowness of the practice that does the business. It is the care with which the learner concentrates on the *kind of response* needed. In working for speed one should practice carefully, and above all, musically. Overstrain is instantly fatal, for it brings in tension and destroys the ordered structure of the movement. Exactly the same ideas apply also to endurance and accuracy, which depend on the same foundation as speed.

4. Everything we have said implies that the attack upon technique through drill on formal exercises is entirely wrong. It is based directly upon a conception of learning as habit building, and of skill as a mechanical structure of movement habits. Even if this kind of work is pushed to the extreme limits found in some European conservatories, it only results in empty acrobatics unless the pupil is musical enough to feel the full meaning of what he does, and in this way is able to overcome the faults of the teaching. But in school music such a method is hopeless, because we have not enough leverage on the pupil to apply it at all. Even if we had, it would be just the wrong way to go. *A technique is not built by working at formal drill exercises, but by creating musical effects better and better.* Where exercises are used at all, the following principles should be controlling: (*a*) An exercise should never be used except in direct connection with a felt difficulty in producing a musical result desired by the pupil. (*b*) An exercise should never be used for its own sake—to

give "a knowledge of double thirds" for instance—but always to give the pupil the right feel of motor control in a movement cycle actually demanded by some phrase in a composition he is studying. (*c*) One should encourage the pupil to invent his own exercises in connection with difficulties in establishing movement cycles, because this tends towards the application of intelligence to technique and a real analysis of the problem involved.

Suppose we take the ideas that some music teachers entertain about technique, and apply them to the process which takes place when a child learns to talk. Of course we must never let him say a whole word. He is sure to get it wrong. He'll be saying "mum-mum" instead of "mother," "icky" instead of "sugar," or "nock" instead of milk, and ruining himself for life. This will not do at all. We must begin with simple formal drills on the proper placement of the tongue and soft palate, using the different vowel sounds, but at first carefully separating them from consonants. Then attention must be given to breathing and breath control, without which effective speech is well known to be impossible. These drills should be rigidly continued till the child is two years and eleven months old, and if we let him talk any sooner, we will spoil things just as surely as we would if we opened a window in a room with alleged mechanical ventilation. Next, coördinations of them all may be undertaken, till the eleventh month of the third year, after which, for one month, practice on consonant-vowel coördinations may be introduced. At the age of three the child may begin on words, starting with the A's in Webster's Unabridged Dictionary. By such methods the really lamentable speech defects of our population may be overcome, and the intellectual level of the American people raised from a mental age of thirteen to one of three-and-a-half!

5. Growth in technique should always be thought of and dealt with as growth in musical mindedness. Little by little the pupil comes to differentiate and recognize the various tonal and rhythmic elements in the phrase, which we have discussed. They gradually come to mean motor adjustment to him. *Just as fast as possible he should be encouraged to work definitely for finer and better tone quality, surer pitch placement, subtler dynamic shading, finer management of modulations and changes of key, more delicate molding of the phrase and melodic curve, and a better and surer structured enunciation of the rhythm.* These are the things we strive for in working for technique. They are also the essentials of musical-mental development and the foundations of appreciation. The great question for the pupil in building a technique is always *"How can I make this sound better, more meaningful, and more beautiful?"*

6. All this leads directly to the next chapter, where we point out that really and vitally, working for technique may be thought of as working for expression, and that the best means of establishing technical control of a phrase is often to stress its expressive demands and nuance.

### Summary: Outcomes of This Chapter

1. Technique is defined functionally as the ability to produce intelligible and beautiful musical results by the use of a given medium.

2. We make a distinction between technique and mechanics. Every instrument, including the human voice, requires a certain repertoire of movement types for its proper actuation. These constitute its mechanics. Technique is the musically and rhythmically-structured play of movement within these requirements. The mechanics of an instrument

should be rationalized, and taught from the very first. However, this does not involve habit building.

3. Human skill always means intelligence expressed in action. The conditions of its development are the establishment of the movement cycle as a whole, the establishment of economical control, the establishment of relaxation, and the establishment of free posture.

4. Technique cannot be built up by formal drill processes. Its acquisition is simply one side of acquiring musical mindedness.

5. Technique has an essential place in progressive music education. Properly understood and properly taught, it is a means of musical development, and not an obstacle to it.

6. As a final outcome of our discussion we would say that the difficulty of technique is commonly much exaggerated, due to misunderstandings as to its nature, and wrongly directed educational effort.

### Questions for Discussion.

1. Show that our account of the development of technique really implies a learning process by analysis and synthesis.

2. Show that the use of formal drill exercises for technique implies the idea of habit building.

3. Why does one's appreciation of a composition advance as one studies its technical problems?

4. In the light of our analysis, suggest ways of dealing with note errors made by pupils.

5. What is the analogy between the grasp of a musical phrase, and a swing at golf?

6. Examine some elementary course, either for the piano or for the violin, and see to what extent it emphasizes and brings out *(a)* problems of technique *(b)* problems of mechanics.

7. Why should singing be the basis of instrumental technique?

8. Discuss the commonly held notion that school music has "nothing to do with technique."

9. Should one ever use scales, exercises, vocalizes, etc., in school music work? Why?

10. Have you ever been told that a certain pose is essential for some instrument? Give details. Discuss the idea.

11. In what way is posture similar to movement?

12. Is it correct to think of relaxation as "looseness of the wrist," etc.?

BIBLIOGRAPHY.

1. MURSELL, JAMES L., *Principles of Musical Education,* The Macmillan Company, 1927, ch. 8.
2. STETSON, RAYMOND H., The Mechanism of Different Types of Movement, *Psychological Monographs,* 1923, vol. 22, whole no. 145.

For further references on technique see the bibliography for Chapter Three and particularly the references dealing with motor learning and skill.

## Chapter Ten

# *Expression*

### The Place of Expression in Music Education

In thinking about expression in music education the fundamental thing to see is that we are not dealing with something that is arbitrarily imposed upon music at the whim of the performer,—something that can be put in or left out just as we like. *Expression is demanded by the structure of the music, and every expressive nuance aims merely at liberating the beauty and meaning of the musical structure.* Once we clearly see that music is not a mass of notes, but a pattern of meaningful elements, the most significant of which are the phrases, the logic of expression becomes unmistakable, and from it follows its proper treatment in music education. We have exactly the same problem in realms other than music. Expressive speech is simply speech in which the structural elements of language,—the phrases and sentences—are shaded in loudness and speed in such a way that their meaning is brought out. A picture, again, a visual pattern, demands a certain treatment of light and shade, to make its structure and significance more apparent. Musical expression is nothing but the light and shade required by the pattern of sound.

This idea has a number of far-reaching and interesting implications. One is that a great interpretive artist does not arbitrarily choose the sort of expression he will use in a particular passage. Always his work is in the nature of a discovery of the demands of the musical structure. Then again, it becomes evident that there is such a thing as wrong, as well as right, expression. In speaking one can make a sentence sound ridiculous and almost meaningless by wrong emphasis. In music a phrase can be made nonsensical and deprived of all beauty, either by false expression or by none at all. Finally, it is possible to formulate principles of expression. This has been done quite exhaustively by Czerny, Lussy, and Christiani, whose works, listed at the close of this chapter, will repay careful study by every music teacher. Duncan McKenzie, too, has some very helpful suggestions in this direction.

But it is the direct implication for music education of our conception of expression that is of paramount interest for us. Clearly that implication is that expression has a central place in music education. It should, we believe, begin with expression. This means the singing of simple rote songs with proper expressive management. Always we should work towards a better and better grasp of the expressive factor, for this simply means a better and better grasp of musical verities.

Some music teachers hold that expression should come as the final element in musical learning, and that factors of note accuracy, time, rhythm, and tone color should be developed first. We believe that this position is based upon some very fundamental misconceptions. (*a*) It seems to arise from a note-wise rather than a phrase-wise approach to music. As soon as the phrase is properly understood and firmly and intimately grasped, a demand for expression is set up. One cannot feel the phrase as a unit without becoming aware that it ought to be shaded and molded. (*b*) It also seems to involve the idea of expression as something that we can just add on to the music. Teachers who take the attitude we have described argue that one cannot require the little child to pay attention to questions of nuance imposed and superadded by fiat, without compromising the learning process. So much we may admit. But expression ought to grow out of the child's direct feeling for the musical structure. Certainly we do not want to teach expression by a sort of imitative drill, in which the child is told what to do and then forced to try to do it. We want to teach it by giving him such a clear apprehension of the meaning and the beauty of the music that it will be natural for him to want to sing with some shading. Arbitrarily-imposed expression is wrong. Against this our whole argument is directed. (*c*) Furthermore the idea of postponing expression seems to involve a notion of learning as habit building. First we teach the notes, then we teach the rhythm, then we teach tone quality, and then last of all expression. (This may not be the particular sequence recommended; we use it merely to illustrate the point.) Learning is not like this. Everything develops together, though we give analytic attention now to one element, now to another. We do not put in expression right at the end of the construction of a long sequence of habits. *As the music becomes meaningful, it becomes expressive.*

So we would strongly insist that there is no point in music education where expression can be ignored, just as there is no point in music education where it can ever be arbitrarily imposed by fiat. In speech work, one does not drill the pupils on pronunciation, voice production, etc., and then later on teach them to say their sentences expressively. Furthermore, one never does what the old fashioned elocution teachers used to do,—drill the pupils on expressive utterance imposed arbitrarily. In speech the meaning of what one has to say creates its own expression. This is exactly the case with music.

## Factors in Music Upon Which Expression Depends

We must now carry our exposition of the general logic of expression further into detail, and try to show its educational implications.

1. **How the musical structure determines expression.** *The phrase is the heart of musical expression.* The pupil's ability to sing or play expressively will depend directly upon his feeling for the phrase unities. We have seen that the phrase is not at all a sum of separate notes, but a functional totality, which must be sensed and treated as such. The mere fact that one keenly feels this totality makes one immediately want to shape it up, and to give it out with a certain distribution of intensity, a certain speed, and a certain kind of tone quality. Moreover, the various constituent factors within the phrase all contribute to its expressive requirements. (*a*) The rhythmic structure of the phrase calls for expressive treatment precisely because it is not a mathematical pattern of time values. We have seen that while a rhythmic conception always translates itself into a time sequence in music, this timing is never regular nor quite accurate as measured by the clock. Always it involves processes of speeding up and slowing down, as well as a subtle system of accentuation. This holds true of rhythm in the dance, where we have what Jaques-Dalcroze calls the "pathetic movement," *i.e.,* a departure from absolutely strict timing to make the motor swing more intelligible and better placed. It holds true also of music. When a rhythmic structure is properly treated, it looks right (as in the dance), it feels right (as in both music and the dance), and it sounds right, in spite of some departure from rigid timing. (*b*) The melodic curve of the phrase also creates an expressive demand. The rise and fall of pitch will suggest perhaps a hurrying or a slowing down, an increase

or a diminution of intensity. The expressive reading of a melody means the subtle molding of its curve so that its meaningfulness and beauty shine out. (*c*) The tonality elements in a phrase also set up an expressive demand. As one approaches the tonic, certain changes of intensity or speed may be suggested. If one has a phrase ending elsewhere than on the tonic, it needs to be molded in another way. (*d*) Finally, harmonic sequences clearly set up expressive demands. If one simply marches through a series of chord effects, without the least change of intensity or speed, one certainly loses much of their beauty and meaning.

So to sum up our point, Matthay's requirement that no pupil ever be allowed to "sound a series of sounds" without being made aware of their musical "shape" directly implies that the series of sounds must be given out with an intensity, a speed, and a tonal quality such that their "shape" is recognizable. This is exactly what we mean by expressive performance, and it arises from an apprehension of the structure or shape of the music. *So in striving for expression, we should work for an intimate grasp of the phrase, with its rhythmic, melodic, and tonal constituents, and its harmonic background.*

2. **Why the musical structure determines expression.** We have here a question which pertains more closely to musical aesthetics than to music education. And yet it will repay at least a brief discussion here. *Musical structure sets up expressive demands because we feel and apprehend it through the responses of our bodies.* Music is not tonal geometry. If we only *hear* music, we never fully apprehend it. Music enters into us, possesses us, permeates us, and molds and modifies all our physical responses. The case of Sutermeister illustrates the power of tone, and its direct appeal

to human nerves and muscles. Diserens has given much attention to this question, and has found that listening to music has profound bodily effects. It increases metabolism, alters muscular energy, accelerates respiration and makes it less regular, has a marked effect on blood pressure, and produces a keener sensitiveness to other stimuli. In fact, it produces just those very bodily conditions which are known to be exceedingly important in emotional experience as such. Again we have explained that rhythm is not something we see with our eyes, or hear with our ears, or think with our minds, but something that we feel with our bodies. We remember also that Bingham has shown that the unity of a melody is always sensed physically, and Thurstone's argument that the up and down of pitch is due to a bodily feeling of reaching upwards and downwards.

The reason why a musical structure demands expressive treatment is that we always experience it as a sequence of excitements and relaxations, and through the swing and sweep and pulse of rhythmic response. *Expression in music is a translation into tone of the bodily apprehension of the music.* The human body is the basic musical instrument. We are responsive to music because of the nature of our bodies. The great aim in all music education is to help the child to identify himself with the sweep and flow of music,—not merely to hear it with his ears, or to understand its theory with his mind, but intimately and profoundly to feel it in all his tissues. Just in so far as he does this will he feel also the need for expression in music. And just in so far as this is achieved, will he be musically educated.

3. **Educational implications.** Now let us try to state just what our position means for practical music teaching.

(*a*) Basic training in musical expression is really training in grasp of the tonal and rhythmic verities in music. Of course this does not mean that we must never call the pupil's attention directly to an expressive requirement. The teacher should always sing the phrases of a rote song he is handling, as expressively and beautifully as possible, to reveal beauty as a standard of accomplishment. As the work goes on he may suggest a certain shading of the phrase the pupils are learning. In this way they become increasingly aware of expressive opportunities. This means reciprocally, that they become increasingly sensitive to the musical pattern which furnishes these opportunities.

(*b*) It is always wrong to teach expression by an elocutionary method, that is, by simply telling the pupils to sing or play in a certain way. This is probably what those teachers have in mind who argue that expression ought to be postponed in musical learning. The real reply, however, is that such a postponement implies an entire misconception of the nature and place of expression in music.

(*c*) Every musical effort of the child, including the earliest, should involve the element of expression. Inexpressive music is musical nonsense. It is music whose structure,—and this means its significance and beauty—is being ignored. We do not teach a child to talk by having him practice saying everything on one level tone without any shifts of intensity. Expressionless singing means singing that approximates the musical utterance of the monotone. We cannot get away from this too soon or too completely.

(*d*) As the child develops musically in the school, the surest sign of his progress is that he becomes much better able to perceive the opportunities and needs for nuance in his performance. It is perfectly true that we should never expect a first grade child to interpret a song in the way that a high school glee club might. The reason is that the first grade child has an entirely different apprehension of the music. But it is just as true that the child should always be encouraged to capitalize every expressive opportunity that he naturally perceives. The attitude of the teacher should always be to help the child to make aesthetic discoveries. This is the vital thing in all music education.

(*e*) Every musical effort should have expression for its goal. That is, we should always be working for a musical effect rather than for the singing or playing of certain notes. Such a point is obvious and inevitable as soon as we see that music is simply a structured pattern of tonal effects. *So our claim after all means no more than that the child should always be directed towards music as such.*

(*f*) These premises demand that the materials of school music work must offer genuine expressive opportunities. *Music that "says" nothing is educationally sterile.*

(*g*) They also mean that the teacher must have enough musical perceptiveness himself to recognize an aesthetic opportunity when he sees it.

From this aspect of expression we now pass on to discuss the proper educational treatment of the three great expressive devices or media,—dynamics, tempo, and tone quality.

### The Expressive Devices in Music:—I. Dynamics

The first means of expression in music is dynamic choice, that is, the loudness or softness, the intensity, with which we give out the music. Always we shall find that such choices depend absolutely upon the apprehension of the musical structure, and particularly of the phrase; and also that they arise, not from an intellectual understanding but from a direct physical apprehension of that structure.

1. **The general problem.** As soon as we approach the question of musical dynamics in the light of scientific findings, we come upon a very striking and extremely instructive paradox. We cannot deal with loudness and softness directly in terms of loudness and softness at all. There are few more illusive psychological problems than that of the intensity of sound. This may be illustrated in many ways. Thus a speaker who shouts often becomes unintelligible in spite of producing quite loud sounds, whereas we clearly hear another who talks much more softly. Again, a moderate *forte* coming after an extreme *pianissimo* sounds far louder than it would if it came after a *mezzo forte*. Extreme dissonances usually sound much louder than consonances, even though the actual size of the physical vibrations is just about the same. So if we want practical guidance, we must think in other terms than those of loudness and softness direct. *We shall have to think about dynamics always in terms of the kind of physical reaction produced in the performer and in the listener.* Here we see a special case of our general proposition that expression depends upon the bodily feel of music, rather than upon the hearing of it, pure and simple.

2. **Dynamic level.** The first thing to discuss in connection with loudness and softness in music, and their proper treatment, is dynamic level. By this we mean the general degree of intensity with which a composition or a phrase is given out.

(*a*) First, we have the question of the choice of a dynamic level. When we are teaching a song, should we tell the children to sing it loudly? Should we tell them to sing it softly? Or should we say nothing at all? The underlying principle which determines our answer to all these questions is found by turning from intensity as such to its meaning and effect in bodily response. *The choice of a proper dynamic level should be determined by bodily freedom and motor ease.* If we let the children just yell a song, their bodies are working so hard and so wildly that all the responses are blurred, and it becomes utterly impossible for them to feel the structure of the music. Their whole sense of the phrase pattern degenerates, and is very likely to be completely nullified. But if, on the contrary, we keep telling them to sing very softly, we bring about another abnormal, nervous, and muscular condition. They are under a constant inhibition, a blocking of the full, free, natural sweep of response. Once more their bodily feeling for the music is bound to degenerate. The thing to work for is neither loudness nor softness, but motor placement and physical ease. In singing we must capture the head voice, as will be explained in the next chapter, for this at once guarantees correct and free vocal action. Then we help the children to decide the mood and meaning of the song, and sing it with whatever grade of intensity it seems to them to demand. Always we criticize their dynamic choice, not directly, but with reference to the mood and meaning of the music. Always we watch for lapses from proper vocal placement and production. In this way they find it increasingly possible to sense physically, in and through the vocal action, the structure of the music and the swing and sweep of the phrase. We may be sure that physically correct singing, with attention properly directed to what the music aims to express, will sound dynamically appropriate and beautiful. In instrumental music, exactly the same principle holds good. We do not force extreme softness, nor permit violent loudness. We set up and seek to maintain correct and free response. As soon as this breaks down, the musical structure is lost in a jumble of physical inhibitions and anxieties. And dynamic control and appropriateness is lost with it.

(*b*) Then we have the question of maintaining the dynamic level. Failure to do this may, for instance, take the form of beginning with a moderate intensity and ending with yelling. This must not be corrected directly so much as indirectly. It is a symptom rather than a disease in itself. We should first see to it that the right motor placement is not lost as the child sings or plays. For instance, if the voice slips back or down, the vocal motor feeling for the musical pattern and the phrase is compromised. Much the same thing is to be found in instrumental work, where motor control begins well, but is soon lost. Secondly, we must control any tendency to pass from a moderate intensity to a yell by recalling attention to the mood of the music. Thus in the whole control of the dynamic level, we return again and again to the music as the regulating principle. *It is the music that dictates the dynamic level for the child, not the teacher.* Furthermore, it is the music sensed in and through facile, clear response.

3. **Dynamic Changes.** The structure of music always demands a shifting of intensities. This directly involves a shift of bodily tensions, both in the performer and in the listener, upon which the whole aesthetic effect depends. An increase in intensity carries a heightening, and a decrease in intensity a lowering, of tension. In this way the structural unit of music is outlined and sharply apprehended. Such dynamic changes may be gradual or abrupt.

(*a*) First let us consider gradual dynamic changes, that is to say, *crescendo* and *diminuendo*. We must remember that the natural effects of these changes are in the first case a gradual increase, and in the latter a gradual decrease of tension.

A number of points at once arise bearing upon the handling of these factors of expression in music teaching. (1) *Crescendo* and *decrescendo* must always be made to refer to the phrase structure. In shaping the phrase, the natural thing is for it to begin on less than its maximum intensity, increase to a crisis, and then diminish again. Sometimes there will be a type of phrase which demands a different kind of treatment. But this is the normal effect. We should notice that this at once defines and outlines the phrase as a unit of physical response and apprehension. (2) The normal relationship of *crescendo* and *decrescendo* to the melodic line is for intensity to increase as pitch rises, and fall as pitch falls. This is because rise in pitch and increase in intensity, and fall in pitch and decrease in intensity, both mean the same thing. The first two mean increase in bodily tension, and the second two mean its decrease. However, as Christiani is careful to explain, expressive effects are often produced by a reversal of this normal relationship. The important principle for us is that intensity changes of this sort have a direct relationship to the melodic curve, and are not to be introduced arbitrarily. (3) In teaching *crescendo* and *decrescendo,* one should always have in mind a movement towards a point in the melodic curve, not just a process of getting louder or softer. We wish, as it were, to dramatize the phrase and the melody, and to give the pupil a clearer sense of its rise and fall. (4) The proper placement of *crescendo* and *decrescendo* will often amazingly clear up the whole technical attack upon a phrase, and will also help in the matter of good tone and note accuracy. This is because it is based upon, and attention to it may produce, just the sort of intelligible motor sensing of the phrase structure on which both its enunciation and feeling depend.

(*b*) Now let us consider abrupt changes in dynamic level.

Here we have definite breaks in the level of bodily tension, both in performer and in listener. As Christiani has pointed out, there may be an abrupt intensity transition downward within the phrase, but scarcely ever upward. The latter effect nearly always produces an impression of the grotesque. It is a breach in the continuity of the phrase, a violation of the continuity of bodily tension through which we sense it. The most typical cases of abrupt change are those between contrasting phrases. Some song collections for school music contain excellent instances of such work. Always there are two things to bear in mind in dealing with it. First, the child must sense the two phrases which contrast. Second, he must feel the need of the dynamic contrast in and through the mood and meaning of the phrases. Ordinarily this means that the words connected with such phrases should be such as to emphasize the contrast, and make its desirability evident.

In closing this account of dynamics, we should call attention to one very excellent way of helping the children to a consciousness of the intensity factor. This may be done through physical rhythmic activity. The children may be stepping the phrase rhythm or the beat of a song in the way we have described, and may be taught to increase or decrease the length of the step as the music becomes louder or softer. This method, which is strongly recommended as entirely practical, is a fine illustration of our whole psychological conception of the relation of dynamics to music. Increasing power means increased vigor of action, and *vice versa.* This is directly sensed when the rhythmic activity becomes more vigorous with louder and less vigorous with softer music. Furthermore, it definitely connects rhythm and the feeling for rhythm, with the expressive device of dynamics, which is just as it ought to be.

## The Expressive Devices in Music:—II. Tempo

Here we have two problems: first, that of absolute tempo; second, that of *tempo rubato*. In both cases we shall see that tempo control depends on rhythmic grasp, and that the real function of tempo is to clear up and make intelligible the rhythmic structure.

1. **Absolute tempo.** Schumann has said that it takes a genius to set a tempo. Certainly it is a point where many school music teachers fail. We sometimes hear school singing which is spoiled by intolerable dragging. Sometimes, in the effort to be spirited and lively, a bright song is rushed so that it becomes a gabble. How shall we go about choosing a proper tempo? On what principle shall the teacher himself rely when he has to make a decision as to tempo? If he wishes to build up in his pupils a feeling for proper tempo, where shall he turn for the psychological foundations of this sense?

The answer is clear and indubitable. *Tempo depends primarily on the rhythm of the beat.* To set a tempo, we must sense the beat. Miss Hallock has done a piece of work in this connection that is of unusual interest and helpfulness. She carefully studied the tempo indications in four standard editions of the Beethoven Sonatas. These indications, of course, represent a long tradition, in some cases going directly back to Beethoven himself, and embody much musicianly insight. She found that it was always possible to identify in them a "true beat," and that this invariably fell between 60 and 80 per minute, given on the metronome. Moreover, a questionnaire sent to seventeen well known conductors revealed that they always set their beat between 64 and 72 per minute. This conception of the true beat needs to be understood in connection with our previous discussion of the *Takt*. It is not always indicated directly by the metronome marks.

For instance, in the first movement of the Appassionata, the true beat, the real swing which permeates the music, would be a dotted half note at a speed somewhere between 60 and 80 mm. This is the way a good conductor would beat it; and this is the way a music student ought to feel it. Moreover, the true beat is not always well indicated in the time signature. According to our analysis, the first movement of the Appassionata, which is written in 12/8 time, actually swings in groups of two's. Miss Hallock has pointed out that the true beat always lies between these limits, both for slow and fast music. Her illustration is that both the Doxology and Yankee Doodle have exactly the same basic swing, but that the former has usually only one note to the beat while the latter has as many as four. Or to take an instance from Beethoven, since he has already been mentioned, it would be perfectly possible to set the metronome at 60 and go right through the three movements of the so-called Moonlight Sonata without a single change. The tempi would not be ideal, for the last movement would be a little slow. But they would not be bad,—there would be neither dragging nor scrambling—and the effect of the music would come out. An instance from school music may help to clinch the point. Take the song "Feathers" given in figure 7, page 219, and the song "Swanee River." We could put both these through very nicely with the metronome somewhere between 60 and 80, and at the same point for both. To repeat, all music, fast or slow, has the same swing. The difference lies in the number of notes to the swing,—in the phrase rhythm.

This true beat, between 60 and 80, is an immensely significant rhythmic phenomenon. Notice that it is precisely the natural pace of marching men. When it is exceeded or slowed down, one is hurrying or dragging. It is the natural, normal swing of the human body. After all, there ought to be such a natural tempo of response, just because we are all about the same size. If men were as tall as trees, the true beat would be slower. If they were as small as gnats, it would be faster. Its speed depends on our nature. *In order to set the right tempo, it is necessary to sense and catch the true beat.* Our advice would be, not to be guided primarily by the time signature, which is a mathematical convention rather than a direct rhythmic indication, but to sense the music as laid out on a swing falling somewhere between 60 and 80. This is the true *Takt,* and if we keep this going, it will do just what *Takt* was invented for,—organize the whole structure of tone, and carry it through for us with effect.

So we reach a series of practical conclusions about handling absolute tempo in school music.

(*a*) Absolute tempo is an expression or result of the true beat. What we must do is to give the child a feeling for the underlying swing and surge of the music. In other words, we approach tempo through rhythm. Here again we see the supreme importance of large physical response.

(*b*) The two great faults of dragging and rushing can spoil the aesthetic effect and the pleasurableness of any composition. But we should not think of either directly, nor try to deal with it as something that exists in and for itself. Each fault is due to failure of rhythmic grasp. Both indicate that neither teacher nor class have felt clearly the imperious and controlling swing of the true beat. *When a song drags or scrambles, what we want is not so much more or less speed, but more and better rhythm.*

(*c*) We should always deal with tempo in terms of musical expressiveness. That is, we should not bluntly and unimaginatively tell the children to sing slowly or quickly. We should have them feel the mood of the song, and learn how this mood is embodied and enshrined in its swing and sweep, and arrive at tempo through this.

(*d*) It ought not to be necessary to say—but it probably is—that the choice of tempo is something that should have the attention of the music teacher from the kindergarten onward, simply because of its vital rhythmic meaning. *Bad tempo destroys rhythm, and without rhythm, music perishes.*

2. **Tempo rubato.** Here we have one of the most celebrated of all musical "mysteries." Yet our conceptions make it very easy to explain. We have seen that the phrase is a tonal and rhythmic unit. We have also seen that the phrase rhythm does not depend on, or demand, absolute accuracy of timing. Indeed, the reverse is true, for there is a natural tendency to dwell on accentuated elements, and shorten those that are unaccented. This rhythmic shading is universally recognized by everyone who has given any serious attention to the matter. For instance, with Jaques-Dalcroze it takes the form of the "pathetic movement," *i.e.,* the movement out of strict time, but correct in rhythmic feeling. *"Tempo rubato" is nothing more than this shading of the phrase in accordance with the demands of its rhythmic structure.* It is not something arbitrarily imposed, but arises from the logic of the phrase rhythm itself. It has just as real a place in the proper playing of Bach and Mozart as in the proper playing of Chopin. The only difference is that the phrase structure of Chopin is so complex that a more far-reaching use of *rubato* is demanded. *It should appear also in the simplest rote song, if this is to be enunciated in a musically and rhythmically-meaningful way.* We should never impose it by fiat. But, like the natural slowing-down and speeding-up of speech, it should come out of the child's apprehension of the meaning and unity of the musical phrase. Just as was the case with

appropriate dynamic treatment, proper tempo shading will often clear up the technical problem of a phrase. In both cases, we have the same basic factor operating. Both dynamic shading and tempo shading arise from the demands of the phrase structure, sensed in and through bodily reaction and response.

### The Expressive Devices in Music:—III. Tone Quality

Here again we begin with a paradox. For there is really no such thing as "good tone" or "ideal tone." The distinction in terms of physics between good and bad tone is exceedingly relative and uncertain. In the orchestra we have innumerable varieties of perfectly "good" tone, all quite different. Moreover, a given tone quality may be excellent in one connection, and atrocious in another. As Sir John Stainer says in his celebrated book on the organ, to give out a fugal subject on the tuba would be the height of bad taste, in spite of the fact that the tuba has a superb tone quality for some purposes. We seem forced, then, to regard good tone as *appropriate* tone, and in two senses.

1. Good tone is appropriate to the medium in which it is produced. A beautiful vocal tone comes from a free, facile, and perfect vocal placement and action. A naturally lovely voice is one in which all the factors of voice production work together with perfect ease and harmony. When we enjoy the tone quality of a singer, we are not enjoying an abstract, depersonalized beauty. We are not just enjoying the particular distribution of overtones above the fundamental that he produces. We feel in ourselves the rightness, the perfection, of his action, and this makes possible to us an indescribable comfort and ease in listening to the contours of the music he creates. The same is true with the violin. When we

listen to good violin tone, we are subconsciously, yet really aware of the perfect unity between the violin and the player. We feel in our bodies an intimate sympathy with the rightness and ease of his action. Once more, the lovely tonal coloring of a perfect violin in the hands of a master comes from our sense of the perfect rightness of the whole action, the complete absence of all impediments and obstacles, the facility and placement of the whole performance. So we would claim in general that good tone is always determined by its appropriateness to the medium of production.

This means that we should make the child tone-conscious through proper motor placement. We help the child to capture and use his head voice, and we get him to attend to the tone produced. The rightness of the feel of his singing, and of its sound, are two aspects of exactly the same thing. They both work together, and one checks up and sustains the other. The properly placed voice enables the child to enunciate the whole musical structure with ease and certainty. When he does this, the music sounds right and meaningful to him, both as regards tone quality and otherwise.

2. Good tone is appropriate to the composition. This idea has little bearing on school music work, and we mention it for the sake of completeness. A composition wrongly scored for orchestra, or wrongly registered on the organ, sounds wrong, even though the very same orchestration or registration might be good elsewhere. It sounds wrong because we have made a choice of tone quality which cannot do justice to the musical pattern that is to be given out.

### General Points in the Pedagogy of Expression

1. In teaching expression what is wanted is always to produce in the pupil an attitude of *aesthetic problemizing* towards

music, which grows more and more thorough and far-reaching as he develops and grows older. This means that we want to give him the sense of a composition as a whole, or of a single phrase, as something to be "put over," as calling for a definite effect, not just as something to be gone through more or less correctly.

2. We should emphasize expression from the very first, in rote song work. Always we should seek to achieve a feasible dynamic level, proper dynamic shading, an expressive tempo, proper tempo shading, and good free vocal tone. Thus the rote song, from the very first, is made beautiful and meaningful, as music.

3. Always approach every new song or instrumental composition in and through its aesthetic meaning. In other words, every performance project should be approached in the spirit of appreciation, as something worth doing for its own sake, as an opportunity for the creation and enjoyment of beauty.

4. Never be content with an intellectual analysis of the phrase structure, the rhythm, the tonality, and so forth, of a piece of music. Always make such analysis the opportunity for creating beauty and properly using expressive nuance.

5. Remember that the example of the teacher in the treatment of expression is of paramount importance. The teacher is not a model to be copied, but a source of inspiration and revelation in these matters. He should be able to show the pupils directly what expressive singing really means.

6. Direct suggestion and criticism in matters of expression is not only desirable, but necessary. But always the aim should be to help the pupil to perceive better and better the demands of the music, and the opportunities for beauty and pleasure that it offers. So the teacher should not try to control the expression of the children through *ex cathedra* demands, arbi-

trarily imposed, and followed out only because he insists upon them. The teacher must lead and reveal. He must not dominate.

7. The creative reviewing of old songs is a most valuable aid in developing interpretive insight, and so a better grasp of the musical verities. A song should always be learned as artistically as the pupils can manage at any given stage. But it should never be regarded as wholly learned. The discovery of new possibilities in familiar music is one of the greatest agencies for musical growth. Notice again that this implies the use of music good enough to stand creative reviewing—music in which there really are rich possibilities for beauty.

### Summary: Outcomes of This Chapter

1. Expressive nuance is not something arbitrarily imposed upon music. It is the logical outcome of its structure, and analogous to the light and shade of a painting. It is derived primarily from the phrase pattern, with its constituents of rhythm, melodic curve, and tonality.

2. For this reason we cannot agree that it ought to be introduced only at a late stage in musical learning. Rather all musical learning involves a constantly deeper insight into the expressive possibilities and demands of music.

3. The proper approach to the three media of expression—dynamics, tempo, and tone quality—is always through a physical apprehension of the musical structure. The aesthetic power of music depends upon the fact that we can and do feel and apprehend it through our nerves and muscles.

4. One of the larger outcomes of this chapter is the intimate connection between technique and expression, on which we have commented. We have seen that a technical problem is often clarified when we set up proper dynamic and tempo

treatment. The reason is that expression and technique both have the same foundation. Both come from the physical, the bodily apprehension of the musical structure. Thus our psychological analysis reveals the identity of what is often thought to be the most mechanical element in music with the most spiritual. Our discussion of expression really supplements and confirms our discussion of the spiritualization of technique.

## Questions for Discussion.

1. What theory of the nature of expression is involved in the claim that little children should not be taught expression?

2. Take a few children's songs and show that their expressive rendering always depends on the molding of their phrases.

3. What is the relationship between our treatment of expression, and our analysis of ear training and rhythmic training?

4. What is the relationship between our treatment of expression, and our analysis of appreciation?

5. Why should every musical undertaking have expression for its goal? What other goal might conceivably be set up?

6. Comment on the statement that children should always be required to sing softly.

7. Would it be a good plan for the teacher to have the class mark in the *crescendos* and *diminuendos,* and then drill them on these points? Give reasons for your answer.

8. Should we cure a dragging tempo merely by speeding it up? Do you find any significance in speaking of an unduly slow tempo as "dragging"? What "drags"?

9. Why do we say that there should be *tempo rubato* in playing Mozart, and even in singing a rote song? Why is this different from the ordinary viewpoint? What is the basis and meaning of *rubato?*

10. How would you go about making the child tone-conscious through the use of the voice?

11. Discuss ways in which the teacher may lead and inspire, without dominating, in teaching expression.

12. Explain the identity between technique and expression, and comment on some of its wider implications for music education.

Bibliography.

1. Christiani, Adolph F., *The Principles of Expression in Pianoforte Playing,* Harper and Brothers, 1885.
2. Diserens, Charles M., Reactions to Musical Stimuli, *Psychological Bulletin,* 1923, vol. 20, pp. 173-199.
3. Diserens, Charles M., *The Influence of Music on Behavior,* Princeton University Press, 1926.
4. Hallock, M., Pulse and Rhythm, *Popular Science Monthly,* 1903, vol. 63, pp. 425-431.
5. Jaques-Dalcroze, Emil, *Rhythm, Music, and Education,* tr. Harold F. Rubinstein, G. P. Putnam's Sons, 1921.
6. Kullak, A., *The Aesthetics of Pianoforte Playing,* 3rd Ed., tr. Theodore Baker, G. Shirmer, Inc., 1893.
7. Lussy, Mathis, *Musical Expression,* H. W. Gray Company.
8. McKenzie, Duncan, *Music in the Junior School,* Oxford University Press, 1929.
9. Matthay, Tobias A., *Musical Interpretation; Its Laws and Principles and Their Application in Teaching and Performing,* 3rd Ed., Boston Music Co., 1913.
10. Mursell, James L., *Principles of Musical Education,* The Macmillan Company, 1927, ch. 5.
11. Schoen, Max (Ed.), *The Effects of Music,* Harcourt, Brace and Company, 1927, ch. 9.

Chapter Eleven

# *Singing*

## The Place of Singing in Music Education

As a mere matter of practical necessity, singing must nearly always be the core of school music work. But this is also logically and psychologically desirable. Song is the basic musical activity. Those who have not developed it are bound to be more or less lacking musically. Surette[1] has well said "Singing beautiful songs prepares children by the best possible means for an intelligent understanding of the compositions of the great masters, which for lack of this preparation many adults never comprehend." So our basic aim in school music is not singing for the sake of skill in singing, but singing for musical development, and for growing joy in music. A word of advice given by Schumann to music students is here in point. "Try to sing at sight without the help of an instrument, even if you have but little voice; your ear will thereby gain in fineness."[2]

The application of science to the problems of vocal work in the schools is peculiarly valuable. The tradition of song and its pedagogy is confusing, and of very dubious aid to the school music teacher. There are few fields of work in music where one finds a greater profusion of impossible ideas, or wilder clouds of mythology. The judgments of experts on

[1] Surette, Thomas Whitney, *Music and Life,* Houghton Mifflin Company, 1917, pp. 70-71.

[2] Agnew, Marie, The Auditory Imagery of Great Composers, *Psychological Monographs,* 1922, vol. 31, No. 1, Whole No. 140, pp. 279-287.

points connected with vocal performance are most extraordinarily varied and unreliable. One of the studies made at the University of Iowa on the vocal *vibrato* quotes the comments of distinguished critics on a musical performance, in which they absolutely contradict one another as to the presence and amount of *vibrato,* some saying that there was far too much, others that there was none. Although we do not know nearly everything about the voice and its management, we do know something. So the value of psychology in this connection is that it gives us a clear formulation of indubitable and ascertained facts about the voice and the conditions of its use. On this we may base our teaching. We shall find that the general outcome of a scientific approach, here as elsewhere, is that singing must be motivated by appreciation, and that it is a primary means of deepening appreciation.

## The Act of Song and Its Nature

One of the most authoritative and illuminating expositions of the nature of singing is that of Stumpf, who is an outstanding figure in music psychology. In the article by him, listed at the close of the chapter, he says that the vital distinction between song and speech is that in the former we introduce definite, separated steps of pitch, while the latter involves a continuity of pitch. He particularly emphasizes the point, which some previous workers had questioned, that the distinction between speech and song is only relative and not absolute. Thus, to repeat, the only essential difference between the use of the voice in speech and in song is the introduction of definite pitch steps, with the various elements of mechanical control that this implies.

This analysis gives us a most important insight into the essentials of vocal instruction. Clearly a great many of the ideals of the pedagogy of speech will apply to both. Modern work in speech does not deal primarily with the mechanics of voice production, nor with the labored elaboration of studied effects. Rather it aims to encourage expressiveness, arising out of an understanding of and feeling for the meaning of what is being said. Expressiveness, of course, involves subtle and delicate inflections of the speaking voice. It has been shown that the inflections of the speaking voice have a close and direct relationship to intelligence. The stupid person's voice is apt to be flat and level, while the intelligent person's voice is highly inflected. So we might say that a great aim in elocution is to get intelligence into the voice.

Since speech and song are similar processes in most respects but one, this same idea can be taken over by the music teacher. *What we want is to develop a musically intelligent singing voice, rather than a mechanically trained instrument.* Just as the intelligent speaking voice follows with nuance and fine inflection the meaning of the words, so the musical singing voice will follow with nuance and fine inflection the musically-meaningful phrase sequences. Now this is a principle that applies to *all* vocal work, whether in the studio or the classroom. Greatness in a singer does not turn on the ability to do tricks with the voice, but on the ability to express music with the voice. The ability to do tricks may be there, but it is incidental, and incidentally acquired. But above all, our principle is essentially important in dealing with the singing of the child.

This has many far-reaching consequences, some of which we shall try to indicate in later sections of this chapter. But we should pause to consider some of its more general implications. They are in fact the basic conditions for a program of school singing which is to fulfill our requirement of musical development through song.

Our idea of developing a musically intelligent singing voice as the chief aim of school song at once imposes upon us the following requirements. (*a*) We must have a wealth of songs of high emotional and aesthetic value. It is better to have a song somewhat ahead of the child aesthetically than to have one that is devoid of musical meaning and interest. The introduction of musically worthless songs to teach reading, or to drill on voice control is definitely antagonistic to our leading principle. (*b*) We need songs where words and music are fused into an appealing unity. The words of a song are extremely important. They set the mood, and they offer one of the best opportunities for teaching rhythm and a sense for musical structure. (*c*) *We need singable songs.* By this we mean songs where the voice has something musical to say which is suited to its peculiar genius. Davison has strongly attacked the use of instrumental melodies as songs, and certainly whenever this means the use of an unsingable, vocally awkward melody, the criticism is wholly just. However, we would rather hesitate to put it exactly as he does, just as we would not go as far as he does in recommending the employment of folk music. Every song should be judged on singability, irrespective of its origin. (*d*) We should always teach songs on a broad basis of suggestion and imagination, and emphasize and work for interpretation and beauty rather than for note accuracy. School singing should capitalize every enriching connection with art, literature, history, geography, etc., as we explained in the chapter on appreciation.

In the preface to the Glee Club Book for Girls[1] has been

[1]GLENN, MABELLE, *Glee Club Book for Girls,* Oliver Ditson Company, 1928.

formulated much the same set of ideas, in explaining the basis on which the songs to go into the book were selected: "In choosing each song, we have kept these questions in mind: 1. Is the subject matter of the poem such that it will make a desirable appeal to a girl in her early 'teens? 2. Has each melody sufficient charm to hold interest on its own account? 3. Are the harmonies interesting without bringing any great difficulty to any part? . . . 4. Is there a well defined highest point in each song where there is opportunity for a significant climax? . . . 5. Does each song offer an opportunity for a wide range of dynamics? 6. Is there a good swing? Whether slow or fast, is there a decided rhythmic pulse? . . . 7. Is there something of interest from the beginning to the end of each song? 8. When the melody ceases to be the outstanding element, is there something else to hold the interest of the listeners? 9. Is every selection well proportioned from an emotional standpoint? . . . Let us always remember that the words are the most important element in holding interest; therefore, they must be given every possible advantage in making the song an experience of beauty."

In general, then, *we must give the child something to express in his singing, and help him to express it. This is the foundation of vocal education.*

## The Voice and Its Control

Let us now turn to a more detailed consideration of the vocal action in singing, and its proper control. We follow rather closely the very excellent summary account of Erickson, listed at the close of the chapter.

1. **The operation of the voice.** Here we should understand in a general way the nature of the vocal apparatus, and the way it operates in producing musical effects. (*a*) The

vocal apparatus may be divided into three parts. First we have the bellows, consisting of the trachea, the bronchi, the lungs, the diaphragm, and the thoracic and abdominal muscles. Second, we have the vibrators, consisting of the larynx and vocal chords. Third, we have the resonators, which are of two kinds, fixed and movable structures. The former consist of the cavities, *i.e.,* the vestibule, the pharynx, the buccal cavity, the nasal cavity, and the sinuses. The latter consist of the tone velum, the lips, the cheeks, and the jaw. Our aim is not a complete anatomy or physiology of the voice. As a matter of fact this can be a snare and a delusion, for it may lead us to concentrate all our attention on the training of some muscle rather than on expressive song. But we should have a clear working picture of the operation of the voice. We should understand that the act of singing, in all its phases, consists of an exceedingly complex coördination of all these structures. (*b*) This coördinated control is never, and can never be, purely mechanical. We know that pitch control is by no means mechanically determined by the length and condition of the vocal chords, so that the difference between a tenor and a bass is no simple difference in these structures. The control of intensity, again, is highly intricate, and essentially purposive rather than mechanical. It depends on such factors as sub-glottal pressure, amount of breath, pitch, duration, vowel quality, and resonance. Tone quality, once more, which of course depends on the distribution of the overtones, involves an intricate coördination and control of the resonators and the vocal chords. What we call general vocal stability depends on the consolidated coördination of the whole mechanism.

All in all we could not have a better illustration of the absolute hopelessness of the mechanical theory of learning based on habit building. To try to analyze vocal action into its constituent habits would be an utterly impossible task. We have a complexity of structure, and an intricacy of relationship which would certainly defeat us, even were unitary habits present at all. All that we know of vocal action assures us that its proper management must be from the side of synthetic experience—of having something to express—rather than from that of concentrating and drilling on constituent habits.

2. **The neural control of the voice.** When we raise the question of how this complex mechanism is controlled by the nerves, we get a still further impression of an intricacy which cannot be resolved into constituent habits, and find still more reason to believe that training must be in terms of spirit, meaning, and expressiveness, rather than mechanics. We know that the larynx is directly connected, nervously, with incoming and outgoing impulses to and from the diaphragm, the ear, and the facial muscles. So if the breath support at the diaphragm is inadequate this may mean "stiffening in the throat," *i.e.,* it may compromise the free action of the larynx. A failure properly to hear a standard tone which is to be sung may reflect instantly in the form of insufficient breath support by the diaphragm. A rigid facial pose may compromise the control of both the breath and the larynx. In other and more general words, every part of the vocal mechanism acts and reacts most intimately upon every other part. No part can do wrong alone. *No part of the mechanism can possibly be trained alone.* Furthermore, it is pointed out as indubitable that ultimately the control of the voice involves the whole of the cerebral cortex—the highest and most general coördinating agency in the body. This conclusion means that it involves the whole personality. Once more we see how impossible as a guide to education is the mechanical theory of learn-

ing, and how essential it is to proceed always in terms of meaning, feeling, and expression. We have here further insight into our idea of musical technique as being in essence the embodiment of intelligence and purpose in action, rather than a mechanical structure of definite, separable habits.

So in helping the child to sing, we are helping him to master and use a wonderfully sensitive and far-reaching mechanism—a mechanism which transcends mechanism. *The singing "instrument" is the entire personality, physical and mental. It is not the child's voice that sings. It is the child who sings.* With all this in mind, we emphatically disagree with those plans of school music work which sacrifice natural musical expressiveness for the sake of "preserving the voice." For instance, we have the proposition that children must always produce a hushed tone if their vocal development is not to be compromised. Our criticism is that such a requirement substitutes a formal rule for musical expressiveness. Nearly always this results in bad vocal action, for the subdued, unnatural tone is very likely to be breathy. Certainly it results in weakened musical development, for we gravely diminish spontaneous pleasure in song. Of course we must guard against vocal overstrain, but this is quite a different thing from saying that singing should always be quiet. Indeed, soft singing itself leads to the most vicious errors in vocal action, unless the pupil can really control intensity quite well—which in the grades he certainly can not. Of course too, we must produce proper vocal placement, but this is not difficult. Once we establish a reasonable type of vocal action, the idea that the child will do himself some sort of mysterious harm if he enjoys himself spontaneously may be dismissed as utterly preposterous. *Vocal training that is not in terms of human values, meanings, and desires, is condemned without any further trial. The child must sing because he loves to sing, or not at all.*

## Factors on Which the Control of Song Depends and Their Management in School Music

We cannot be too careful never to disturb or distort by stupid instruction and crude pseudo-teaching the exquisitely sensitive configuration and coördination of the child's singing voice. Thus we need to know definitely and in detail what elements to stress in helping him to uncover, possess, and enjoy to the full the golden treasury of his capacity for song. Here again we are guided by psychological research.

1. **Motor factors.** While we do not completely understand the motor elements in the control of voice, three points emerge as important, and on these we may confidently build. These are breath control, control of the facial muscles, and vocal placement.

(*a*) *Breath control.* In establishing breath control, two points need to be observed. First we must secure good positional freedom, the importance of which was discussed in the chapter on technique. We should not make a fetish of some particular pose, and fuss and fret about its details. In requiring the children to sit or stand upright, or to hold the books or place their arms or hands in some position, we should remember that it is not the outward shape but the inward muscular freedom that is essential. So our requirements in the matter of pose should be directed towards this end, and when it has been achieved we should be satisfied. Secondly, we should work for control of the breath by a phrase-wise attack. Breathing exercises should be used very sparingly or not at all; and if used, should never be formalized, *i.e.,* set up as something to be learned for its own sake, without a perceived relationship to musical expressiveness. What we want is to have the children feel the phrase on the breath, and to achieve this we should call attention to the phrasing rather than to the breathing.

(*b*) *Freedom of the facial muscles.* This means a free posture of the cheeks, tongue, and jaw. Primarily it should be approached by setting up a pleasurable and interesting situation, to which it is the natural response. When the child is presented with a new song which charms him, it is natural for his whole facial mechanism to relax into the condition of smiling. A rigid jaw and a set expression are concomitants of unpleasant situations, which call for exacting effort. They are the concomitants of drill and driving. Of course we must sometimes work more directly for the result we want, as for instance when we deliberately tell the children to let the jaw fall wide open. Some school music teachers encourage the children to sing with a smile. But any direct attack that we make on facial rigidity must have the support of those pleasurable conditions that favor relaxation. Here again we see the importance of capitalizing the meaning and the beauty of a song. It definitely favors proper vocal motor response.

(*c*) *Vocal placement.* Many kindergarten and first grade children cannot sing because they have not learned to listen properly. Cases of *absolute monotones* are indeed few. With those children who have not learned to listen consciously, the most successful results can be accomplished by individual help, which should occupy at least a third of every lesson period in the first grade.

The child cannot sing properly until he has found his

"head voice." To show clearly what is involved, we here describe the type of procedure followed in some primary grades, for this purpose.

### Suggested Helps

1. Use for imitation, calls or phrases chanted on one tone, *starting on a high pitch.* (Some of the children will use only high tones, others will sing only low tones. Sometimes the only way to get good results is by taking the child's tone and working up or down from this pitch.)

2. Games of "train" and "boat" may be used. The "choo-choo" must be matched for a ride on the train. "Too-too" must be matched for a boat ride.

*Note:* A child with a clear, sweet voice may act as teacher to a pupil with an unmusical voice, or the musical children may keep the call going on a light tone while the latter tries to make his voice match their tone. A conversation may be carried on between teacher and pupil, thus: Teacher sings (on a high pitch) "Did you see the robin?" Pupil replies on same pitch, "Yes, I saw him fly away."

*Note:* Raising his hand as high as he can is often an aid to the pupil in lifting the voice. Give him the mental concept of something "high."

Up we go—(*do mi so*) (As high as possible)
Blow—wind—blow—($\overline{do}$ *so* $\overline{do}$) (Can't you sing higher?)
How are you?—(*do mi so*)
See-saw—(octave with high *do* first)
Teacher sings—Jim-mie
Pupil sings—I'm here (*so* $\overline{do}$)
Teacher sings—Cuck-oo
Pupil sings—Cuck-oo (*so mi*)

Teacher sings—Bob-white

Pupil sings—Bob-white (*do* $\overline{do}$)

Teacher sings—Cock-a-doodle-doo

Pupil sings—Cock-a-doodle-doo (*so so so so* $\overline{do}$)

These intervals are merely suggestions. The teacher may use any interval desired, remembering that at first it is difficult for a child to sing the smaller intervals.

One further point should be mentioned. The thing to avoid is straight line singing. In every phrase of poetry there are important words to be brought out and other less important words connecting the important words. To sing all words with equal stress, whether with vigorous tone or hushed tone, is bad singing in primary grades or in the high school.

In concluding this account of the motor factors in school singing, two points should be made. We see that the factors consist of breath control, freedom, and placement. So long as these conditions are maintained, we need have no fear at all of vigorous singing. It is almost inevitable that if we begin to insist on quietness, we shall destroy the whole motor pattern by compromising breath control, producing facial rigidity and a partial closing of the jaw, and driving the voice inward and downward.

Secondly, the control of the motor factors should be indirect rather than direct. This has been brought out under each point, and it is an essential idea. We should never try to drill formally and in separation from music making on breath control, facial looseness, or placement. Any little work we do in this respect should always be treated as part of the analytic phase of an actual performance project. Because our aim is the development of motor skill and control, we must not proceed by means of mechanical work.

2. **Sensation and imagery in vocal control.** Considerable research has been done to investigate the extent to which the control of the voice depends on various kinds of sensations and images. The outstanding findings are that the sound of one's own voice is the most effective guide in attacking a new tone, that tonal imagery is very important in guiding song, and that the muscular and motor imaging and sensing of a tone furnishes a cue that is particularly valuable for the beginner. From this there arise a number of practical suggestions. (*a*) It is exceedingly important to have the child listen to his own voice, for pitch and for tone quality. (*b*) Have the child listen carefully to a standard tone—have him really attend to it, and "fill his ears with it"—and then sing it. (*c*) Have him listen to a standard tone, taken as *do,* and then immediately sing *mi, so,* etc., above it. This procedure can be widely varied. (*d*) Make a definite break between the listening to a standard tone, and the singing of that tone or a related tone. Postpone the response by singing until a signal has been given. This encourages tonal imagery. (*e*) If errors in pitch, or bad tone quality occur, have the child image what has been done, and make his own correction.

Once more, these procedures, and similar ones that can readily be invented, should not be handled as formal drills. They should be used in the actual learning and singing of rote songs, as parts of the study phase of the learning. Here too, we see the intimate relationship between vocal development and ear training, on which we have several times insisted.

3. **Imagination and association in vocal control.** Erickson puts this point as follows: "As artistic singing is to be essentially creative, so it calls for a mind that is enriched by a vivid imagination. The singer's power should transcend

the mere imaging of tones to be produced, and picture the ideals and sentiments that tones are intended to convey." (*op. cit.* p. 105.) Thus in teaching any song, its setting, meaning, mood, and expressive demands should be discussed and considered with the class. We must remember that the desire for a certain kind of effect is one of the chief agencies for producing it. So, as we saw in our chapter on expression, the child should not approach a song as a number of notes to be sung, but as a musical and aesthetic project to be carried through. In doing this, the associations of the song, and its suggestions to the imagination need to be capitalized.

4. **Emotional factors in vocal control.** These are enormously important. It has been shown beyond any doubt that states of feeling reflect themselves very directly and powerfully in the accommodations and adjustments of the body. Unpleasant feelings tend to produce tenseness, and a preparation, through certain glandular secretions and other changes, for violent action. Pleasant feelings, on the other hand, have a harmonizing effect upon the body, and result in relaxation and motor ease and freedom from strain. These are no metaphors nor fancies, but demonstrated facts. So it is evident that a state of pleasant feeling is all-important for such a subtle, far-reaching set of free coördinations as are required in singing. Cannon, one of the most distinguished investigators of the physical effects of emotion, has spoken of certain states of feeling as placing the organism on a "war basis." This we emphatically do not want for effective song. On the contrary, we need relaxation, ease, and fluency of response. *So anything that interferes with the pupil's pleasant feeling tone in the act of song, works against proper voice control.* Clearly there are many implications that may be derived from this, and its bearings upon educational practice are legion. We

shall be content with just one comment along this line. Evidently we have here a principle which disallows any sort of formal or mechanical treatment of the voice, for this operates towards boredom and disgust, which are the enemies of song. Our principle is in effect a demand that all singing shall be done for joy. Once more, any such requirement as a perpetually hushed tone, set up for mechanistic reasons as it ultimately is, will be bad from this standpoint.

5. **Intelligence in relation to voice control.** We have no evidence that an intellectual knowledge of the anatomy and physiology of the voice in any way helps singing. But it is true that the singer ought to have sane and just notions about vocal action. With children these should be developed, not by anatomical charts and drill on technical names, but by giving them the feel of the correct vocal response, throwing in an occasional comment which will enlighten actual experience.

6. **The effect of a standard.** The teacher's own singing for the class is a very important agency in the establishment of proper vocal control. Here the essential thing is not so much a great vocal technique, but the musical and aesthetic quality and intelligence of the teacher's singing. We should remember once more that standards work in education through revelation rather than imitation. If the teacher can demonstrate tonal and vocal beauty, he will have done far more than set up a model to be copied. He will have set up an inspiring ideal.

## Voice Building and What It Means

Will Earhart, in his survey of public school music made over ten years ago, remarks with regret that comparatively few systems report any definite plan of "voice building." Probably a different situation now exists. But the whole question is so interesting and important that we must discuss it at some length.

What is "voice building," and how should one go about it? We may say that its aim is never mechanical precision, but always flexible control which results in musical intelligibility. Thomas Alva Edison, in a very interesting article, presents with much force a view of the voice and the ideals of its cultivation, which seems to us misleading in important respects. His great complaint is that the human voice lacks the steadiness and sureness of an instrument. Now this is perfectly true. Extensive experimental work has been done in vocal control at the University of Iowa. Under Dean Seashore, methods and devices have been developed which make it possible actually to photograph the tone as it is produced, and to record and make plain to the eye every tiny variation in its pitch. This work is so interesting and valuable that it well repays study by any music teacher. Full references to it will be found at the close of the chapter. For us, its outstanding finding is that the very greatest singers, including even coloratura sopranos, never achieve a mechanical precision of vocal management. Always there is quite a considerable variation of pitch on a sustained tone. Always there is a pronounced *vibrato*. Instead of the *vibrato* being diminished by musical training, it is often increased. One study showed that the only voices which had no *vibrato* were those of monotones, classified as very unmusical, and producing a flat and painful type of tone. Our clear inference is that while the voice does not possess the mechanical precision of an instrument, this is really not a defect, and that *vocal development is not towards mechanical precision, but towards flexible and intelligible control. When we listen to and enjoy good singing, we are not enjoying a mechanically-perfect device, but the creative utterance of a musical personality.* So in a sense we would be inclined to criticize such an expression as "voice building," and to substitute "voice discovery."

Let us now indicate some of the practical consequences of this leading idea.

1. The vital thing in voice building is to aim always at finer and finer musical effects,—to work for nuance and always more nuance. We should develop the voice in and through actual song material. In dealing with it we should stress *legato* singing, good tone quality, control of intensity, and above all, fine phrasing. We should work for beauty and expressiveness, and joyous vitality.

2. Drill has an extremely minor place in voice building. When scales, vocalizes, and other types of study exercise are used, they should always be made definitely contributory to a musical effect the children are trying to create, and they should always be musical in themselves. A vocalize should not just be a number of notes, but should be treated as a beautiful phrase in its own right.

3. In dealing with the monotone, we should think in terms of personal rather than mechanical development. His inability to carry a tune is really a symptom of some maladjustment in musical mindedness, which may be quite trivial, but possibly is far-reaching. So there are two things to be borne in mind in considering treatment. (*a*) The broad motivational agencies of music education, particularly along the line of appreciation, are extremely important for the monotone. We need to organize for him a situation where he will want to sing, for if the desire is not present, the case is hopeless. (*b*) The various devices discussed in Chapter Two should be used in order to help him achieve his desire, and release his voice.

4. The intensive and careful study of worthy song material is the best and most central means of voice building, which means making musical voices, and through them, musical children. Quantity work, where a great deal is run through

and nothing really finished, is entirely wrong. What we need is a growing repertoire of familiar songs in which vocal ease has been achieved, to which we can return for creative reviewing and additional nuance. Through such re-working and re-creating of song material whose first difficulty and unfamiliarity have disappeared, we have one of the very finest agencies for making musical voices. The reason is that the pupil is wholly free to attend to the music, and to make his singing expressive and finely shaded, which is the true direction along which to work for control. As for those teachers who say that children cannot achieve nuance, first, we would refer them to our chapter on expression; secondly, we would ask them if they have ever seriously tried to develop expression in a group of normal children, using some sane and possible scheme of work; and thirdly, we would inquire if they can recognize nuance when they hear it.

5. The vocal problem of the adolescent boy should always be thought of as personal rather than mechanical. The idea that there is an inevitable break in the voice and a period during which singing must stop, is exceedingly questionable. The natural tendency of the voice is to sink little by little to a lower range, and if the boy is forced to continue singing on high pitch too long, a break will certainly occur. But we should blame our management rather than nature. The dogma of the breaking voice comes from a choral tradition in which the boy soprano is at a tremendous premium, and where accordingly he is kept singing soprano just as long as possible, without any regard to the strain and peril involved, —in a word, it comes from a tradition and practice which exploits the boy as a person for the sake of a musical effect.

Such a viewpoint has absolutely no place in school music. Many excellent teachers who have abandoned this false philosophy of music and of song, have found that they have also disposed of its inevitable consequence,—the broken voice. If we set up a situation in which the boy can shift downwards according to need, and always guard him from attempting too much range, we shall usually make a transition from the boy's to the man's voice without a break. This is a point on which expert management is needed. The classification of voices from the sixth grade onwards depends not only on pitch, but also on quality, which tells the experienced judge and teacher a great deal about what to do.[1] We may here cite a passage dealing with this problem. "Usually boys from ten to twelve sing either soprano or alto, a soprano not higher than five line F and an alto not lower than middle C, being perfectly safe. At thirteen these lovely, floating, high voices should be coaxed down a few tones, though the same quality should be held. Exercises should start no higher than four-space E, and this quality should be carried down the scale, first with humming, then with a loose *loo*, and later with the syllable *nah,* on scale or chord exercises. This soprano quality of the eleven and twelve-year-old boy will develop into a light alto at thirteen and into a rich alto-tenor at fourteen or fifteen. The range of the alto-tenor of fourteen is likely to be from two line G to G below middle C. At fifteen the same boy reaches E below middle C and retains a light tone on G above middle C. The junior high school bass sings only a few tones lower, his easiest tones being in the C octave. When the boy voice is led into man voice through careful use, there is no 'break' and therefore no cessation from singing."[2]

[1]On this important topic the reader should turn to the discussion by Beattie, McConathy, and Morgan in their *Music in the Junior High School,* listed at the close of this chapter, for much practical advice too detailed to be included here.

[2]GLENN, MABELLE, Beautiful Singing in Our Elementary and Junior High Schools, *The Musical Observer,* October, 1928, vol. 27, pp. 11, 12, 29.

By such means we are able to carry the boy along with an unimpeded joy in music making through song. It is brought about simply through the expert application of our notion of the voice as an affair of the personality, and of expression, rather than as a machine to be handled mechanically.

6. All this of course bears very importantly upon part-singing. The great mistake here is to work prematurely for a complete and stabilized vocal ensemble in the school. We want part-singing in the grades for the sake of the musical pleasure and the musical experience that it offers. These values become richer in the junior high school, where more extensive part-singing can be developed. *But we should not work for a stabilized chorus effect until we have voices that have established themselves.* Work in music that is quite proper for mature persons may be exceedingly bad for those in process of growth. Always the personality, the individual need, must come first in our minds, and we must suit our musical activities to its interests.

### Educational Values in School Singing

In closing this chapter we may bring together its wider implications in a discussion of the educational values to be derived from school singing, properly directed.

1. It should create a feeling for phrase. This is one of its most central values for musical development. Again and again we have seen how essential phrase-wise grasp is. Its natural point of generation is in grade school song.

2. It should create a feeling for pitch, tone quality, and melodic curve which instrumental music can hardly bring. All these factors are more intimately involved and directly sensed in singing than in any other type of music making.

3. Through part-singing it should build up in the pupil

harmonic sensitivity along much sounder lines than is easy, for instance, with the piano.

4. It should develop power and refinement of tonal imagery, for the control of the voice depends to a considerable extent on the imaging of tone, which should be deliberately cultivated.

5. It offers natural and ready opportunities for rhythmic training, partly because large physical activities are more readily carried on in connection with singing than with instrumental music, and partly because one actually senses the phrase rhythm more immediately with the voice than in the action required by any instrument.

In general, singing is the natural basis for a complete musical education. It very definitely functions along the line of deeper and richer appreciation, and as we have seen, it is an activity which to an unusual degree needs to be motivated by appreciation and the love of music. We must insist however, that these values will not be obtained accidentally. We must teach singing with a purpose, and understand what means to use to achieve it, or all we shall have will be twenty or thirty minutes daily of note spelling, and no real music education at all.

## Summary: Outcomes of This Chapter

1. Singing differs from speech primarily in the introduction of fixed pitch levels. Otherwise it is similar, and so modern vocal education must be based on expressiveness, and interest in expressing something, like modern speech pedagogy.

2. The voice involves an extremely complex coördination which cannot be built up piecemeal out of its elements, but must be developed through expressive use.

3. The nervous control of the voice is so extensive and in-

tricate that it really involves the entire personality, which is the true agency of song.

4. Thus our approach to all vocal problems should be personal rather than mechanical.

5. All the various factors on which the control of the voice depends, indicate a personal rather than a mechanical approach. Even the motor factors of breath control, facial looseness, and placement should be handled through interest in the creation of musical beauty rather than by direct and formal drill.

6. Voice building, or better, voice discovery, should not aim at mechanical precision, but flexible control dictated by musical conceptions.

7. In dealing with the voice of the adolescent boy, the principle of personal approach is of special significance, for otherwise we may sacrifice his musical interests for the sake of ensemble effect, and ruin his voice.

8. School singing is the natural foundation of music education, and has very wide educational values.

### Questions for Discussion.

1. Comment on Schumann's claim that singing will improve the ear. Why is this true?

2. From a comparison between the intelligent speaking voice and the musical singing voice, could we infer that the monotone has a musically stupid voice?

3. Discuss Davison's criticism of the use of instrumental melodies in songs.

4. Why does our account of the nervous control and the anatomical structure of the voice seem to make a mechanical theory of learning to sing very hard to believe?

5. Should one give children exercises to develop some particular vocal muscle or to refine some particular habit of enunciation?

6. Discuss our criticisms of hushed, soft singing.

7. Suggest methods of capitalizing voice control through sensation and imagery in addition to those mentioned.

8. Show just how you would take advantage of association and imagination in teaching two or three specific songs. Why should such an approach actually help the vocal action of the child?

9. Can you suggest any methods for arousing the pleasurable mood which we saw was so important for singing? Why should such a mood affect vocal action?

10. Discuss Edison's idea of vocal training and its aims. What sort of practices in school music would this seem to imply?

11. Discuss the idea that the break in the boy's singing voice is due to exploitation. What unfortunate consequences for music education result from the breaking of the boy's voice?

12. Can you suggest any further educational values in school singing besides those considered here?

## Bibliography.

1. Bates, James, *Voice Culture,* Part 1, H. W. Gray and Company, 1907.
2. Beattie, John W., McConathy, Osbourne, and Morgan, Russell V., *Music in the Junior High School,* Silver, Burdett and Company, 1930, ch. 11.
3. Beaunis, H., Muscle Sense in Singing, *American Journal of Psychology,* 1887-1888, vol. 1, p. 205.
4. Edison, Thomas Alva, An Interview with Thomas Edison Concerning the Imperfections of the Human Voice, *American Magazine,* March, 1921.
5. Erickson, Carl L., The Basic Factors in the Human Voice, *Psychological Monographs,* 1926, vol. 36, No. 2, Whole No. 168, pp. 82-112.
6. Evetts, Edgar T., and Worthington, Robert A., *Mechanics of Singing,* Oxford University Press, 1928.
7. Glenn, Mabelle, Beautiful Singing in Our Elementary and

Junior High Schools, *Musical Observer,* October, 1928, vol. 27, pp. 11, 12, 29.

8. KNOCK, CARL J., Visual Training of the Pitch of the Voice, *Psychological Monographs,* 1922, vol. 31, No. 1, Whole No. 140, pp. 102-127.
9. KWALWASSER, JACOB, The Vibrato, *Psychological Monographs,* 1926, vol. 36, No. 1, Whole No. 140, pp. 84-108.
10. METFESSEL, MILTON, What Is the Voice Vibrato? *Psychological Monographs,* 1928, vol. 39, No. 2, Whole No. 178, pp. 126-134.
11. SCHOEN, MAX, An Experimental Study of the Pitch Factor in Artistic Singing, *Psychological Monographs,* 1922, vol. 31, No. 1, Whole No. 140, pp. 230-259.
12. SEASHORE, CARL EMIL, A Base for the Approach to Quantitative Studies in the Aesthetics of Music, *American Journal of Psychology,* 1927, vol. 39, pp. 141-144.
13. SEASHORE, CARL EMIL, Phonophotography in the Measurement of the Expression of Emotion in Music and Speech, *Scientific Monthly,* 1927, vol. 24, pp. 463-471.
14. SEASHORE, CARL EMIL, and JENNER, E. A., Training the Voice by the Eye in Singing, *Journal of Educational Psychology,* 1910, vol. 1, pp. 311-320.
15. STEVENS, F. A., and MILES, W. R., The First Vocal Vibrations in the Attack in Singing, *Psychological Monographs,* 1928, vol. 39, No. 2, Whole No. 178, pp. 200-220.
16. STUMPF, KARL, Singen und Sprechen, *Zeitschrift für Psychologie,* 1924, vol. 94, pp. 1-37.
17. TAYLOR, D. C., *The Psychology of Singing,* The Macmillan Company, 1908.
18. WAGNER, ARNOLD H., An Experimental Study in Control of the Vocal Vibrato, *Psychological Monographs,* 1930, vol. 40, No. 1, Whole No. 181, pp. 160-212.
19. WHITTAKER, W. G., *Class Singing,* Oxford University Press, 1925.

CHAPTER TWELVE

# *Instrumental Music*

## LEARNING TO PLAY AN INSTRUMENT

*Learning to play a musical instrument is essentially a voyage of discovery in music making.* The instrument offers a vast wealth of possibilities for unique and delightful musical effects. When the child goes to work with it, what ought to happen is that, with the teacher's sympathetic and expert help, he discovers for himself more and more of these possibilities. The instrument should be, for him, an opportunity for self-expression, for the creation of satisfying beauty. His zeal to play it better, and to master its intricacies more perfectly, is a zeal to enjoy more fully the musical opportunities it affords. Our aim in instrumental music must be to teach the instrument through music and for the sake of music, and to use the instrument to refine, define, and make more ardent, the music-making impulse.

The great bugbear of much instrumental instruction is the approach through mechanics rather than through music. We have here, of course, a perfectly genuine problem, which must be faced, understood, and solved. But too often this problem is not dealt with intelligently, or in accordance with basic psychological principles. In much studio work, for instance, we have an overwhelming and most unfortunate emphasis upon mechanical technique, acquired by formal drill, and made an end in itself. We find the child loaded down with exercises, scales, and studies, which have positively no relationship at all for him with actual musical projects. A great deal of instrumental class work is open to the same criticism. In general, the instrument is treated as a mechanical problem, and not as a musical opportunity. Such an approach is wholly unsound. The true solution of the problem of mechanics is to make it incidental to the creation of musical effects. This means that we do not lay out a sequence of formal exercises as a separate unit in our work. Rather we encourage the pupil to try to produce musical effects, and when he finds that he cannot do what he would like to do, we give him just the specific help he needs, then and there. But it may be said that this will lead to a great deal of very bad playing, and will compromise the pupil's development. Shall we, for instance, let him try to play music that may be interesting to him, but technically somewhat beyond him? Ought we not rather to hold him down to a routine which may be dull, but which will build up in him the "right" repertoire of movements and habits necessary to master the instrument? Our reply is that here once more we encounter the fallacy that all learning must go from the simple to the complex, at the expense of meaning and reality. One does not acquire mastery of an instrument, or anything else, by a nicely graded sequence of habit building. One acquires mastery through meaningful, potent, authentic experiences. What if the pupil does fail? He will have learned and enjoyed something in the attempt. He will have caught at least some vision of the exacting and inspiring demands which make music a great art, and a great medium of human education. It is in this way that power is won, and not by a meticulous adding of line upon line and precept upon precept. An external success with mechanics, won at the expense of abandoning interest, appeal, value, and reality, is what really compromises development. The accursed thing in music education is not the pupil's immediate failure to achieve all he hoped or all we could wish in his performance. *The accursed thing in music education is musically unambitious performance.*

So our aim in this chapter must be to show just what is involved in learning to play an instrument essentially through projects in music making.

### The Instrumental Program and Appreciation

In instrumental music, as everywhere else in music education, appreciation must be both the motive and the goal. Let us briefly consider the two facets of this proposition. Appreciation must be the motive in instrumental work. That is to say, the child must approach the instrument with a longing to release for himself, and to enjoy, the wealth of musical possibilities which are locked up in it. This should be one of the great outcomes of the listening projects. When a child has heard thrilling and beautiful effects produced on some instrument, and then comes to study it for himself, he brings to it a favorable dynamic background. He has the makings of a genuine will to learn. He may, indeed he will, discover that the road is steeper and the struggle harder than he had expected. But there is all the difference in the world between a struggle to create and enjoy something he feels to be worth while and desirable, and a mere arid, meaningless wrestling with mechanical difficulties. Hence the spirit of appreciation must carry over into the instrumental classroom as motive. Anything which blocks this is not merely wrong, but fatal. The desire to create musical beauty is really the only effective motive in instrumental instruction. If we lose this, we lose the will to learn. The teacher becomes a drill master, and the learning process stops.

Then appreciation must be the goal and outcome of proper instrumental instruction. The instrument is not only a musical opportunity, but also a musical revelation. As the pupil learns to play better and better, he comes into more intimate contact with a wider and wider range of musical effects. He has studied these effects in detail. He has worked for, and observed them with care. In this way his whole feeling for music develops and expands. The true aim of the instrumental class is something far wider and better than mere skill in the manipulation of a mechanical device. It is a firmer grasp of music, and a more understanding love of music, gained by music making in a given medium.

The claim that instrumental instruction must proceed in terms of appreciation involves certain more specific consequences, which we will now try to indicate.

1. *We must use interesting, worth while music from the very first.* We have insisted again and again that without this there can be no genuine musical development, for the child grows musically only through musical projects. This is a proposition which really cannot be contested. Yet we find instrumental music teachers who pooh-pooh playing "pretty tunes." We can only wonder what sort of motivation these people think they are setting up. Usually the actual situation reflected by such attitudes is one where pupils go mechanically through the motions under pressure from the instructor. More fundamental still,—we have yet another expression of the idea that learning comes by mere doing, and that if the pupil repeats and repeats, all is well. The exact opposite is the truth. *The child learns to play an instrument only by*

*trying to play music that he loves. He learns through internal will, not external repetition.* If we provide him with music for which no human creature could conceivably feel an enthusiasm, we kill his instrumental development.

2. *Whenever possible, we should adopt the procedure of the creative project in the instrumental field.* This has been done, notably, by Jaques-Dalcroze, much of whose elementary work in piano takes the form of improvisation. There is no reason why undertakings along this line cannot be greatly extended. For instance, the class might make a song in the way already described, and then learn to play it. The value of such undertakings is, that, although from a technical standpoint the music produced may be faulty, it has living meaning for the children,—a situation that is just what we want.

3. *We should always take pains to create the spirit and interest of a musical project in every undertaking.* A good deal of instrumental work is extraordinarily devoid of any definite purposiveness or interest in the making of music. Once more, it relapses into the sort of teaching and learning (*sic*) where the pupil languidly and without zest goes through certain motions because the teacher tells him to. If this cannot be overcome, the situation is hopeless from the educational standpoint. What we want is that every new composition taken up shall be presented and undertaken as a project in the realization of musical beauty. Always the aim is expressiveness and effect. What was said about the learning of a new song applies precisely here. The pupils are not just playing notes. They are creating effects imbued with certain moods, and filled with meaning. Thus the pupils should have the experience of listening to the composition they are to learn to play. There should be free aesthetic discussion of its interest and significance. Its constituent phrases should be picked

out and listened to with care. It should be learned phrase-wise.

4. *We should deal with note errors not in isolation, but in their musical setting.* As soon as we have the child anxiously watching for and thinking about a particular note which he has been told to correct, we have removed his attention from the meaningful phrase-unit. This is just what we want to avoid. We want the pupil to feel the wrongness of the mistakes as a weakening of an otherwise enjoyable musical effect, not as a disobedience to mysterious orders. This means that ordinarily we should not stop immediately when a wrong note is played, but go on to the end of the phrase at least, and then ask the pupil to re-think, and to play it again. An unduly meticulous, or still worse, a scolding attitude in regard to mistakes tends directly to produce a painful anxiety about accuracy as an end in itself, rather than as a means for creating beautiful effects. Real accuracy is the result of confidence which comes from phrase-wise sweep and grasp.

5. *We should work definitely for expression in tone quality, in dynamics, and in tempo.* But expression should come from the pupil's inner, personal grasp of the music, and not from arbitrary requirements set up by the teacher. This should involve two things. (*a*) The pupil should be helped to develop attitudes of self-criticism in regard to tone quality, dynamics, and tempo. That is, he should be helped to listen with care to his own music, to think about the effect he wants before trying to produce it, and to think about the effect after it has been produced. We should have him work for expression by imaging and grasping the musical verities with which he is dealing. (*b*) Creative reviewing has an essential place in instrumental work. This, to repeat, means far more than just sometimes playing through familiar pieces. It means

trying to create something new in familiar pieces. As we have seen, this is one of the primary agencies of musical growth.

One great value in working for expression is that through this, technique is clarified. We have seen the surprising and intimate connection between technique and expression, due ultimately to the fact that both depend on the intimate physical sensing of the musical structure. We strongly believe that if elementary instrumental teachers worked always to have their pupils play beautifully and expressively, and to have them do so because they felt the musical demand for the expressive device, the bogey of mechanical technique would be largely dissipated.

### Integration of Instrumental Work with Vocal Work

*Our central claim here is that the proper background of approach to any instrument is by way of properly directed vocal experience.* There are certain definite musical-mental abilities which are best initiated in the vocal field, and which should be carried over into instrumental work.

1. *Phrase-wise grasp should be developed in the vocal field, and carried over into instrumental work.* Instrumental instructors usually pay at least lip service to the importance of the phrase in music, and most of them would probably agree that technical expertness really depends on a movement cycle organized and guided phrase-wise. But in spite of this, they are very apt to teach music note by note. The mechanical constitution of the instrument has a strong natural tendency to cramp attention down to the individual notes. So it is far harder to feel the phrase as a unit on any instrument, than with the voice. The result is that when we listen to many an elementary instrumental class, we cannot dodge the conclusion that they are playing notes rather than phrases. Still,

the instructor will quite agree that this is wrong, that it is a misfortune, and that many difficulties would clear up very quickly if only the children could be taught to play phrases. But he is apt to think that this cannot be done, and perhaps faintly hopes that the feeling for phrase will come somehow or other, by Heaven's mercy, to the more talented children.

But if we have children whose vocal work has established and consolidated in them a phrase-wise approach to music, the whole educational situation is altered. The problem then is one of projecting their phrase consciousness into the instrumental performance, to give them the same phrase-wise response and feeling in instrumental music making that they have in vocal music making. Specifically this indicates procedures along the following lines. (*a*) The new instrumental composition should be taught phrase-wise, by rote and by score combined. If we teach wholly by score, it is likely that attention will be unduly fixed upon the individual notes, and that none will be paid to the phrase unities. This is true because with an elementary instrumental class, the pupils will hardly have achieved such a mastery of the score that they see it in phrases in spite of the strong tendency of the instrument to hold them down to note spelling. (*b*) In teaching a piece phrase-wise, the pupils should listen to it before they play, *and also sing it before they play.* The phrase should be heard and sung as a unit, and then the attempt should be made to play it. In making corrections and working for improvement, there should be a return again and again to the total phrase, which should often be re-sung as a whole. The tendency of corrections note by note is obviously away from the consciousness of the phrase. The systematic use of singing is probably the most practical and valuable single agency for making a transfer of ability from the voice to the instrument.

(*c*) The children should be brought silently to think the phrase, both before it has been played, and afterwards. We must remember that learning does not go by "trial and error," by blind, unenlightened stumbling and staggering. Learning depends on a thoughtful isolation of what we want to do, a careful and yet direct attempt to do it, and then a thoughtful criticism of one's results. By measures such as this, the sense of phrase generated in vocal work may be carried over into the instrumental field.

2. *Rhythmic grasp should be developed in the vocal field, and carried over into instrumental work.* It is usually a fixed item in the instrumental teacher's *credo* that if only pupils had a good sense of rhythm, their development would be enormously easier. This is absolutely true, because an instrumental technique, from the motor side, consists quite largely in rhythmic action set up within the mechanical limitations imposed by the medium.

But once again, a sense of rhythm is best developed in vocal work. This is true for the following reasons. (*a*) We cannot build rhythmic grasp properly unless we work in and through large physical movement. Activities of this kind should be initiated long before the child is ready for any organized instrumental work. Jaques-Dalcroze gives children a year of eurythmics before starting them on the piano. Most school music teachers, with much more meager opportunities for intensive rhythmic training, would prefer a considerably longer period. If there has been a proper program of activities of the general eurythmic type from the kindergarten onward, then by the time instrumental instruction is begun, the child should have developed a precise feeling for the rhythmic structure of music. (*b*) Phrase rhythm is sensed very intimately with the voice. Thus vocal work offers the best opportunity for giving the child a feeling for the pulse and swing of the rhythm of the phrases. (*c*) Analysis of rhythm patterns can be made an integral part of learning songs. The disturbing difficulties created by an instrument are here at an absolute minimum. Vocal experience should have resulted in the child's possession of a keen awareness of the rhythmic structure of music.

Once more the educational problem defines itself as one of transferring rhythmic grasp from the vocal to the instrumental field. If the child is accustomed to sensing and "realizing" rhythm through large physical movement, there is no reason why something along this line cannot be done in the instrumental class, when a new piece is being learned. Of course we must be on our guard against doing things that the child will regard as silly, or as "too young" for him. But as a matter of fact, such rhythmic realizations are carried on by quite advanced pupils at times, and with beneficial results. Then again, the child should have considerable experience in singing and thinking the phrases before and after playing them. His attention should be called to the rhythmic pattern of the music he is learning.

We would regard counting, foot tapping, and the minute study of temporal durations as open to question. As to counting and foot tapping, these are poor ways of generating a sense of rhythm. Instrumental instructors who build wholly upon them ignore the previous rhythmic experience set up in the vocal program. (Of course in some vocal work, no sense of rhythm is built up, and then there is nothing to transfer.) What is wanted is not a sense of one-two-three-four, etc., etc., but a sense of the swing of the music. This ought to be carried over from the background of vocal experience along the lines suggested. As to attention to durational values, this should be treated as a consequent, not an antecedent, to rhythmic grasp. Once more, we do not approach rhythm through time, but time through rhythm. We may work so hard for mathematically accurate time values, that the pupil thinks of nothing else, and completely loses hold of the rhythmic swing. The way to work for time accuracy,—for precision in attack and release—is first to transfer the sense of the rhythmic swing and structure, and then to put the pupil into an ensemble situation where inaccurate attack and release spoil the effect. Timing is very difficult when taught *directly*. When taught in and through rhythm, it becomes easy, because this is its natural setting.

3. *Mastery of the score should be developed in the vocal field, and carried over into instrumental work*. It is much harder to teach the score as it should be taught in connection with an instrument than in connection with the voice. The instrument at once ties us down to notes. It makes it very important to know the names of the notes, and their positions on the staff, and to understand the detail of key signature. But as we have seen, these are not the fundamental elements in the musical symbolism at all. The score should never be regarded as primarily a system for dotting down notes, but as a picturization of a musical structure. We want the pupil first and foremost to see the phrases, the musically-meaningful elements, and only little by little, by a continuous process of analysis and synthesis, to become accurately aware of notational detail. This is the real basis of good reading. The reason why there is so much bad reading among musical people, is that in their young days the whole direction of their attention was towards the individual notes, and this has made them musical cripples ever since.

When an instrumental instructor complains that the pupils

come to him from the vocal work without knowing the names of the notes, or their positions on the staff, it is apt to be a sign that he misconceives his real educational function and problem. Of course, if they come knowing absolutely nothing about the score, he has just ground for criticism. But it is quite possible, nay even probable, that a child may be able to look at a piece of music, and instantly perceive its phrase structure, without being able to tell the name of a single note in it. We would even be inclined to say that this ought to be just about his situation at the end of the third grade. This means a *functional* as contrasted with a *formal* mastery of the score. If we approach the score *formally,* we may get the ability to name and spell the notes, but virtually no ability to read music. As we have demonstrated, it is certainly far easier to develop a *functional* mastery of the score with the voice than with an instrument, simply because there are no everlasting problems of picking out keys and using certain fingerings,—problems which instantly mean attending to notes rather than phrases. *Hence, the problem of the instrumental instructor here, is to take the child's functional mastery of the score, gained in vocal work, and add to it just those special elements required for instrumental performance.*

Once more the general procedure would be to have the children sing phrase-wise, and then learn to play the phrases. Little by little, the instrument itself will define the notes for them. They discover by experimentation that it is necessary to go a bit further in the analysis of the score. If functional mastery is already established, the further steps ought not to be difficult.

The reader will probably have noticed that what we have said about approaching instrumental music through vocal experience is, in a sense, an amplification of our claim that instrumental work should be fused with the spirit of appreciation. The real function of the vocal background is always to transform the instrument from a mechanical puzzle into an opportunity for music making, and always to set up each new piece as a true musical project. In other words, our whole plea is that when the instrument is properly taught, we do not merely develop skill with the instrument, we teach music through it.

### The Attack Upon Mechanics

The self-same idea applies also to the specific problem of dealing with mechanics.

1. *Approach mechanics through music.* We should always remember that the real controls in human skill are mental and purposive. The expert golfer is not going through an elaborate sequence of carefully planned movements, to every detail of which he must give anxious attention. He is hitting a ball. So when a child plays an instrument, he is not fingering in a particular way, holding a stick in a particular way, or keeping a mouthpiece in a certain position. He is making music. This must be in the forefront of his consciousness. It is the music, not the instrument, that ultimately must tell him what to do. This is why we contend that when he starts out to play a phrase, he must have just as clear an idea as possible of the effect he wants, and that when he is led to criticize his own execution of that phrase, his self-criticism should always be along the line of comparing the effect he produced with the effect he wants. It also explains why we should work for expression,—for beautiful tone, for dynamic shading, and for shading in tempo. Working for expressive intonation of the phrase is exactly the same thing as working for motor

control of the phrase. Moreover, the skill refines itself, and wild, crude, hopeless movement organizes itself into precision and beauty, by keeping in mind always the goal of the skill rather than concentrating on its constituent elements. *Technique comes not by mechanical repetition and drill, but by listening to, and thinking about the music one makes and would like to make.*

2. *Rationalize and minimize mechanics.* Far too much has been made of the mechanical difficulties and problems of musical instruments. This is due to unclear thinking. As a matter of cold fact, the mechanical requirements for getting music out of an instrument are not so very forbidding. Of course, if a pupil holds a violin against his chest, or grasps the bow in the palm of his hand, or places the mouthpiece of a cornet to one side, he will defeat himself. But is there anything here that a good instructor cannot very easily remedy? Is there anything here that cannot be taught as an incident to music making? Is there anything here that demands endless formal technical drill? We really cannot see it. What the instrumental teacher needs to do is just to list the ultimate mechanical A B C of his instrument, and he will not find himself compelled to go beyond the fifth letter of the alphabet, if as far. We have allowed ourselves to be too much overawed by the alleged difficulty of instrumental mechanics. A direct, business-like, rational attack upon the whole problem, will dissipate a great many of these ideas. Difficulties have been created where none or only a few exist. The obstacles to dealing with instruments as musical opportunities rather than as manipulative puzzles have been enormously exaggerated.

3. *We must avoid overstrain.* Overstrain always blocks motor learning. Anything which causes overstrain is bad,

whether traditionally venerable or not. Two typical causes of motor overstrain are premature working for speed, and working for extreme range. It is not the speed as such, or the extreme range as such, that is bad. It is its effect in setting up motor tensions and anxieties. Speed and control are the outcomes of ease. Once we permit stress and strain, we break down the whole course of learning. We want the pupil to sense and feel the music in the rhythm and pulse of his reactions. As soon as anxiety and stress creep in, his motor apprehension of the musical structure is utterly lost.

## Selection of Pupils for Instrumental Work

The problem of selecting pupils for instrumental instruction is two-fold. It includes attracting those who are desirable, and weeding out those who are not.

1. Let us consider first the factors which should attract desirable pupils to instrumental work.

(*a*) The first of these is the inspiration and interest of the work in the elementary grades, with its strong and central emphasis upon appreciation. Clearly one fruit of this work ought to be a strong desire on the part of many pupils to continue with music. Because we have seen that interest is in general indicative of ability, a live program of music in the grades is a selective agency of no mean value. On the other hand, a poor and formalized program not only fails to correlate specifically with instrumental work, but does not elicit interest in the able pupil.

(*b*) The second agency which brings pupils into instrumental work is the prestige of the instrumental ensemble work, --bands and orchestras. This agency is considerably less likely to select talent. If we find a boy coming to instrumental work merely because he wants to qualify for a uniform and a place in the high school band, we may certainly accept him and do our best for him, but at the same time there may be some questioning in our attitude.

2. Now let us consider briefly the factors which should determine the choice of pupils for instrumental work.

(*a*) First there is the rating in singing. The kind of work the pupil has done in this connection will give us at least a fair idea of his musical status. At least it will be reasonably clear that some pupils are exceedingly bad instrumental risks.

(*b*) William Larson was able to show that as one goes from the elementary instrumental classes to the junior high school preparatory orchestra, and thence to the junior high school advanced orchestra, and thence to the senior high school advanced orchestra, one finds a steady and significant increase in ratings on the Seashore Tests. The averages he obtained for all six tests are as follows: Elementary instrumental classes, 52.1; junior high school preparatory orchestra, 49.1; junior high school advanced orchestra, 66; senior high school advanced orchestra, 73.2. This certainly is a significant advance, and on the basis of it he has suggested that we may select promising candidates for the orchestral ensembles by giving the Seashore Tests in the elementary instrumental classes, and perhaps even earlier. If further investigation should definitely show that success in the advanced orchestras was closely associated with high Seashore Test ratings, the value of these tests for such selective work would be demonstrated. As it is, we cannot accept this as more than an interesting and perhaps useful suggestion. The numbers in the advanced groups investigated by Larson were small. Moreover, he did not take a group of pupils in elementary instrumental classes, and follow them through to senior high school, to find whether those with low Seashore Test records tended to drop out.

(*c*) The last basis of selection which will be mentioned here is that furnished by the attitude of the pupil. If we have an attitude of persistent interest, and a strong and evident determination and desire to continue, it should be taken strongly into consideration, for many reasons. Such pupils are just the ones most likely to succeed, when others, who may perhaps seem to us more natively musical, will fail because of lack of will. After all, music in the schools is for the sake of the pupil, and not *vice versa,* and if a pupil has a keen interest in it, then for his own sake he should, if at all possible, be allowed to follow his bent.

### Summary: Outcomes of This Chapter

1. The essential thing in instrumental work is to teach the child to make music through the instrument. We are teaching music, not instruments.

2. This involves penetrating the whole instrumental program with the spirit of appreciation, which should be both its motive and its goal.

3. Many musical values may be captured for the instrumental program if we correlate it closely with the vocal work. This gives the pupil ideal musical development in many ways, and facilitates and humanizes his whole approach to the instrument.

4. Instrumental mechanics cannot, of course, be ignored. But they ought to be handled incidentally to the actual experience of making music. This becomes perfectly possible if we rationalize and minimize the mechanical factor, and avoid overstrain.

## Questions for Discussion.

1. Discuss any concrete instances that have come to your notice of instrumental teachers who have emphasized mechanics in their work.

2. What kind of attitudes do you find existing on the part of instrumental teachers to vocal teachers in the schools? Why?

3. Have you ever heard instrumental teachers make skeptical comments about music education organized on progressive lines? Discuss any such statements.

4. Why do so many instrumental courses for beginners contain a great deal of absolutely uninteresting music? What effect has this on the pupil?

5. Can you think of any other musical-mental abilities developed in the grades that ought to be of value in instrumental work besides those we have mentioned?

6. Can you think of any instances of tension and overstrain produced by teaching practices in connection with any instrument? What is the effect on the pupil?

7. Discuss the saying "work for speed slowly."

8. Try to work out the A B C of some instrument with which you are thoroughly familiar.

## Bibliography.

1. Beattie, John W., McConathy, Osbourne, and Morgan, Russell V., *Music in the Junior High School,* Silver, Burdett and Company, 1930. ch. 13.
2. McConathy, Osbourne, Morgan, Russell V., and Clarke, H. T., *School and Community Band and Orchestra Series, Manual,* Oliver Ditson Company, 1928.
3. Maddy, J. E., and Giddings, T. P., *Instrumental Technique for Orchestra and Band,* The Willis Music Company, 1926.
4. Woods, Glenn, *School Bands and Orchestras,* Oliver Ditson Company, 1921.

# *PART FOUR*

# *Measurement, Materials, Aims*

## Chapter Thirteen

# Tests in Music

### The Place and Value of Tests in Music Education

It is important for the school music teacher to have some knowledge of the existing tests in the field, which are now being rapidly developed. The testing movement in education in general has led to some very striking results, and we may hope much from its extension into the field of music. The aim of this chapter, however, is not to give specific and detailed instructions for the actual use of music tests of various kinds, nor to discuss technically and at length the principles of test construction, and the character of tests and test batteries in music. What we shall try to do is merely to give the music teacher the basis of an intelligent attitude towards testing, to indicate how tests ought to be evaluated, and to sketch in a very general and cursory way, the main achievements to date of the testing movement as applied to music.

Perhaps the best way to think about the value of tests in education is as follows. We all know that in the work of teaching we constantly undertake to make comparisons on the basis of quantity. For instance, we say that one child is more or less musical than another, that one child has made more or less progress than another, that one educational method produces greater or smaller results of some kind than another, or that normally we expect a certain average advance in some ability or attainment as we move upward from grade to grade. Of course a great many important decisions are based on such quantitative judgments and comparisons. For instance, we may give a boy a certain bit of vocational advice because of our opinion as to the amount of talent he possesses; we may select or reject a certain pupil for our high school orchestra on the ground of the amount of his attainment as compared with another; or we may decide to use a certain classroom method for the reason that we believe it accomplishes more extensive results in a given time than some other. All that tests undertake to do is to remove these judgments of amount, of greater and less,—these quantitative judgments, in short, that are so important in education—from the realm of guess into the realm of reasonable certainty. Absolute certainty we can never have, and we should never criticize a test because it is not infallible. The real question is whether it is less fallible than our unaided judgment. This in exactly the value of tests in other fields, where they have had strikingly beneficial results, and we may hope for just the same kind of development in music.

In particular, we would like to urge upon the reader the unwisdom of taking extreme attitudes on this question of music tests. On the one hand we have extreme attitudes of negation and rejection. For instance, Davison rather rhetorically says that when it is possible to measure a child's love for his mother, then, and not till then, it will be possible to measure his love for music. But this is not a fair statement at all, for most people who believe in music tests do not have in mind anything so extensive. All they claim is that there are many very important factors in musical ability and training which can be measured, and with valuable results. On the other hand, we have those who want to make music testing the foundation for the entire scheme of school music.

But again we have an untenable position. If our tests in music were as excellent as those in some other fields of education,—if we had anything really comparable with the Stanford Achievement Tests, or the Stanford-Binet Scale—then there might be something in such an idea, although even then test results are not permitted to decide everything, without the consideration of other factors. But such tests have by no means been developed in music. *Our position is that existing tests may be very helpful, that their further development is very desirable, and accordingly that everyone in music education should have at least a general understanding, though not necessarily an expert knowledge, of what is offered.*

In closing this section we will briefly mention some of the values which the working teacher may find in the existing music tests.

1. Tests may give us considerable help in deciding as to the innate musical ability of the individual pupil, or at least they may help us to decide upon the extent to which he possesses certain abilities, such as a keen sense of relative pitch, a developed feeling for tonality, and so forth, that seem important constituents in musical ability.

2. Tests may help us to foretell the probable musical development of a child better than we could without them.

3. Tests may help us to select from a large group of pupils those who are very musical, and those who are relatively unmusical. A test may do this in far less time than would be possible in any other way. No doubt an experienced teacher, after perhaps a semester's contact with such a group, will have formed pretty reliable judgments. But a good test may give us a judgment as reliable, or even more so, with the expenditure of only an hour's time.

4. Tests often discover ability. Frequently the most experienced teacher will fail to recognize the presence of outstanding ability in some shy or stubborn child. If we can discover this by a good test, it may be the basis of helping the child to a better orientation to school and to life by capitalizing the ability he is shown to possess.

5. Tests may help us to diagnose the secret of certain weaknesses or defects which appear in the child's musical development. For instance, we may have a child in a violin class who seems incapable of playing in tune. If by a test we show that his sense of relative pitch is defective, we make one sort of decision. If on the other hand our test shows that his sense of pitch is excellent, we make quite a different decision. In the first case we transfer him to a piano class. In the second, we look for the source of trouble in his mechanics.

6. Tests may help us to evaluate certain methods of teaching, by giving us an exact account of the results these methods achieve, which we can somewhat confidently compare with the results of other methods.

7. Certain kinds of tests may be used for motivation. This is possible with tests of achievement, but never with tests of innate ability. For instance, we might give pupils a sequence of sight-singing tests which would show them their own progress in an interesting way.

*Educational and vocational advice and decisions should never be given solely on the basis of test results.* This is not done even when the very best intelligence tests or educational tests in other fields are in question. Always such elements as the teacher's judgment, personality factors, home background, etc., are taken into account. There is no magic in any test. But it can be an extremely valuable aid when applied with discrimination.

## How to Judge a Test

We have seen that the aim of a test is to make quantitative judgments about human beings more certain and exact. What then are the criteria of a good test? On what points ought we to try to judge any test?

1. *A good test is objective.* This means that its result is not merely the outcome of some person's private viewpoint. If we were to raise the question as to whether Mozart was a greater composer than Beethoven, we might argue about it endlessly and fail to agree. But if we ask whether Mozart wrote more consecutive fifths than Beethoven, we could work out an answer to which everyone would agree. In the one case we have mere subjective opinion. In the other, we are dealing with an objective, real situation. Again, if we ask whether pupil A reads better than pupil B, and if so how much, every music teacher who has worked with the two may have a different opinion. But if we give both A and B the same passage to sing, and A makes 5 mistakes to B's 9, we have an answer, which, for whatever it may be worth, cannot be questioned. It is this quality of being entirely removed from the personal opinion of the examiner that constitutes objectivity in a test. We achieve it by defining with great care exactly what we are testing, and then creating situations such that the pupil's responses will be confined within definite and narrow limits. For instance, the Seashore Test of Sense of Pitch is highly objective. It consists of 100 comparisons between the pitch of two tones, and in each case the subject is called upon to decide whether the second tone is higher or lower than the first. Always he is bound to be either right or wrong. When we score the test, our personal opinion has absolutely nothing to do with the result. We see here an illustration of our two conditions. There is no doubt as to

what is being measured; it is the ability to discriminate differences in pitch. The pupil is placed in a situation where he must make responses which cannot be otherwise than right or wrong. The test in the new Kwalwasser-Dykema battery, however, in which the subject has to pick out the better of two different terminations of the same melody is probably not so objective,[1] for clearly there might be a real, expert difference of opinion as to which of two such endings really was the "better." Thus the pupil's response is not so certainly right or wrong as in the former case. We should notice that objectivity is a matter of degree, and that the best tests do not always have 100% objectivity, though they always rate pretty high in this respect.

2. *A good test is reliable.* We say that any measuring device is reliable in so far as it gives us the same result when applied twice to the same facts. A tape measure made of elastic would be extremely unreliable, and so is one's guess at the weight of a suitcase. There is no such thing as a perfectly reliable measuring device. A fine automobile engine is accurate to within one two-thousandth of an inch, because the gauges are reliable to that point. But it is never absolutely accurate. When we measure mental processes, and the results of education, unreliability is much greater. How important the reliability of a test may be, we can see from an illustration in general education. Suppose we set up a test for college entrance that is quite unreliable. Eighty per cent of our candidates pass it. But when we say that it is unreliable, we mean that if all the candidates took it again, we could not be in the least sure that the same 80% would pass

[1] We state this as a probability on general grounds. The proof and measurement of objectivity is a statistical process which we shall not here describe. So far as we know it has not been applied to this particular test.

again; and that, in fact, they probably would not. So whether a person is failed by such a test will depend very largely on chance. It is just as if we proposed to admit people to college if they came to a certain height, and then measured their height with an elastic tape measure. Once more, college entrance would be a matter of luck, for some of the tall people might get a short measurement and *vice versa.*

So we would give this piece of practical advice to the music teacher. *Always have reservations about any test whose reliability you do not know, and never base important decisions on the results of any test unless you know it to have a high reliability.*

But this raises the question: How is reliability determined? Reliability is expressed in what is known as a *coefficient of reliability.* This is obtained by giving the test twice to the same group (probably as two equivalent forms of the same test), and comparing the scores of individuals in the two cases. The coefficient measures the amount of agreement between the two sets of test scores. If it is $+1$, then each person has made exactly the same score each time, and the test is perfectly reliable. If it is $-1$ then the order is precisely reversed, the person with the highest score on the first testing making the lowest on the second. If it is zero, then there is simply no relationship between the testings, the test is said to have a zero reliability, and the score obtained by any person on it is a matter of pure chance and so quite meaningless. We would say that any test with a reliability much below .60 is not very valuable educationally, for if it is repeated, there is a chance that any given individual will very greatly modify his record, and the element of luck is altogether too great.

Among the many causes of unreliability we will here mention only the most important one, and that is shortness. The longer the test, the greater the reliability. For instance, if we want to measure a person's sight-reading ability, or his power to discriminate consonance and dissonance, or the keenness of his choice among melodic endings, and only give him one or two tries, it is obvious that all sorts of things may arise to disturb him. He may be temporarily astonished at the form the test takes; or the instances we choose may be especially hard for him; or one or more other disturbing circumstances may be present which prevent his doing his best. Or, on the other hand, for some reason, he may be able to do far better than his average,—for instance, if he happens to know the passage we choose for sight reading, or to have studied the few dissonances we present, or to be familiar with the melody in question. But if we give him enough instances, all such special factors tend to cancel, and we get a much fairer picture of his real ability. Trying to judge a person on a very short test is like trying to find out the constitution of the ocean floor by scooping up just one bucket-full. The more samples we take, the more accurate our ideas become. Hence, if the teacher wants to make a test, it should always consist of a considerable number of situations,—the more the better—calling for relatively brief responses.

3. *A good test must be valid.* That is, it must really measure what it purports to measure. For instance, we have heard music teachers complain that the Kwalwasser-Ruch Test of Musical Accomplishment does not measure innate musical ability. This is a perfectly true statement, but a very stupid one. The battery undertakes to measure certain items of musical knowledge and skill. For these it is valid. But it has no validity for innate musical ability, and does not pretend to have.

The question of validity may be a very subtle one. For instance, we may make a test calling for the writing down of certain grammatical forms in a foreign language, and run it with a time limit. We may find that some person who actually has a very good knowledge of the language does far worse than another person whose actual language mastery is quite mediocre. The reason may be that, instead of language mastery, our test is really measuring the ability to write down grammatical responses very fast, and with a minimum of cogitation, in a given situation. Or again, some ordinary essay type examinations are really much better measures of a pupil's ability to fill several blue books in two or three hours, than of his mastery of the subject. So this raises the question as to how we determine validity. We mention here the two most common methods. (*a*) By the judgment of experts. The test items in the Kwalwasser-Ruch battery were selected on the basis of a study of the most representative courses of study in music, so that, within its limits, this test series represents expert opinion on what the music pupil ought to know. (*b*) By correlation against criteria. For instance, we may take a group of pupils, give them the six Seashore Tests, and then have a teacher who knows them well make estimates of their musical ability. After this we may determine the degree of relationship between test scores and ratings of ability. If this relationship is close, we would say that the Seashore Tests are valid measures of musical ability as estimated by a music teacher; if the relationship is remote, we would say that they are not.

Thus, we pass on once more to a word of practical advice. *In using any test, find out if possible exactly what abilities it measures, and what it does not measure, i.e., its validity. And also find out the degree of its validity.* The degree or amount of validity is expressed, again, in a coefficient, in the same way as reliability. But this time the coefficient expresses the relationship between the test and the criterion, *e.g.*, the relationship between ratings on the Seashore Tests, and estimates of talent by the teacher.

4. *A good test must be easy to administer.* Robert Seashore has devised what is probably the best of all rhythm tests, from the standpoint of objectivity, reliability, and validity. But it takes intricate apparatus, and technical skill, to administer it. So the test has no value in the schools. One difficulty with sight-singing tests is that no one has yet been able to devise any means of giving them simultaneously to a large group. They are all individual tests, and thus less usable than they otherwise might be. If a test calls for intricate statistical methods in rating, it is bad. The same is true if the rating depends on the group judgment of experts.

5. *It is a great advantage to have published norms for a test.* A norm is simply a statement of the levels of performance of considerable groups taking a test. For instance, we may have a norm for all sixth grade children throughout a city system, a state, or the United States, or a norm for all ten-year-old boys or girls in a system, etc., etc. Norms, in short, are stated in a great many different ways. They are useful for purposes of comparison. Without them, our test results are much less meaningful and suggestive. But they should never be crudely used as standards. For instance, if a given grade or a given individual does not come up to a national norm, this is not necessarily a sign of deficiency. For the whole scheme of education in the particular system may be such that while it produces low standings in the particular test under consideration, it may compensate for this by producing high standings elsewhere.

These five points are very useful to have in mind in evaluating tests. They should serve to show the music teacher why the makers of tests use the forms they do. They should help the teacher to avoid using poor tests. They are characteristics which should be present not only in published and "standardized" tests, but in homemade classroom tests as well. They are nothing more than the obviously necessary conditions for carrying on any sort of meaningful measurement, and interpreting its results.

## A Description of Some Music Tests

We shall not attempt to make any exhaustive survey of all the music tests now available, or to discuss the extensive technical literature dealing with them. To do this would call for a whole book in itself. Moreover, we make no particular classification of tests. All we want to do is to give the teacher some idea of what there is in the field, and to characterize some well recognized tests that have been used in school work.

1. **The Seashore Measures of Musical Talent.** This is one of the oldest, and probably the best known, set of music tests. It consists of six tests which are given by means of the phonograph. (*a*) *Sense of Pitch:*—This test consists of 100 pitch comparisons of varying difficulty, the subject being required to decide whether a second tone is higher or lower than the first. (*b*) *Intensity Discrimination:*—This consists of 100 comparisons of two tones differing more or less in intensity, the subject being required to decide whether the second is louder or softer than the first. (*c*) *Sense of Time:*—This consists of 100 comparisons of the length of two time intervals marked off by clicks. (*d*) *Sense of Consonance:*—This consists of 50 comparisons between pairs of two-tone clangs, the subject being required to judge whether the second

clang is better or worse than the first on the basis of smoothness, purity, and blending. (*e*) *Tonal Memory:*—This consists of 50 comparisons between two sets of unrelated tones, one tone in the set being changed on repetition, the subject being required to identify the changed tone. (*f*) *Sense of Rhythm:*—This consists of 50 comparisons between pairs of rhythm patterns, the subject being required to judge whether the second pattern is the same as, or different from the first.

No brief summary can do justice to the extensive literature on these tests. But the following seem salient points. (*a*) This test battery measures innate ability, and ratings are not affected by musical training. (*b*) With the exception of the consonance test, the objectivity of the measures cannot be questioned. (*c*) The six tests have a medium to low reliability. (*d*) As to validity, a simple statement is not easy to make. It has been shown that there is some relationship between success in these tests and continuance in certain schools of music. William Larson has shown that pupils in the more advanced instrumental ensemble work in the schools seem to show higher than average ability on the tests. On the other hand, Brown has shown that there is almost no relationship between success on the tests and musical talent as estimated by a music teacher in school work, and one of the authors of this text (Mursell) has demonstrated the same lack of relationship for a conservatory of music. There seems to be more relationship between the Seashore Tests and various special musical abilities, like sight singing, or singing pitch, than between the tests and general musical ability. (*e*) School music teachers have criticized the battery on many grounds, some of which are not very fair. Probably the most serious criticism is that it tends to treat musical ability as a composite of many special abilities rather than as a functioning unit. The test against which most criticism has been leveled is that for consonance. Many music psychologists do not believe that there really are the specific degrees of consonance and dissonance which the test assumes. (*f*) Our general attitude is that the full uses and limitations of this battery are not yet understood. Clearly we must not expect the impossible from it. We doubt very much whether it will give us a very good index of general musical ability. But it serves various purposes of real value in conjunction with other methods of testing, along the line of predicting and analyzing special abilities and disabilities. As the pioneer test in the attempt to measure talent, it did awaken teachers to the possibilities of knowing definitely whether children possessed talent.

2. **Kwalwasser-Dykema (K-D) Music Tests.** This is a battery of 10 tests, given by means of the phonograph. (*a*) *Tonal Memory Test:*—This test consists of 25 pairs of tonal patterns of increasing length, the subject being asked to judge whether the pair consists of the same or different halves. (*b*) *Quality Discrimination:*—This test consists of 30 trials in each of which a motive is played twice, either by a different instrument or the same instrument, and the subject is required to say whether the tone quality is the same or different. (*c*) *Intensity Discrimination:*—15 pairs of tones and 15 pairs of chords are sounded with a difference in intensity only, and the subject is required to tell whether the second is louder or softer than the first. (*d*) *Tonal Movement:*—This consists of 30 four-tone tonal patterns, which demand a fifth tone for completion, the subject judging whether this fifth tone should be above or below the fourth. (*e*) *Time Discrimination:*—25 items of 3 tones each, with the first and third of equal length, but the second variable, the subject judging whether

the three intervals of every item are the same or different in length. (*f*) *Rythmic Discrimination:*—25 paired rhythm patterns are given, differing either in intensity or duration or both, the subject judging whether the second is the same or different. (*g*) *Pitch Discrimination:*—40 items, in each of which a tone is sustained for three seconds, either with or without a fluctuation in pitch, the subject deciding whether the tone has remained the same or has changed. (*h*) *Melodic Taste:*—This test consists of 10 items which are repeated again, making in all 20 trials. In each item the first phrases of the two melodies are the same, but the second phrases are different. The subject is to judge which of the two concluding phrases is the better, on a basis of congruity with the first. (*i*) *Pitch Imagery:*—25 tonal patterns are given in notation, and the subject decides whether they are the same as, or different from those sounded on the phonograph. (*j*) *Rhythm Imagery:*—25 items are given in notation, and the subject indicates whether the rhythm patterns, as they are produced on the record, are the same as, or different from those on the page.

While much research analysis needs to be done before we can come to final conclusions as to the values and limitations of this quite new battery, it has all the looks of superior excellence. In contrast to the Seashore Tests, it uses actual musical material. The tests are much shorter, less fatiguing, and more interesting. Excellent norms are provided, and the administration and rating of the tests is facilitated by the blanks and scoring stencils that are supplied.

3. **Gildersleeve Music Achievement Tests.** This battery, which has been rather widely used, consists of two forms, A and B, of the same tests, the two forms being of equal difficulty. This is a distinct advantage in administration. The tests measure the following abilities. (*a*) Assigning names

to compositions played by the examiner. (*b*) Detecting changes in pitch, in meter, in key signature, and in meter signature. (*c*) Writing key signatures; locating *la* in 6 different keys; the use of accidentals; knowledge of note values; knowledge of time signatures; transposition of a G clef phrase to the bass clef. (*d*) A multiple response test, containing 15 main questions, which cover in some detail instrumentation, theory, history, and harmony. (*e*) Recognition of compositions from the score.

This is distinctively a test of knowledge about music, and of skill in using the notation in certain ways. It is quite unlike the Seashore Tests, in that it measures the results of training.

4. **Kwalwasser-Ruch Test of Musical Accomplishment.** The aim of this test is to measure musical knowledge from the fourth to the twelfth grade inclusive. It consists of the following separate items. (*a*) Knowledge of musical terms and symbols. (*b*) Recognition of syllable names from notation. (*c*) Detection of pitch errors in the notation of a familiar melody. (*d*) Knowledge of pitch or letter names of bass and treble clef. (*e*) Knowledge of time signatures. (*f*) Knowledge of key signatures. (*g*) Knowledge of note values. (*h*) Knowledge of rest values. (*i*) Recognition of familiar melodies from notation.

The comment made in explanation of the Gildersleeve test applies here also. It is unjustifiable to criticize these tests, as some music teachers do, on the ground that they do not directly measure musical ability or achievement, for this is expressly not their purpose. In some such cases, it is true, the title of a battery is open to objection on the ground that it is misleading.

5. **Torgerson-Fahnestock Tests.** These tests are divided into two parts. Part A deals with theoretical knowl-

edge of items, such as note and rest values, time signatures, pitch and syllable names, marks of expression, repeat bar, slur, major and minor key signatures, natural and harmonic minor scales. Part B deals with ear-training proficiency, and consists of 4 tests. (*a*) Writing syllable names of 12 exercises from aural dictation. (*b*) Writing time signatures and supplying bars for incomplete notation of four given melodic fragments. (*c*) Detecting both pitch and time errors in notation. (*d*) Writing notes on the staff from dictation.

6. **Hillbrand Sight-Singing Test.** This consists of a four-page folder containing six songs. The pupil is permitted to study the notation for a few minutes, and is then asked to sing, without help of any kind. The various errors made by the pupil are recorded on a copy of the songs by the teacher.

7. **Mosher Test of Individual Singing.** This consists of 12 exercises, which contain problems that frequently occur in school music, arranged in order of increasing difficulty.

It will be noted that both these sight-singing tests are individual tests. In fact there are no group tests in this field, and perhaps never will be. However, Mosher has tried to find some group tests which will be a significant index of sight-singing ability, though it may not directly measure it. In doing this he investigated the degree of relationship between performance on his individual test, and on seven group tests. That most indicative of sight-singing ability was found to be the ability to write tonal figures from hearing them (correlation .6212. Multiple correlation between whole battery and individual tests .6771).

8. **Some less formal and developed tests.** Besides the highly-developed published tests which we have described,

and others like them, there are a number of measuring instruments which have never been standardized. But it is very well worth while for the school music teacher to know something about them, for they often suggest valuable informal methods of testing musical ability, such as that mentioned in Chapter Two.

(*a*) **Lowery's tests of Cadence and Musical Memory.** The cadence test consisted of 50 comparisons between cadences in various positions,—perfect, plagal, imperfect, and deceptive—the subject being required to say whether the second cadence of the pair was more or less final. The phrase test consisted of judgments as to whether two tonal sequences were the same or different when the only difference lay in the phrasing. The musical memory test consisted of 10 musical sentences, followed by 5 variations on each one, the variations being interspersed with irrelevant items, and the subjects being required to identify the variations on the theme they had heard from the irrelevant material. In giving these tests, a piano was used. The test items are not published in complete form.

(*b*) **Tests by Révécz.** On the basis of his study of the prodigy Nyiregeházi, Révécz drew up a series of 8 tests of musical ability. (1) Clapping rhythms given either monotonically or melodically. (2) Absolute pitch, tested by reproducing a given tone on the piano. (3) Octave recognition and transposition. (4) Relative pitch, tested by the vocal reproduction of an interval sounded on the piano, with a new note for its bass. (5-6) Harmonic sense, tested by vocal reproduction of the constituent notes of chords. (7-8) Melodic memory tested by ability to sing a melody given, and to play by ear a known tune. He regarded the ability to sing back a melody as most diagnostic of musical ability. He found that the ability to clap a rhythm is not highly diagnostic, but that instrumental reproduction of melody, absolute pitch, vocal transposition of an interval, and ability to analyze chords, are indicative of musical ability in the descending order given. His subjects were 63 boys from 7 to 12.

(*c*) **Rupp's measures.** Rupp undertook to measure eight abilities closely related to musicality. (1) Absolute pitch. (2) Discrimination of small differences in pitch. (3) Ability to recognize successive intervals. (4) Ability to recognize simultaneous intervals. (5) Ability to repeat a melody. (6) Ability to sing and repeat a second part to a given melody. (7) *Takt* and rhythm. (8) Chordal analysis.

(*d*) **Frances A. Wright Tests.** These tests fall into three divisions. FAW 1 tests: (1) List the student's repertoire. (2) Test on performance of one piece selected by the examiner and one by the student. (3) Piano sight reading (from the Laurel Song Book). (4) Singing back a four-measure melody. (5) Writing out notation of a melody given on the piano. FAW 2 tests: Music writing from dictation. FAW 3 tests: Two- and three-part dictation with modulations and difficult rhythms.

These tests are intended for music students, but they are interesting, and practical suggestions may be picked up from them by the school music teacher.

### Summary: Outcomes of This Chapter

1. Tests in music, as in education generally, are simply devices for helping us to make more certain and accurate quantitative statements and comparisons. We should not expect too much from them; nor, on the contrary, should we feel that they have no value or place.

2. Tests should be evaluated on the bases of objectivity, re-

liability, validity, and ease of administration. The existence of published norms is a great advantage. All tests, whether formally published, or made by the teacher himself, should conform to the above four conditions.

3. A comment on the music tests discussed is here in order. They are samples of the available material, and fairly well represent its excellences and deficiencies. Obviously they tend to emphasize the more or less mechanical aspects of musical ability, and to stress knowledge and specialized skill. This in fact is their most serious weakness; and it arises quite largely from the necessity of making them objective. We must remember, too, that progressive music education is a new thing, and that it does not yet wholly understand itself. Its aims are not entirely definite and clearly stated. Moreover, we can construct good tests only when we know exactly what to test for. As the aims of music education progressively define themselves, and the desirable musical-mental processes become more evident, new and better tests will develop.

### Questions for Discussion.

1. What reasons have you heard school music teachers give for opposing the use of tests? Discuss such reasons.

2. What criticism would you make of the suggestion that children should be sectioned strictly on test ratings in music work?

3. Discuss the probable objectivity, reliability, and validity of such an informal test as singing back a four-phrase melody.

4. On the basis of a study of the less formal and developed tests, what suggestions could you make to a music teacher who wanted to know approximately how to pick out musical and non-musical pupils?

5. Suggest definite ways of using any one of these test batteries in school work, or ways of using tests in general.

BIBLIOGRAPHY.

1. ADLER, MORTIMER JEROME, Music Appreciation: an Experimental Approach to Its Measurement, *Archives of Psychology,* 1929, No. 110.
2. BRENNAN, F., The Relation Between Musical Capacity and Performance, *Psychological Monographs,* 1924, vol. 36, No. 1, Whole No. 167, pp. 190-248.
3. BROWN, A. W., The Reliability and Validity of the Seashore Tests of Musical Talent, *Journal of Applied Psychology,* 1928, vol. 12, pp. 468-476.
4. GAW, ESTHER ALLEN, Five Studies in the Music Tests, *Psychological Monographs,* 1928, vol. 39, No. 2, Whole No. 178, pp. 145-156.
5. GILDERSLEEVE, GLENN, *Music Achievement Test,* Bureau of Publications, Teachers College, Columbia University, 1929.
6. HILLBRAND, *Sight Singing Test,* World Book Company, 1923.
7. KÖNIG, H., Über das musicaklische Gedächtnis, *Zeitschrift für Psychologie,* 1928, vol. 108, pp. 398-420.
8. KWALWASSER, JACOB, Third Yearbook, *Department of Superintendence, National Education Association,* 1925, ch. 14, pp. 354-366.
9. KWALWASSER, JACOB, *Tests and Measurements in Music,* C. C. Birchard and Co., 1927.
10. KWALWASSER, JACOB, Tests and Measurements in Music, *Psychological Bulletin,* 1928, vol. 35, pp. 284-301.
11. KWALWASSER, JACOB, and DYKEMA, PETER W., *K-D Music Tests; Manual of Directions,* Carl Fischer, Inc., 1930.
12. LARSON, WILLIAM S., Measurement of Musical Talent for the Prediction of Success in Instrumental Music, *Psychological Monographs,* 1930, vol. 40, No. 1, Whole No. 181, pp. 33-73.
13. LOWERY, H., Cadence and Phrase Tests in Music, *British Journal of Psychology,* 1926, vol. 17, pp. 111-118.

14. Lowery, H., Musical Memory, *British Journal of Psychology,* 1928-1929, vol. 19, pp. 397-404.
15. McConathy, Osbourne, Miessner, W. O., Birge, E. B., and Bray, Mabel E., Tests and Measurement, *The Music Hour, Intermediate Teacher's Book,* Silver, Burdett and Co., 1929, ch. 14.
16. Mosher, R. M., *A Study of the Group Method of Measurement of Sight-Singing,* Teachers College, Columbia University, Contributions to Education, No. 194, 1925.
17. Révécz, Geza, Prüfung der Musikalität, *Zeitschrift für Psychologie,* 1920, vol. 85, pp. 163-209.
18. Rupp, Hans, Über die Prüfung Musikalischer Fähigkeiten, Teil I., *Zeitschrift für angewandte Psychologie,* 1915, vol. 9, pp. 1-76.
19. Schoen, Max, Common Sense in Music Tests, *Music Teachers National Association Proceedings,* 1925.
20. Schoen, Max, Tests of Musical Feeling and Musical Understanding, *Journal of Comparative Psychology,* 1925, vol. 5, pp. 31-52.
21. Schoen, Max, The Validity of Tests of Musical Talent, *Journal of Comparative Psychology,* 1923, vol. 3, pp. 101-121.
22. Stanton, Hazel, *Prognosis of Musical Achievement,* University of Rochester, N. Y., 1929.
23. Stanton, Hazel, Seashore Measures of Musical Talent, *Psychological Monographs,* 1928, vol. 39, No. 2, Whole No. 178, pp. 135-144.
24. Torgerson, T. L., and Fahnestock, Ernest, *Music Tests,* Public School Publishing Co., Bloomington, Illinois.
25. Williams, C. O., A Critique of Measures of Musical Talent, *Music Supervisors Journal,* October, 1929, pp. 67-81, 95.
26. Wright, Frances, The Correlation between Achievement and Capacity in Music, *Journal of Educational Research,* 1928, vol. 17, pp. 50-56.

CHAPTER FOURTEEN

# School Music Materials and Their Evaluation

## THE GENERAL PROBLEM

The ability to assess competently the various collections of musical material for school use is an important part of the professional equipment of the music teacher. If the teacher selects the book, it is obviously desirable that the choice be made on the best and most adequate grounds. If he has to use a book not of his selection, it should be studied according to certain criteria, and from certain definite points of view, in order that it may be used with maximum efficiency. There are certain fairly well-recognized principles of textbook evaluation, which the teacher should know, and which we here propose to apply to the music situation. Before coming to details, however, we should make two qualifying statements. First, there is no such thing as an ideal textbook on the market; hence, the fact that a publication does not measure up to all possible standards is no reason for its rejection. Second, the actual decision to introduce a book will depend on the procedures and educational ideals of the teacher. No set of formal rules of analysis can thus determine the choice of a book to be used in a given school or school system. The most we can do is to show how to go about evaluating any book. So we shall seek to answer the question: What can one rightly look for in a textbook in school music? What should such a book offer the teacher? We shall find that any such book should be evaluated from six points of view. One should take into consideration content, organization, correlation, pedagogical suggestions, format, and collateral factors.

### I. Content

Of all questions to be raised in evaluating a textbook in school music, that of content is the most important. Here we have two basic general considerations, of most pertinent application to elementary school needs:

(*a*) The musical excellence of the materials brought together is of prime significance. It is impossible to teach music properly unless we have the use of good music. This we have seen again and again. The task of assembling music of high excellence and arranging it for children, is certainly no easy one, but it must be performed if the book is to be a success educationally.

(*b*) The range and variety of the materials provided is a second consideration in connection with content. If two books rate about equal in musical quality, that one with the wider variety of material should be preferred,—folk songs, children's classics, art songs, songs by the masters, and songs by contemporary artists. Because of the importance of variety, it is often desirable that more than one book be used in connection with the music program. This becomes especially important after the sixth grade.

With these generalizations well established, let us see what detailed questions the teacher should raise in assessing the content of any textbook, especially for use in the primary and intermediate grades.

1. First of all, does the content provide for all-round musical development through performing, creative, and listening

opportunities? Does the book contain a considerable representation of the work of the great masters of music, even for the younger children? Such work should be in a youthful idiom, and is usually an extract from a longer selection, or a suitable arrangement, at least for the lower grades.

2. Does the book contain a considerable proportion of folk music? We do not agree with the tendency in some quarters to make folk music a fetish. Rather we believe that anything qualitatively good ought to be used. But there is no doubt that folk music is a vital and primary source of school music material, just as from time to time it has been for art song.

3. What proportion of the material has been directly written for the book? Considerable criticism, some of which is justified, has been directed at the song especially written for children. But generalizations on this score are misleading. There are two types of "specially written songs," involving, however, a vast difference. First of all, the supervisor must remember that the recognized composer commissioned to write songs representative of his best work, will permit publication of only those which he considers of unquestioned musical merit. After he has written an artistic song, its assignment in the grading plan of a book is immaterial. Its artistic merit cannot be questioned just because it also has the additional virtue of being useful. If, on the other hand, the specially written song (in many cases not identified as to source) was manufactured obviously and primarily to provide a drill opportunity or sight-reading practice, or to give recognition (in doubtful taste) to an obscure composer, its artistic value is very likely negligible. To those critics who would use only songs sanctioned by immemorial usage we might ask, "How shall the children know the best work of contemporary composers as a definite part of their musical heritage unless

the composer is given an opportunity to write charmingly and spontaneously in their particular idiom?"

4. What proportion of the material consists of instrumental music adapted for the voice? This again has come in for criticism, often only too justly. But once more our judgment will depend on the particular case,—on the instrumental melody chosen, and on its treatment. Still, it is a point against which the supervisor should be on his guard.

5. What kind of words are used in the songs? We have seen the great importance of words as aids in creating a mood, in helping rhythmic grasp, etc. Hence, we should look for words that have poetic meaning and interest; that are natural, unforced, childlike in their whimsicality, and that connect the music with childhood experience. The acknowledged children's poets represented in the book will be a guide to the teacher in questions of literary merit.

6. Are the accompaniments in a separate book for the teacher, especially in the case of elementary school material? Is the accompaniment in the spirit of the text and music? Is it a perfunctory four-part harmonization underlying the melody when the nature of the song demands another type? An interesting and suitable accompaniment has a number of educational values.

7. Is material for toy orchestra, rhythm band, etc., provided from the kindergarten into the third grade?

8. How readily could the book be used in developing rhythm plays and activities? Is there any special music for these purposes? Is the song material such that it would be available? Are suitable directions provided for the proper synthesis of the vocal and rhythm programs?

9. How does the material check up from the standpoint of appreciation? Is appreciation the basic consideration in

the choice of material? Could the material provided readily correlate with a "listening lesson" program? Does the book contain any material to be played or sung to the children? Does every type of song, instrumental selection, or "listening lesson" motivate the child's interest and stimulate his love of beauty?

## II. Organization

Textbook organization means the massing and ordering of the material to present certain problems, to favor certain lines of approach, and to effect certain objectives. Always it represents a pedagogical viewpoint, and it should be studied with this in mind. Again, a number of questions should be raised by the teacher in evaluating the organization of a book.

1. What sort of activities are especially stressed in the book? Some books are organized in such a way that a disproportionate emphasis is placed either on rote singing or on note spelling. In either case we should regard such a book as a defective text.

2. How are the various problematic aspects of music approached and isolated? How does the book deal with phrase, tonality, harmony, rhythm, etc.? Is the sequence followed in presenting the "time, tone, and theory" problems psychologically sound?

3. At what level or grade are the various problems introduced? Remember that there is no *absolute* sequence in which the various aspects of music must be taken up. All we want is some reasonable and feasible sequence (no logical order is possible), so that by the end of the sixth grade a reasonable competence is attainable, and so that the child is all the time occupied with genuine musical projects.

4. Are the various musical problems,—for instance, learn-

ing to recognize the notation of chord figures, *e.g.*, tonic chord and neighboring tones—introduced on an adequate background of synthetic, functioning, musical experience?

5. Does the quality and ordering of the material suggest and facilitate creative reviewing?

6. What sort of a sequence of problems do we find? We have seen that a good sequence is by no means dominated by a rigid simple-to-complex, known-to-unknown order. The rule is always to provide vital, real experiences, arranged so as not to be too hard for the child to master, but still hard enough to be interesting.

7. Is the book so put together that it could be taught from a viewpoint different from that on which it is organized? In other words, does it offer certain flexibility in operation? This is a useful quality. Usually it suggests a wealth of good material which permits alternatives, as well as helpful indexes so that a teacher can easily find his way about.

## III. Correlation

We should assess the book from the point of view of the opportunities it offers for correlating music with other studies. The educator and school administrator looks for the integration of music on the activity and social program basis with other subjects in the curriculum, as one means of judging its educative and socializing values.

1. Does the selection and arrangement of song material suggest correlation with literature?

2. Does the content suggest means of correlation with geography and history? For instance, are the folk songs properly identified as to source, suggesting country or race? Are there suggestions as to the historic periods in which composers lived? Do suitable pictures intensify these correlations and

tend to produce a finer appreciation, and hence more musical performance?

3. Does the book suggest and facilitate correlation of music with art? Does it contain a well organized plan of illustrations,—pictures which mirror the mood of the song, increase the child's sensitiveness to the appeal of the music, and in general assist him to an appreciation of the aesthetic and cultural values in art and music?

### IV. Pedagogical Suggestions

1. Does the book contain any pedagogical helps and suggestions? An elementary school music textbook should by all means contain these, with a minimum of suggestion in the child's book itself, and a complete program in a teacher's manual.

2. How practical and usable are such suggestions? Are they full, explicit, adequate? Do they explain everything that occurs in the book, and show just how to use the devices provided? Or do they leave one in doubt as to what the author thinks ought to be done with some part of his material? How would they work out in the hands of the ordinary grade teacher? How effective would they be in teacher training classes? Would they tend definitely to raise standards of accomplishment?

3. Are such suggestions based on recent psychology, and on really authoritative psychological conceptions? For instance, we find teacher's manuals in which the superseded idea of definite developmental stages of the child's growing-up process, or the discarded idea of music as a mind-trainer, still find a place. Such things need not militate seriously against a book, as their influence may be canceled by its excellences elsewhere. But they ought to be noted.

4. Are there any pedagogical suggestions directed to the pupil himself? There might be instructions as to what to do, and how to do it, etc.,—a workbook plan of procedure.

## V. Format

The question of the attractiveness and usability of the book should expressly be raised in evaluating it. The following points are important here:

1. *Size.* The book should be small enough to be easily handled by the child, but on the other hand should also be large enough to permit adequate display of music and text. The undersized music primers sometimes put into the hands of young children fail wretchedly in this respect and thereby have a harmful effect on the child's earliest contact with music.

2. *Binding.* The binding should be attractive in appearance, but above all for school use, books should be substantially bound to withstand the careless and frequently severe handling by the immature child. In general, a cloth binding constructed over a rigid board cover recommends itself for its greater permanence and durability. A properly bound book should be so constructed as to be held open with reasonable facility. The margins, even in a school book, should be pleasing.

3. *Paper.* Studies in visibility, eyestrain in reading, etc., indicate that the best paper for schoolbooks is a smooth, toned white. It should not, however, have such a high finish as to produce a glossy or glaring effect which is injurious to the eyes.

4. *Typography.* The teacher should pay special attention to the size and visibility of the typography. This appraisal applies particularly to the typography of the music notation.

Most modern music books for little children employ large staves and noteheads, as well as large type for text. As the children become more and more familiar with music notation in reading, the size of the type should show a proportionate reduction.

5. *Layout.* Is the song material for the earlier grades printed phrase-wise; or has some other order been adopted, seemingly for the convenience of the composing room? If the latter, the resultant crowded page sacrifices the appearance and handicaps the child's interest. Those books which provide accompaniments along with the melody (this applies to the lower grades), confuse and distract the child.

6. *Illustrations.* What pictures, decorations, diagrams, etc., does the book contain? Are they merely decorative and conventional, or do they form a vital and integral part of the educative plan? Are they related to the musical and poetic content? Do they provide teaching opportunities?

### VI. Collateral Factors

We now come to certain points of a rather different type. They are points which give us an indirect rather than a direct appraisal of the book. Many school music teachers do not take them into consideration. But in this they are certainly wrong, for here are items which are really significant in many ways. To put it at its lowest, the teacher should make it a matter of professional pride to be able to answer the following questions about any book he is using or has studied with a view to adoption:

1. Who is the author? What is his full name, his present official position, his past experience and professional background, his educational affiliations, and his general reputation in the field for which he is writing? What are his other publications? Such information, to be gleaned from the title page,

the preface, notices in "Who's Who in America," or from educational directories, is of genuine value in helping one to understand a book, to judge the authoritativeness of its suggestions, and to use it with discrimination.

2. Who are the publishers? What other school music material have they put out? Are they new in the field, or well established? What is their general reputation, and what are their affiliations? Have they an established policy of publication which warrants confidence in their program of music education?

3. What is the copyright date? Unfortunately, quite a number of textbooks in school music do not show a copyright date. Get this if possible. If the book before you is not a first edition, what edition is it? If it is a standard work, does it show successive revisions to accord with modern needs?

4. What sort of "front material" is there? Look at the title page, preface, and introduction, if any. What title has the book? Would it be meaningful or attractive to children?

5. Is the stated purpose of the book fulfilled?

6. Can the book be used advantageously to supply a felt need?

7. Where is the book used? Make it a point to learn about recent adoptions from the publisher's announcements. Has the book maintained itself in actual use until it has become a standard work? Learn also about discontinuances of use. Do not take these at their face value until you really know the reasons for them.

8. What is the price of the book?

### Questions for Discussion.

1. Discuss the value and importance for music education of adequate and properly arranged collections of material.

2. Why is it essential in music education always to use material of high musical value?

3. Select and discuss some instances of the two types of "specially written songs" from school music texts with which you are familiar.

4. What is the value of the folk song in music education? Should we confine grade school singing largely to folk song material?

5. Why is it valuable to have more than one book of music material available in school music teaching?

6. Evaluate some collections of school music familiar to you from the points of view here suggested.

BIBLIOGRAPHY.

1. BAMBERGER, F. E., The Effect of the Physical Makeup of a Book Upon Children's Selection, *Johns Hopkins University Studies in Education,* No. 6, 1922.
2. FOWLKES, J. G., *Evaluating School Textbooks,* Silver, Burdett and Company, 1923.
3. FRANZEN, R., and KNIGHT, F. B., *Textbook Selection,* Warwick and York, 1922.
4. HALL-QUEST, A. L., *The Textbook: How to Use and Judge It,* The Macmillan Company, 1917.
5. MAXWELL, C. R., *The Selection of Textbooks,* Houghton Mifflin Company, 1921.

CHAPTER FIFTEEN

# The Aims of School Music

## THE VALUE OF A DISCUSSION OF AIMS

We now come to a point where it is our task to assemble the wider and deeper implications of all that has been said. We have brought together the scientific findings relevant to music education in the schools, and have shown their relationship to practice. We have seen in what ways science can tell us what should be done and how to do it. But a larger question still remains: *What is the meaning for human life of our subject, when organized and taught in accordance with psychological conceptions? What is its ultimate value? What is its final justification? What contribution can it make to the welfare of the individual and of society? What is its ultimate aim?*

Thus we approach the philosophy of music education. But when we say this, it may seem that we are losing contact with solid ground, and passing into a cloudy and unprofitable realm of words. This, however, is a profound misconception. For one thing, a sound educational philosophy must have its roots in science; and as soon as we apply science to education, the outlines of a philosophic view begin to emerge. Besides this, every working teacher vitally needs a wide and general view of the values of his subject. An understanding of aims is an essential part of the equipment of the creative teacher.

Let us see just why this is so.

1. A constructive understanding of the ultimate aims of a

subject inspires and enlightens the actual work of teaching. It makes all essential choices wise and human, and gives them vision and meaning. It offers a criterion for deciding between procedures and materials. It applies intimately to all details of the work. As a matter of fact, all teaching is the application of a philosophy of the subject taught. Sometimes that philosophy is a bad one, and then we always have bad teaching. Sometimes it is a good one, and then the teaching is good and tends to become better. This in fact is the real distinction between good and bad educational procedure. Good teaching is impossible without a constructive philosophy to direct it.

2. Again, a constructive understanding of the ultimate aims of a subject provides an explicit creed, which can be made clear to the layman. Music educators may be, and often are, challenged to say why their subject should be taught at all in the schools, and why money and time should be given to it, and various proposed forward steps taken. Such challenges may come from many sources,—from administrative officials in the schools, from school boards, or from the general public. This in itself is a thoroughly healthy sign. With our crowded modern curriculum, every subject ought to be carefully scrutinized, and be forced to offer justification for its place in the school. And this means that for merely strategic purposes, the music teacher ought to be able and willing to give a reason for his faith. But more than this, such challenges have a deeper value, for they compel the music teacher to think fundamentally and plan wisely, so that he may be sure at every point that he is offering something of real value. So once again, we see the value and importance of a discussion of the aims of music education in the schools.

We shall find that the educational values of music may be

summed up under four points. Music education is a progressive reconstruction of experience. Music education has value as discipline. Music education is an enterprise in fuller living. Music education has an essential place in creative democracy. And always, if such aims are to be achieved at all, work in the field of music must be inspired by appreciation and directed towards appreciation.

### I. Music Education as a Progressive Reconstruction of Experience

John Dewey has defined all education as the reconstruction of experience. By this he means that it is neither the storing up of information, nor the creation of fixed habits. Rather it is the opening up to the individual of new and ever wider avenues for experience and action. Every subject in a curriculum may be educative or non-educative, according to the fundamental philosophy on which its treatment is based. It is educative only in so far as it becomes an opportunity for wider and more characteristically human experience. For instance, if mathematics, history, and literature are taught merely on a basis of information or of skill, they lose their value. Essentially they are great fields of human enterprise and endeavor, wide realms in which men have discovered possibilities of experience and action. Exactly the same thing holds in music. If it is taught as a drill subject, or as an information subject, then it has no real place in the school curriculum. Its justification, and its educative value, depend wholly on its being treated as a field of vital and inspiring experience.

Here we come upon a most important distinction made by Dewey,—that between education and training. Training is the formation of fixed and definite habits, without any particular vision of, or participation in, the ultimate ends which those habits are to serve. The trick animal is the victim of training, because a certain routine is hammered into him, but he himself has no significant part in it, or understanding of it. This is not education precisely because the habits are external. They have nothing to do with the individual's will or purpose. They are not part of his life, and they could be obliterated without his losing anything worth keeping. They do not involve a widening or reconstruction of his inner experience. So training is a static affair. It is directed at fixed goals. When certain definite habits have been formed, its course is run. *Education on the other hand, is dynamic and progressive. As contrasted with training, it is a process which never ends. For its business is not the formation of fixed habits, but the continually greater enrichment of life.*

A great deal of our music education today is really training, —training in note reading, training in technique, training in *memoriter* grasp of definitions and theoretical rules. In this it is analogous to the development of fixed and definite tricks in an animal. It does nothing to widen the individual's horizons, or to provide better chances for enjoyment or fullness of life. We have found many reasons based on psychology, for rejecting this conception of music education and all its manifestations and works. We believe that if such a philosophy of our subject should become dominant, music would inevitably lose its place in the school curriculum, because it would deserve to lose it.

We have said that music education must be a progressive reconstruction of experience. What, specifically, does this mean?

1. It means that all fixed habits shall be regarded as means to an end, not as ends in themselves, and shall be taught always in intimate and evident relationship to the end to be

achieved. On this we have insisted. The ability to read the score, the ability to sing, the abilities represented by the various instrumental techniques, the auditory abilities developed by ear training,—all these are to be created, not at all for their own sake, but for the sake of a deeper and wider appreciation, a wiser and more potent love of music. Furthermore, they are all created, not formally or in isolation, but in and through actual musical projects and undertakings. This is but an illustration of the broad principle that habits taught as ends in themselves are not well taught even as habits. Such a view depends on the mechanical theory of learning, and the myth of neural pathways.

2. The idea of music education as the reconstruction of experience means that excellence in teaching music is not to be achieved by any expertness in the mere use of devices, procedures, and classroom methods. One of the greatest fallacies into which a teacher can possibly stumble is to think that a subject poorly organized from an educational point of view, can be made valuable by a set of psychological tricks. This is a wholly false idea of the relationship of psychology to education. Psychology does not present us with a ready-made, magic method, a talisman which will convert bad and poorly organized content into valuable educative material,—and in general get blood out of stones. *Rather it should show us that the proper organization of the teaching of music is essentially the setting up of opportunities for the actual, functioning enjoyment and creation of music. What is demanded is music education through musical projects.* Nothing short of this will do. Psychology must permeate, infuse, and vitalize the entire music program. When it is confined merely to an external, technical expertness in handling the classroom situation, irrespective of content, it is stultified. There are a

great many subjects where it is very hard to apply any such principle. For instance, it is difficult to create school opportunities for living experience in such fields as mathematics and history. But with music this assuredly can be done. The setting up of musical projects with groups of children is one of the most obviously feasible things imaginable. Consequently, music is exceedingly well adapted to school education, and it offers one of the very finest fields for the application of modern pedagogical conceptions. There is no excuse for a music teacher's failing to organize the subject in terms of actual, growing experience.

3. The idea of music education as a reconstruction of experience leads us directly back to a point on which we have insisted again and again,—namely, that the heart of music education is appreciation. If we fail to create appreciation, we become at once just trainers, mere teachers of tricks, and we cease to be educators. Appreciation precisely means experience with the beauty and the power of music, and we have seen how all parts of the program must be organized to produce just this result.

## II. Music Education as Discipline

While we insist that music education is entirely different from training, so that its chief agency is not drill but appreciation, this does not mean for a moment that we want to make everything easy, to eliminate all challenge, and all stress and strain. To remove essential difficulties from any subject is to vitiate it. But wrongly to understand, and wrongly to handle the difficulties of any subject, is to kill it. What we believe is that the enjoyment and creation of music should be made so attractive, so alluring, that difficulties become challenges, and hard work, a joy. This is the disciplinary value of music, as well as of any other subject.

The precisely wrong line of thought about, and practical attack upon, the difficulties of a subject, are seen in the celebrated theory of formal discipline,—one of the most pervasive and pernicious of all educational fallacies. This is the view that the difficulties in a subject are of value because they "strengthen the mental muscles," train the mind, or develop certain mental faculties, such as reasoning, memory, imagination, perception, the power to coördinate, the power to observe, and the like. This most dangerously false line of educational thinking has been destructively criticized again and again during the past thirty years, until now there is probably not one reputable psychologist who would avow it in its unadulterated form. Yet it is amazing to find it cropping up again, in its most characteristic, naïve, and unabashed shape in some of the recent literature of music education. Thus we find such claims as these: that reading music will develop quickness of perception and accuracy; that the study of the score on a theoretical basis will develop reasoning power; and that music in general improves the ability to coördinate. In view of the vast research on just such topics, and its almost uniformly negative outcomes, the educational psychologist who encounters such statements may be pardoned for wondering whether music teachers really live in the twentieth century or the eighteenth. We feel that such dicta are as serious blemishes on otherwise excellent discussions as a claim that the earth is flat.

Anyone who wishes to look up the literature of formal discipline can readily do so by turning to almost any good standard textbook on the Principles of Education or Educational Psychology. But it may be well to spend a little time in analyzing somewhat more in detail the claims that are made on behalf of the formal disciplinary value of music.

1. Our first criticism is that such claims are made without any factual proof. It would not be particularly hard to submit them to proof or disproof. The technique of such work is thoroughly well established, and has been applied many times elsewhere. Let us suppose we want to find out whether practice in reading the musical score really develops quickness of perception. We would go about it as follows. We would first of all set up a test of quickness of perception. Then we would select two groups of children whose abilities as shown up in our quickness test were exactly equal. Then we would give one of these groups perhaps six weeks' daily practice with the musical score, while the other group had none. Then at the end of the period, we would again test them for quickness of perception. If the group that worked with the score showed a reliable superiority on this second testing, and if we had properly eliminated other influences, we should conclude that practice in reading did produce an advance in quickness of perception. But this has never been done, and all claims along this line are advanced on a basis of the merest guess. As regards transfer to reasoning, there is at least one study whose result is actually negative. Thorndike, in his great investigation of the disciplinary value of high school subjects, found that music was one of the subjects which yielded zero improvement over a period of a year's work, on a reasoning test. This is the only factual investigation on any of these points known to the writers, and its outcome, as we see it, is entirely contrary to the usual claims. As regards the claim that music study will improve coördination (which presumably would mean that it ought to improve our ability to play such

games as golf and billiards), there is perhaps a shade more reason for this. But again, we have something entirely unproved and unsubstantiated by fact. And after all, it is perfectly possible that those who already are endowed with good powers of bodily coördination tend to do well in music, so that their success in coördinational activities outside of music may not be due to musical training, but to natural inheritance. All in all, the claims for a formal disciplinary value in music are exactly on a level with the old notions that Latin and geometry "train the mind,"—notions wholly abandoned by scientific and progressive-minded educators. If we want our subject to retain its value and advance in standing with such educators, it would seem well to stop bringing forward unsubstantiated claims arising out of an exploded educational theory.

2. Formal discipline is not merely wrong. It is dangerous. This is the reason for discussing it here. It is an historical fact that this theory has been used again and again to validate and defend thoroughly bad schemes of education. It has been used to fight the introduction of modern studies, and to retain a strictly classical curriculum. It has been the chief reliance of those who have insisted on much formal grammar study in connection with language work. It has been the great excuse for handling geometry as a drill subject, without any relationships at all beyond itself. It has even been used to block textbook reform, because of the argument that a textbook so badly organized that it made a subject very difficult, was valuable as a means of training the reason and of making the pupil work hard. It is not too much to say that historical wisdom would suggest always suspecting and searching for some concealed weakness, some indefensible element, whenever the disciplinary argument is advanced on behalf of any subject or any teaching procedure.

In music education, the theory runs true to type. Nearly always it is advanced to validate formal and meaningless drill work of some kind,—*to defend some procedure that has no relationship to a musical project.* This is why we say that it is a very dangerous line of thinking for any music teacher. It offers a soothing excuse for bad educational practice, because when we cannot justify a procedure by saying that it contributes definitely to a widening of the child's musical horizon and a deepening of his musical interest, we come out with the argument that it trains his mind. But our business as music teachers is precisely not to develop accuracy, or quickness of perception, or reasoning power, or ability to coördinate. *Our business is to teach music, and our work will stand or fall by our success in this undertaking.* Anything that deflects us from this aim, confuses the clear issue, or blunts the edge of self-criticism on this criterion, is bad and destructive.

Thus we would regard the theory of formal discipline as a fundamental misrepresentation of the true rôle of difficulty in music study, and of the true disciplinary values to be found in music. Discipline in music comes from an association of inspiration with effort. We have it in the sense of something worth doing, but difficult to do, and in the conquest of difficulty for an inspiring goal. If the inspiration, the drive, fails, difficulties become mere obstacles. But on the other hand, if we try to eliminate difficulties rather than to humanize and spiritualize them, then we deprive our subject of all value because we eliminate the very conditions of achievement. The balloon is filled with hot air, and soon sinks. The young shoots wither away, because they have no depth of earth.

It is abundantly clear that such a conception of the disciplinary value of music directly and inevitably implies that music education must proceed in terms of appreciation. Indeed this is no more than a reformulation of the point we have just made. When the child tackles difficulties in connection with music because he is a child, and at the mercy of adults, and without any glimmer of light as to the constructive and fascinating possibilities of what he is dully trying to do, those difficulties have simply no educative value at all for him. Difficulty, indeed, is rich with educative value, but this is only gained when we attack our problem with an urgent sense of something enthralling and delightful to be achieved in its solution. The difficulties of music yield their disciplinary value only when attacked for the sake of music and the love of music—for the sake of appreciation. We must strike the rock in the name of the spirit, and the waters will surely flow forth.

### III. Music Education as an Enterprise in Fuller Living

Another idea on which Dewey insists is that education is not a process of preparation for life. It is life itself. The ultimate justification for music in the schools is not the idea that children will use it at some time in the future, so that it is wise to prepare them for so doing. It is that music properly taught has an immense and potent appeal to the child, that it offers him a wide opportunity, *here and now,* for fuller living, and that this opportunity ought to be his. Notice that we say, music *properly taught.* If it is handled as a drill subject, with primary emphasis on such things as note reading, theory, or technique, it will not have this value. Such an approach always involves two difficulties. (*a*) It means that we have to create interest and motivation artificially, by some sort of sugar-plum incentives, as, for instance, by greatly over-emphasizing social motivation. But when music is taught in terms of appreciation, it tends to become its own motive. (*b*) Instead of having reasons for what we do, we have to invent excuses. The love of music justifies itself. Its value is obvious and undeniable. But the value of knowing note names, understanding musical theory, or developing technique, as ends in themselves, is far from self-evident. So when teachers aim at these things, they have to concoct reasons. The most commonly used of these—the claim that such studies train the mind—has already been discussed and dismissed. But also we have feeble efforts to show that children may sometime, somewhere, use a certain skill or trick,—efforts always dubious and debatable. *Educational procedures which cannot justify themselves in the here and the now, in terms of a happier and fuller life for the child, are always open to the most serious question.* What we want is a program that will not aim at drill, and at the same time will not shirk difficulties; one that will seek to give the child an opportunity to become, at his own level, a *child musician,*—that is, to find in music an opportunity for happiness and a fuller life.

But we may be asked, what about the vocational and avocational emphasis in school music? Should we not hold that school music aims to help some few into professional careers, and to open for many a worthy avocation? Our answer is that school music, just like every other educative subject, has nothing at all directly to do with preparation. *But it has everything to do with helping the child to discover music for himself, and to discover himself musically.* If this is achieved, then the later uses to which music will be put will very largely take care of themselves. The real problem for the vocational adviser is the person who has not found himself, and has no idea of what he really likes, or how he wishes to shape his life. Finding one's self is the basis of finding work and leisure time pursuits.

In a very real sense, an educative process has no aim or end except more education, more growth, more life. We see this in grade school singing, where we said that each song should be at once a goal and a stepping stone. Here we have a principle as broad as humanity, and to it we should cling. Help the child to live music, and you have educated him musically. Train him in a bag of tricks, and you have wasted both his time and your own.

So here for the third time we are brought in our discussion of aims, to the leading concept of appreciation. A scheme of music education that is to be in truth an adventure in fuller living, must center about the understanding love of music, and must be informed in all its parts by the spirit of appreciation.

## IV. Music Education as an Agency for Creative Democracy

Dewey insists that the true essence of democracy is not its political structure. Its vital characteristic is a wide and intimate sharing of experience, a social situation where lives may meet and may mutually refresh, instruct, inspire, and encourage one another. This was exemplified in the most perfect of all democracies, that of ancient Athens, a state where men of many temperaments and many minds, met and mingled together in a rich community of living. In that state too, we see the creative force of the democratic ideal, embodying itself in matchless masterpieces of art, contributed for the common good, and deriving their meaning and vitality from their expression of the common aspiration. But such a creative sharing is simply impossible without a wealth of experience to be shared. This was the true social meaning of the great literary, dramatic, and artistic manifestations of Athenian genius. They provided the means whereby men's minds might come together, the focal points for the community of will and enterprise and patriotic love. Ancient Athens was a democracy founded in part on music, though certainly the art meant less to a classical civilization than it does to us in this age. Today we are beginning to see in music an agency for humanizing and ennobling modern social life, with all its stress and strain, and all its anti-human, anti-democratic subdivisions of function.

We see the social power and richness of music. But we must not think that to capture this power, we must slight music and intrinsic musical value, and emphasize a spirit of "get-together." Davison tells us how, during the war, those camps which emphasized mere "get-together" and let music slip, found infinitely less value in their community singing than those in which musical values themselves were assiduously cultivated. What we mean is that we must have faith in music, that we must make music the main thing, and let it do its own work, which it assuredly will. We see this strange uniting power in music most perfectly in the amateur ensemble group, where each individual finds his work enriched by that of all the others, and where he himself contributes to a corporate undertaking. It is no accident that philosophers have thought of the harmony of the heavens as a celestial music, or that theologians have pictured the chief joy of the redeemed as participation in an anthem old and yet ever new. Music has an enriching and creative mission for democracy in bringing men more closely face to face.

Here too we see the ultimate mission of school music. There have been times when music was an aristocratic art, the peculiar possession of the few. But these have always been decadent times for music. The art has been continually refreshed by the streams of folk music. Its greatest servants have always tended to universalize its appeal. When they have expressed themselves about their lives and work, they have many times shown their intimate sense of a mission to all mankind. Thus we have the stupendous words of Beethoven, —words which no man not conscious of a godlike power dare utter: "I am the Bacchus who presses for humanity the delicious wine of life."

In American school music we see an art movement which is vital because of its true, democratic instinct and impulsion. To have this movement thwarted by drill-masters and led into blind alleys by pedants and technicians would be a tragedy which we ought not even to contemplate. We should have gone far beyond such immaturity and mechanistic crudity. To teach America the achievement of loving music wisely is the ultimate aim of school music. Thus the school music teacher should dedicate himself to the task of conveying the power and glory of music to all the children of our schools, with a creed which is nobly summarized in these words:

"Thou lovely art, my joy and consolation,
Whose wondrous power drives all our care away,
Thou hast my heart throughout my life's duration.
The world rejoices in thy magic sway.

"I've sounded all the forms of human pleasure;
But thou art better than all else to me.
A foretaste thou of heaven's richest treasure.
Thou holy art, I give my life to thee."

QUESTIONS FOR DISCUSSION.

1. What arguments for the value of school music would you present to *(a)* a superintendent of schools; *(b)* a high school principal who was disinclined to allow enough time for music; *(c)* a member of the public who questioned whether music had any real place in the schools?

2. Show that the application of psychology to music education does far more than merely determine classroom "method."

3. Show that a proper philosophy of music education leads the teacher to formulate wise practical decisions.

4. What improper practices in music education might be defended by an argument based on the idea of formal discipline?

5. Show how our conception of the real disciplinary value of music applies to acquiring *(a)* technique; *(b)* reading ability.

6. Show that Dewey's idea of education as a reconstruction of experience is in harmony with our account of musical learning.

7. Show how the teaching of music with a central emphasis on technique, theory, or note reading threatens the future of our subject in the schools.

8. Why does our conception of the aims of music education imply that appreciation is the central thing in music education?

9. What kind of music program must we develop, and what kind of materials must we use in order to realize the aims discussed in this chapter?

10. What characteristics and training must a school music teacher have to give effect to the aims here discussed?

BIBLIOGRAPHY.

1. BEATTIE, JOHN W., MCCONATHY, OSBOURNE, and MORGAN, RUSSELL V., *Music in the Junior High School,* Silver, Burdett and Company, 1930.
2. BIRGE, EDWARD BAILEY, *History of Public School Music in the United States,* Oliver Ditson Company, 1928.

3. DAVISON, ARCHIBALD T., *Music Education in America,* Harper and Brothers, 1926.
4. DEWEY, JOHN, *Democracy and Education,* The Macmillan Company, 1916.
5. FARNSWORTH, C. H., *Education Through Music,* American Book Company, 1909.
6. GALE, HARLOW, Musical Education, *Pedagogical Seminary,* 1917, vol. 24, pp. 503-514.
7. SAYERS, E. VERN, *Educational Issues and the Unity of Experience,* Contributions to Education, No. 357, Teachers College, Columbia University, 1929.
8. SURETTE, THOMAS WHITNEY, *Music and Life,* Houghton Mifflin Company, 1917.

# INDEX